MW00483891

THE MEN FROM MIAMI

THE MEN
FROM MIAMI

AMERICAN REBELS ON BOTH SIDES OF
FIDEL CASTRO'S CUBAN REVOLUTION

CHRISTOPHER OTHEN

Biteback Publishing

First published in Great Britain in 2022 by
Biteback Publishing Ltd, London
Copyright © Christopher Othen 2022

ISBN 978-1-78590-686-2

10 9 8 7 6 5 4 3 2 1

A CIP catalogue record for this book is available from the British Library.

Set in Minion Pro and Trade Gothic

Printed and bound in Great Britain by
CPI Group (UK) Ltd, Croydon CR0 4YY

MIX
Paper from
responsible sources
FSC® C171272
www.fsc.org

CONTENTS

PROLOGUE

MISSING OVER CUBA: $25,000 REWARD

On 24 September 1963, Alexander Irwin Rorke climbed into a small twin-engine aeroplane at Fort Lauderdale airport and took off on a flight across the Caribbean Sea. He was never seen again. When the handsome 37-year-old with black hair and blue eyes failed to return, Rorke's panicky wife telephoned New York for help. Her father had influential friends.

Sherman Billingsley owned the Stork Club, three storeys of white tablecloths and potted palms just east of Fifth Avenue. In the club's glory days, big-name actors from Hollywood had drunk its overpriced cocktails and pranced around to the band while a fourteen-carat gold chain across the door kept out ordinary folk. These days the Stork was looking a lot less glitzy. A picket line protested outside most nights over Billingsley's refusal to unionise and the celebrities had been replaced by anyone with $1.99 to spare for a burger and fries.

Despite his club's decline, Billingsley still had important contacts on both sides of the law. Jacqueline Rorke begged him for help finding her husband. Alex's friends Frank Sturgis and Gerry Patrick were organising a search party, but they were penniless members of the Miami political underground. She needed professional help.

It was a tough sell. Billingsley had always hated his son-in-law and refused to allow him into the family mansion on Park Avenue. When Jacqueline brought their son Alex III around for visits, Rorke had to wait outside in the car. Billingsley was convinced the marriage was just an act of rebellion by his favourite daughter, and it was only when Jacqueline began sobbing down the telephone from Florida that he realised how much Rorke meant to her.

'Oh my God, you really loved him,' said Billingsley in surprise.[1]

He reached out to some friends in the Federal Bureau of Investigation. They already knew all about Alex Rorke. Agents had been keeping an eye on Billingsley's son-in-law ever since he first got mixed up with Fidel Castro and the Cuban Revolution.

• • •

Cuba was 42,000 square miles of sunlit archipelago floating in the Caribbean Sea. It had entered modernity as a Spanish colony and remained one until the end of the nineteenth century. With independence came choices to be made about trade, investment and the free market. Cuba settled on exporting sugar cane and importing tourists, especially those who liked their cocktails strong and their morals loose. Havana transformed into a Shangri-La of sin whose economy was built around providing visiting Americans with sex and booze and every other sensual pleasure under the sun.

By the 1950s, the American Mafia controlled most of the city's fleshpots. Gangsters had been in Cuba for decades, but their presence metastasised under the shamelessly corrupt rule of glossy-haired tyrant Fulgencio Batista. The relationship with organised crime became so symbiotic that when Batista began awarding a free gaming licence to every new hotel costing over $1 million, it only ever seemed to be Mafia developments that got the green light. The resulting construction boom benefited the gangsters, the government and the urban elite, but the rest of the country remained a neglected backwater where subsistence farmers struggled to feed their families. On paper, Cuba was the richest country in Central America, but the top 20 per cent of the population earned 55 per cent of the island's income and the poorest 20 per cent took home only 5 per cent.[2] There was a racial angle too: the rich tended to be white or light-skinned and the poor mixed race or Afro-Cuban, although Batista complicated any easy socio-political analysis by coming from a peasant family with indigenous and African ancestry.

Cuba's northern neighbour America disapproved of the corruption piling up only 250 nautical miles from its shores but refused to intervene. Batista had declared himself an ally in the Cold War, an ongoing series of proxy battles that had been raging between the West and the Soviet bloc since the late 1940s, and the powerbrokers in Washington were prepared to tolerate any amount of bad behaviour as long as Cuba's leader was fighting beside them in the geopolitical trenches. Ordinary Cubans, less invested in Cold War stratagems, seethed as their government got rich while they stayed poor. In 1956, the young and the radical followed an unsuccessful lawyer called Fidel Castro into the mountains to launch a guerrilla war against the Batista regime.

At first no one in Havana took the uprising seriously, and neither did most Americans. That changed in February the next year when Herbert Matthews of the *New York Times* got an exclusive interview with Castro that convinced readers the bearded revolutionary wanted nothing more than free elections, justice for all and an end to tyranny. Matthews's reporting turned Castro into a hero of US popular culture: the beard, the cigar, the green army fatigues, the struggle against a dictator. It was a caricature of a complex man, but an effective one. Popular pressure forced President Dwight Eisenhower's government to suspend military aid and left Batista to fight off the rebellion on his own.

Around twenty-five Americans smuggled themselves into the Cuban mountains to join Castro's struggle. One was Alex Rorke's future friend Frank Sturgis, a bar-owning tough guy from Virginia who got his mind wrecked fighting as a Marine in the Pacific and returned home unable to cope with regular life. His real name was Frank Fiorini, although people also knew him as Frank Campbell, Frank Attila or any of the other fake names that came in useful for a man always operating on the borders of legality. Patriotic, Catholic and no one's idea of an intellectual, Fiorini had gone ricocheting through peacetime looking for a cause. He found it in 1957 when relatives in Miami introduced him to a group of Cuban exiles assisting Castro's efforts from abroad. Fiorini helped fly weapons into the Sierra Maestra mountains and returned home convinced the bearded guerrilla leader was a fellow anti-communist patriot. It was a serious misjudgement, but few people outside Castro's inner circle were in a position to realise that at the time. Fiorini set himself up as a full-time gunrunner before joining a rebel column to fight against Batista's troops.

A stream of other American misfits and adventurers had already signed up, including a trio of teenagers from the Guantánamo Bay naval base, a Staten Island street rat who wanted to be a hero, a handful of American military deserters, some soldiers of fortune looking for a payday, a sleazy ex-con who liked underage girls, and at least two future murderers. Some had genuine mental health issues ('kill-crazy' in one volunteer's words)[3] and Korean War veteran Neill Macaulay coolly watched his Cuban comrades lynch unarmed prisoners. Others had more to offer. One-time jailbird William Alexander Morgan became so respected by a rebel faction that they made him comandante of a column.

Some American volunteers stayed only a few weeks. Others fought for months against Batista's forces and were part of the triumphant guerrilla army of January 1959 that rode jeeps into Havana through a rain of flowers tossed by cheering supporters. The American government immediately sent a message of congratulations to Castro. Washington's political elite felt quietly confident that Cuba's new leader would take his place on the Cold War chessboard as a loyal ally, just like his predecessor. Castro seemed to agree. Within a few months of his victory, he made a goodwill tour of America, full of crowd-pleasing gestures like wearing a Stetson to a Texas rodeo.

In return, a wave of Americans came pouring into revolutionary Cuba looking for work. Among them was Gerald Hemming, or Gerry Patrick to the FBI and anyone else he pestered with pseudonymous telephone calls about the need to fight communism and smack around beatniks who threatened the American way of life. He was a 6ft 6in. former Marine in his twenties, never able to stick at anything long enough to make it a success. Hemming ditched a promising military career to bum around California then turned up in revolutionary Havana as a military volunteer for the new regime. He didn't care about politics or the Cold War. Cuba just seemed the right place for a fresh start.

As 1959 got into its stride, the island was buzzing with hope and opportunity and a sense that good had triumphed over evil. The revolutionary euphoria wouldn't last. It never does.

• • •

The first to slip away into Miami exile were the Batista loyalists. No one was surprised to see men with guilty consciences flee the firing squads, but soon former Castro lieutenants were joining the exodus, disillusioned by the authoritarian tone of the new regime. Thousands more would follow over the coming months as government rhetoric became more extreme and the food scarcer. Soviet advisers were seen in Havana. Marxism–Leninism became the official state ideology.

Almost all the Yankee adventurers who had fought with Castro in Cuba would leave in the next year or so, some voluntarily and some at gunpoint. A significant number changed sides to fight against the man they had helped put in power. William Morgan worked undercover in Havana for a counter-revolutionary group while Neill Macaulay trained Cuban exiles in the expanse of Florida wetlands known as the Everglades. Others ran guns, flew bombing missions over Havana or launched guerrilla raids across the Caribbean.

Frank Fiorini was one of the most prominent turncoats. He ditched the revolution in the summer of 1959 after watching the new government get packed full of communists, then moved to Miami and submerged himself in a festering swamp of right-wing resentment and private armies. Out in the Everglades, exiled Cuban nationalists were training to take back their country alongside gangs of unemployed American adventurers who gave themselves grand names like the Cuban Revolutionary Army of Liberation and the International Anti-Communist Brigade and paid the rent by donating blood every two months.

Reporting on and often working alongside these men was Alex Rorke, who soon became one of the most familiar faces in Miami's

Little Havana. He styled himself a freelance foreign correspondent, a job that mostly involved lugging a camera around potential hotspots in the Caribbean and selling the results to NBC. Rorke had first got mixed up in Cuba back in August 1959 after receiving a tip about a potential coup d'état from some gangsters anxious to reclaim casinos closed by the revolution. The coup failed to happen and the Cuban police jailed him for a week. Deported back to America, Rorke became a fanatical anti-communist who often blurred the lines between being a journalist covering a story and an active participant fighting Castro.

Rorke, Fiorini and the rest were amateurs at regime change compared to the experts in Washington. President Eisenhower was convinced Cuba had become a tentacle of the Soviet bloc slithering through the Caribbean, and he ordered the Central Intelligence Agency to replace the Castro regime with something more friendly. CIA agents recruited an invasion force from exiles training in the Everglades, while veteran spies held discreet talks with Mafia hit men in pastel-coloured hotel bars about the prospects of wiping out Fidel in a gangland hit.

Some exiles tried to launch their own invasions of Cuba ahead of the Americans. The most prominent was Rolando Masferrer, a former communist who had fought with the International Brigades in the Spanish Civil War but slid to the other end of the ideological spectrum as a death squad commander under Batista. Masferrer's reputation was so toxic the CIA froze him out of its own operations but couldn't stop him organising an ill-fated landing in Cuba with a ragbag of fellow exiles and some American soldiers of fortune, one of them an asthmatic carpenter well out of his depth. It didn't end well. CIA agents told the exile community to let the professionals handle things in future.

The Cold War had arrived in Miami, a tourist city where everyone seemed to be wearing plaid shorts and sun hats and smoking cigarettes as they got in and out of fin-tailed cars. A Little Havana district bloomed around South River Drive and restaurants all across town ordered up Spanish-language menus. The exiles convinced themselves their stay was only temporary.

• • •

Early in the morning of 17 April 1961, the CIA landed its official invasion force at the Bay of Pigs, a beach-lined inlet surrounded by swamp. The agency expected an easy victory, but their exile troops walked straight into the waiting guns of the Cuban militia. American assessments of everything from Castro's popularity to the suitability of the landing point were proved fatally wrong. The fighting went on for two more desperate days and when it was over, there were 100 dead from the brigade and 1,000 men in a Cuban prison. Recently elected President John F. Kennedy denied any official US involvement, but no one believed him.

In the aftermath, hundreds of red-blooded American boys with buzzcut hair and hard eyes flooded into Florida to drink beer, shoot guns and wave the Star-Spangled Banner in the face of those Godless Reds. The CIA didn't need their help and the local police tried to run them out of town, but these would-be soldiers of fortune were determined to show the world that the USA didn't lose wars. Among them was a familiar face: Gerald Hemming had changed sides after being thrown into a Havana prison for getting too friendly with some Nicaraguan revolutionaries. He formed a group called the Intercontinental Penetration Force and announced he would personally lead the charge to liberate Cuba. Hemming connected with Frank Fiorini through their shared hatred of communism and a common background as former military men. Rorke made it a trio, even if he annoyed the others with his habit of hogging the limelight.

America's war against Castro continued, in a more covert manner, and the three musketeers of anti-communism watched in frustration as their government threw money at any Cuban group with a boat and a gun but refused to give them a taste. The CIA had no interest in funding amateurs. Rorke's wife helped him financially while Hemming lived off food scrounged from local Cuban businesses and Fiorini got a job selling used cars. When an exile leader donated $100 as a gesture of solidarity, it felt like Christmas. The trio eventually managed to scrape together enough cash for their own private operations. In 1961, Fiorini and Rorke scattered anti-Castro leaflets over Havana by plane and tried to establish a presence in Guatemala while Hemming's Interpen found themselves a base out at No Name Key, a desolate wilderness of snakes and alligators, where they trained anyone with enough cash to pay for a weekend of survival instruction.

In October 1962, the Cuban missile crisis changed everything. The presence of Soviet nuclear weapons on the island pushed Kennedy and Nikita Khrushchev into a tense showdown that took the world to the brink of war. Eventually, both sides backed down. The missiles were removed and, in return, the Americans promised to halt any more aggression against Cuba. Most of the Miami scene listened, but Rorke and his friends ignored the threat of nuclear holocaust and kept fighting their own private war. They made night-time boat trips to the island for guerrilla missions and launched air raids over Havana; Hemming's Interpen nearly started the Third World War with an ill-timed commando raid on Cuban territory. Hard-faced CIA agents told them to stop, or at least be discreet, but Rorke went straight to the newspapers after every successful mission. The reporter was never keen on keeping his mouth shut.

'By his own admission [he] is somewhat garrulous,' noted a CIA report.[4] 'He did not appear to be a sharp operator.'

His wife last saw Rorke in late September 1963 when he kissed her goodbye and climbed into the car, talking about visiting Central America for an import–export business. The plane set off from Fort Lauderdale, refuelled on the Mexican island of Cozumel, then filed a flight plan for Honduras. No one ever saw the blue-and-white twin-engine Beechcraft again. Sherman Billingsley was one of many who assumed the Honduras destination was a bluff and his son-in-law had diverted east for a mission over Cuba. He held a press conference at the Stork Club and offered a $25,000 reward for Rorke's safe return. Fiorini and Hemming were already searching for their missing friend.

Rorke was yet another casualty of the fight for, and then against, Castro by a miniature army of American adventurers. Some got shot in mysterious circumstances. Some went to prison. Some blew up in planes over Havana and could only be identified by their dental records. When a sniper assassinated President Kennedy in Dallas, conspiracy theorists decided the surviving adventurers must have been involved and forced them to spend the rest of their lives denying everything. Frank Fiorini became a Watergate burglar and inadvertently brought down another US President. The really unlucky ones held on to their Miami mercenary dream and joined an invasion of 'Papa Doc' Duvalier's Haiti, sponsored by CBS in exchange for exclusive television rights and overseen by a ghostly voodoo guide channelled from the spirit world by a Cuban witch.

That invasion was doomed from the start. Haiti may have been a nightmare of dictatorship and death squads, but it was also an ally of Washington in the Cold War and the invaders had forgotten to get official approval before they sailed.

The men from Miami saw themselves as warriors in a titanic battle between opposing historical forces – liberty versus despotism, democracy versus communism, West versus East. Sharper minds pointed out that the battle would never have begun if American tourists hadn't enjoyed drinking and getting laid in 1950s Havana so much.

PART I

¡REVOLUCIÓN!

1

THE CITY OF SUPERMAN

HAVANA, EARLY 1957

Superman had a fourteen-inch penis and performed nightly at the Teatro Shanghai for tourists and local perverts. Welcome to Havana.

Girls in bikinis opened the show with a mambo dance down the sticky theatre aisles before handing off to a repertory company so wooden they made the average ventriloquist's dummy look like Orson Welles. The actors mumbled their way through a few skits rammed full of double entendres then gave way to a naked chorus line that shuffled on for some sweaty high-kicks. Management lowered a screen during the interval and projected a scratched-up hardcore pornographic film through the darkness to keep everyone in their seats. Finally, Superman appeared with his member flapping between his legs and had disinterested sex with a girl or two until the red velvet curtain came down.

The Shanghai's star attraction was a lean 6ft Cuban with some African blood and a unit that inspired lust, envy and a regular pay cheque. No one knew Superman's real name, but neighbours in his working-class district called him Enrique la Reina (Enrique the Queen), although never to his face. He had a temper and a knife. For many foreign visitors, Superman was Havana's main tourist attraction, a phallic monument in a corrupt city throbbing with clubs, casinos, brothels, bars, restaurants, shows, tanned flesh and cheap drinks, where it was all part of the fun when a gay man had sex with bored girls for money in front of 800 patrons three times a night.

So many Americans visited the Shanghai in search of cheap thrills that it was hard to find a Yankee tourist who didn't buy a ticket. In the spring of 1957, one miraculously appeared, wandering the streets of Havana and doing his best to look inconspicuous. Frank Fiorini was a 33-year-old war veteran searching for a cause. He'd tried the peacetime army, the police and the nightclub business but found only late nights and broken marriages before Cuba came along and gave the damaged ex-serviceman something to fight for. He was in town on an undercover mission to help anti-government rebels up in the mountains.

The Havana police, usually alert to smugglers and undercover activists, missed him completely. Fiorini had taken care to look just like all the other American visitors who poured in daily to spend their post-war boom money on glorious sensual excess far from the repressive buttoned-down world of Eisenhower America. In Havana, the hotels were full, the sun shone hard and sex was everywhere. Showgirls swayed in elegant formation at the Tropicana nightclub. Dancers shimmied across the floor at Club 66 and the flocks of prostitutes who posed in doorways across the city, day and night, hid the sadness in their eyes behind bright smiles. It was heaven on earth for degenerate tourists with fat wallets and, unlike Fiorini, most of them found time to visit the legendary Teatro Shanghai at least once.

The Shanghai had begun as a straight entertainment venue for the local Chinese community back in the early 1930s. It was the wrong time to invest in traditional Mandarin drama. The place had barely opened before Cuba got hit by a global recession that originated in the crash of the American stock market and spread to every corner of the world. Businesses collapsed and banks went under. Cuba's President, the silver-haired ex-military man Gerardo Machado, soon discovered that sugar cane revenues and tourism weren't enough to pay the bills. His mishandling of the situation got him got chased out by an unholy coalition of far-right students, underpaid plantation workers and leftist intelligentsia. His replacement only lasted three weeks.

Glossy-haired strongman Fulgencio Batista y Zaldívar took power at gunpoint and spent the rest of the decade pulling the strings of a series of puppet Presidents. Even Batista's enemies had to respect the unstoppable ambition of this working-class, mixed-race Army sergeant who cut straight through the traditional Cuban hierarchies of class and race like a machete through a cane stalk. Under his authoritarian rule, the island wobbled through the Depression and came out the other side poor but intact.

Frank Fiorini had been a child in Virginia back then, a pupil at a Catholic school run by nuns who smacked his knuckles with a ruler for every act of disobedience. He was born in a port town called Norfolk to Italian-American parents one generation removed from the old country of wine and olives and poverty. Fiorini retained a few vague memories of his breezy hometown on the Chesapeake Bay before everything changed and life became a crowded blue-collar household in Philadelphia with no sign of his father or older sister. It was a while before he fully understood that his sister had died in a fire and the resulting trauma destroyed his parents' marriage.

He and his younger sister Frances grew up with his mother, her parents and Aunt Katherine and her son Joey living all over each other in three narrow storeys of red brick. At mealtimes, everyone yelled across the table in English and Italian as the serving dishes passed from hand to hand. On Sundays, the household trooped off to the local Catholic church for Mass. Fiorini served as an altar boy. He liked to prank worshippers by spiking the communion wine with vodka, but religion was the moral centre of his life.

'Before the war I had strong leanings towards becoming a Catholic priest,' he said.[1] 'And, if the war hadn't come about, I would have.'

On 7 December 1941, swarms of Japanese fighter planes screamed out of the sun over the Hawaiian naval base at Pearl Harbor. When the attack ended, at least 2,400 Americans were dead and eight battleships had gone down into the oily water. The next year, Fiorini dropped out of his senior year at high school and joined the Marines. He was black-haired, 5ft 10in. tall and seventeen years old. The school measured his IQ at ninety-six. He was an average American from an average city going off to fight for his country.

• • •

Three years later, Marine Corporal Frank Fiorini was sitting in an Oregon psychiatric ward with shell shock. The service had sent him to the Pacific theatre, where he hunted Japanese soldiers across Guadalcanal, New Georgia Island, Emirau Island, Guam and Okinawa. He got shot in the wrist and bayoneted in the foot. By the summer of 1945, it was all too much and the Marines sent him to a psych ward back home to lie on a bed and stare blankly at the ceiling. Talk therapy and sodium pentothal turned him into something close to a functioning human.

'Naturally, during wartime you're brainwashed to a point psychologically where you have to kill the enemy,' said Fiorini.[2] 'But now that the war is over, you have a trained professional man who's been trained and cannot adjust to civilian life.'

Cuba was making its own painful adjustments to the post-war world. In 1940, Batista had left the shadows and easily won the presidential election, although enemies grumbled about missing ballot boxes and rigged polls. Four years later, he was kicked out of power by voters sick of the way he pandered to American mobsters. Mafia men from Chicago and New York had turned Havana into a gangster's paradise which milked dry any tourist who liked to gamble, drink or watch a floorshow. Even the owners of the Teatro Shanghai ditched the Mandarin drama and introduced burlesque shows full of dancers in ostrich feathers. Batista's removal brought in a lot of fine talk about eliminating corruption, but the Mafia just rerouted its bribes to the new intake of politicians and nothing much changed. Within a few years, a presidential decree would exempt the nation's hotels, most of them gangster-owned, from paying taxes.

Fiorini heard all about Cuban politics from a new perch in Miami. His mother had remarried to a man called Sturgis, divorced, then moved to Florida to live with her brother. She married for a third time, to a bus driver, and seemed happy. Fiorini spent time there after demobilisation and, thanks to Uncle Angelo's contacts with the local Cuban scene, heard plenty of talk at the dinner table about Batista, corruption and hope for the future. Away from the house, Fiorini indulged his more basic instincts, chasing girls and hanging out in strip joints. He fell in love with a prostitute named Betty, married her and returned to his barely remembered birthplace of Norfolk. His father's family had enough influence up there to get him a job in the police force. The ranks and uniform seemed reassuring after the war.

Fiorini lasted four months. In his version, the casual corruption disgusted him and he quit after a confrontation with the sergeant at roll call. Friends thought his wife still working as a prostitute played an equally important role in ending his police career.

For the next few years, Fiorini rattled around Norfolk looking for peace but rarely finding it. A short career as a cab driver ended with an arrest for drinking. He became manager of a bar called the Havana-Madrid that catered to foreign sailors who regularly needed their heads cracked open with a baseball bat when the inevitable brawl broke out. Fiorini joined the Naval Reserves to spend his weekends in uniform training to pilot light aircraft. In a rare moment of clarity, Fiorini realised he no longer liked his wife or current life very much. He joined the Army in August 1948 to get away from both. The military posted him to Berlin, where East and West were fighting over the carcass of Adolf Hitler's Germany.

• • •

The heart of the German Third Reich had been a hunk of burning rubble and desperate people at the end of the war. Three years later, it was back on the front lines of another conflict after a post-war land grab had divided Germany between the victorious Soviets and the Western Allies. The division was replicated in miniature with Berlin, until Soviet dictator Joseph Stalin shattered the fragile status quo with a blockade intended to starve out the other occupiers and take the capital for himself. An Allied airlift kept Berlin alive but intensified the Cold War between East and West while the world looked on, praying the confrontation would not lead to another global conflict.

Frank Fiorini played a minor role in the geopolitical drama. He led a tense but uneventful life escorting an American general around Berlin at the height of the crisis until a pointless squabble over a local girl saw him transferred out to an intelligence unit. Friends back home were told tall stories about femme fatales and top-secret clearances, but the truth was a dull secretarial job in the typing pool and a deepening scepticism towards communism. After nine months in uniform, he quit, claiming his mother needed his financial support, and went back into the Norfolk bar business.

Fiorini had never got over his shell shock from the Pacific War and in those days a killer rage was always close to the surface. One night he beat his wife so badly the police intervened. The charges were dropped, but Fiorini found it wise to join the Merchant Marine and sail back and forth to Europe for a while. He came home with tales about helping beautiful Jewish spies smuggle out secrets for Israel that may have been true but which no one in his hometown believed.

After the Merchant Marine, Fiorini returned to bar management with a place called Café Society, where the owner liked him enough to partner up and go halves buying into the Top Hat nightclub. Fiorini had a talent for the business of glad-handing and complimentary drinks that were essential elements in the business, along with a .45 automatic kept by the cash register. In his free time, the former Marine studied at the College of William & Mary for a semester or two until he got bored, then became a flight instructor in the Civil Air Patrol. His cousin Joey died in the Korean War and Fiorini's dislike of communism flamed into an almost pathological hatred.

Around this time, he legally changed his name to Frank Sturgis. Explanations ranged from being pushed into it by his mother, who may still have been using the name of her second husband, to an attempt to tidy up the bureaucracy of having been underage at the time of that marriage. Friends thought there might be another reason.

'He was going by the name of Frank Sturgis 'cause his real name had a Mafia twang to it,' said a customs officer who knew him.[3]

The years ticked by and Fiorini seemed to have settled down into the rougher end of civilian life, the kind that lived at night and saw the law as something to be negotiated rather than obeyed. He was separated from his wife Betty by 1954 when a fellow prostitute shot her in the heart during an argument. Fiorini didn't seem especially troubled by the loss and was already seeing a new girl called Juanita. The relationship led to a marriage that almost immediately became as troubled as his first one. The couple would take regular long, squabbling car trips down to Miami, where Fiorini's Uncle Angelo lived with a new Cuban wife whose family had been driven into exile by the recent upheavals in the homeland. Angelo's in-laws remained loyal to former President Carlos Prío Socarrás, a smooth but ineffectual politician whose main interests in office had been looting the Treasury and breeding prize-winning chickens. He stood no chance when Fulgencio Batista swept him aside in a well-organised military conspiracy.

'They say that I was a terrible President of Cuba,' said Prío.[4] 'That may be true. But I was the best President Cuba ever had.'

Prío fled to Florida and became a big noise in the exile scene while Batista turned himself into the kind of President who talked about democracy but gave American mobsters official positions in his government. Havana got even sleazier, but that only seemed to encourage the huge numbers of American tourists who arrived daily by the boatload. Now the Shanghai held 300 in the balcony and 500 on the floor and sold pornographic books in the foyer. The burlesques had become stripteases, the comedy routines turned into nude tableaux and Superman was having sex on stage. Signs on the walls in Spanish and bad English told patrons to leave the girls alone. *No las molestes.* The tabloids out of New York pretended to be outraged.

'If you're a decent guy from Omaha, showing his best girl the sights of Havana,' said scandal rag *Suppressed,* 'and you make the mistake of entering the Shanghai, you'll curse [the manager] and will want to wring his neck for corrupting the morals of your sweet baby.'[5]

A lot of Cubans felt the same. For them, the Shanghai was an ulcerating lesion that symbolised how their virgin land had been defiled by foreign pimps. Up in the Sierra Maestra of Oriente province, a rebel group under the command of lawyer turned revolutionary Fidel Castro were plotting to overthrow the government and bring about a new dawn for Cuba. Their struggle had been kick-started by a $50,000 donation from Prío Socarrás, but now the former President was hearing disturbing rumours that the rebels had dismissed him as a relic of the past and were pursuing a more radical direction. He asked around for someone reliable to go undercover in Cuba and find out more about Castro's plans. The name Frank Fiorini kept coming up as a trustworthy foreigner who'd been involved in exile circles for the past few years.

The Top Hat nightclub had passed into other hands by now and Fiorini was scraping a living selling real estate in Norfolk. A trip abroad promised action, an escape from a failing second marriage and a chance to see Castro's operation up close. The rebel leader had become a popular hero in America thanks to an interview given to a *New York Times* journalist in the mountains a few months earlier which had surprised a lot of people in Havana who thought Castro was dead. Fiorini took the job.

2

INVENTING A CARIBBEAN PARADISE

SIERRA MAESTRA, FEBRUARY 1957

Ángel Castro y Argiz would have happily lived his whole life without leaving the green hills of north-west Spain, but the Army needed conscripts to protect the empire and his name was on a list. In 1895, the Galician peasant with thick black eyebrows and a permanent frown found himself in Havana obeying orders to put down a nationalist uprising.

The island had become Spanish 400 years earlier when a Genoese explorer called Cristoforo Colombo made landfall at Guantánamo Bay. His three ships of half-mutinous sailors had set off looking for a new route to the East Indies but instead sailed into the previously unknown waters of the Caribbean. Colombo disembarked to be greeted with shy smiles and gifts of fruit by placid native farmers whose only vice was tobacco. The old world met the new. European diseases killed off the natives inside three generations.

Cuba became a Spanish colony powered by imported African slaves who sweated in the sugar cane plantations to make their white owners rich. By the nineteenth century, slavery was fading out and the Cubans felt separate enough as a people to fight Spain for their independence. An 1868 revolt failed, but another effort twenty-seven years later succeeded when the American government backed the nationalist rebels. Ángel Castro y Argiz found himself a cavalryman on the losing side and returned home to Galicia humbled but fascinated by the newly independent island and the opportunity it offered. In 1906, he and his brother immigrated to Cuba as the island celebrated its freedom with a few small-scale civil wars. None of that distracted Castro from the business of making his fortune.

He started off as an employee of the American United Fruit Company then set up his own timber business. The money rolled in and Castro invested it wisely. By the First World War, he was a landowner with a sugar cane plantation and a wife who gave him five children before forcing her husband to sleep in a separate bed. Castro remained fertile as a Mesopotamian flood plain and enlisted a young mistress called Lina Ruz González to give him seven more children, including a son born in 1926 whom they named Fidel Alejandro Castro Ruz.

Twenty-six years later, all but one of Castro's children were well into adulthood and Cuba was a very different place. Batista had clawed his way back into power, the Mafia owned half of Havana and Superman was performing nightly at the Shanghai. Batista called himself the father of the nation and thought he could rule for ever this time.

On 26 July 1953, leftist guerrillas opposed to his dictatorship launched an attack on an Army barracks near Santiago de Cuba in the drooping east of the island. It went badly wrong and left bodies from both sides scattered across the landscape. Batista's men tracked the 26-year-old guerrilla leader to a mountain hideout and dragged him off to a show trial. It was Castro's son, Fidel Alejandro Castro Ruz.

•   •   •

Students at the University of Havana took their politics seriously. They held regular demonstrations and did enough macho gangster posing with guns that Al Capone could have been a varsity mascot. Gunfights between opposing factions were better attended than lectures and the tougher students hired themselves out to Havana's crooks during the holidays as gangland killers.

It was here that political dogma first entered Fidel Castro's life. Leftist classmates took the law student under their collective wing and taught him a whole new way of looking at the world. Class struggle and the alienation of the workers made immediate sense to a young man who, despite his background, had not grown up in luxury. Castro's father had hidden away his illegitimate second family among the servants on the estate then farmed them out to underpaid tutors and tough Jesuit schools. Fidel preferred sports to studying but got good enough marks to enter the University of Havana, where he soon became an enthusiastic partisan of an ideology where the rich were always to blame for something.

Castro joined leftist demonstrations, raged against US foreign policy and carried a pistol to class. The reform-minded Partido Ortodoxo offered a political home for a while but proved too mainstream for a law student who had come to regard himself as a man of action. In 1947, Castro joined a paramilitary group that called itself the Caribbean Legion and was prepping to invade the neighbouring Dominican Republic, whose moon-faced dictator Rafael

Leónidas Trujillo Molina held his country in an iron fist so encom-
passing that even drinking fountains carried signs reading 'Trujillo
Gives Us Water'.[1]

Despite high hopes, the legion never left Cayo Confites port.
American officials, who preferred any regime change to be organised by themselves, pressured the Cuban government into calling
off the invasion and the police raided the legion's ships. Fidel Castro
enhanced his political reputation by diving overboard to escape
arrest, but foreign observers remained unimpressed by his heroics.

He was 'one of the young, "student leaders" in Cuba, who man-
ages to get himself involved in many things that do not concern
him', noted a CIA report.[2]

After the Dominican disaster, Castro married a wealthy philosophy student, honeymooned in the America he distrusted so much
and made some anti-government speeches rabid enough to get his
face in the newspapers. He drifted further to the left and was flirt-
ing with Marxism by the time he graduated in 1950, convinced the
world was only one violent revolution away from proletarian paradise. His wife begged him to drop the politics, but Castro defiantly
set up a law firm that fought capitalism by specialising in clients
too poor to ever pay their bills. Poverty inevitably followed. The
birth of a son looked as if it might nudge him towards a more conventional life, but then Batista's military coup came along in 1952
and reawakened the man of action. Castro formed an underground
revolutionary movement and launched his botched attack on the
Moncada Army barracks.

At the resulting trial, Castro's oratory about equality and the rule
of law made him a hero to fellow opponents of Batista but resulted
in a fifteen-year sentence. His wife left him and took their son. The
government released the rebel activist two years later in a general

amnesty but immediately regretted it when Castro set up a new group called the Movimiento 26 de Julio (M26J) and returned to the fight. In December 1956, he and eighty-one companions sailed in from their training ground in Mexico to bring guerrilla war to Oriente province. Their 61-foot wooden cruiser boat had been paid for by Carlos Prío Socarrás.

An ambush by Batista's troops killed or captured all but twelve of the rebels and news of Castro's death quickly spread. In America, the veteran journalist Herbert Matthews wrote a front-page story for the *New York Times* about the collapse of the rebel movement and dismissed any efforts to overthrow the Cuban government.

'Could anything be madder?' he wrote.[3]

Most Americans agreed. They didn't welcome any disruption to an island regarded as the unofficial fifty-first state of the Union, albeit one whose only purpose was to provide a vacation spot for the other fifty. In 1956, over 350,000 Americans visited Cuba, making up 85 per cent of all foreign tourists. They came by car ferry (departing from Miami, Key West and New Orleans), cruise ship or aeroplane (sixty-five minutes from Miami or a five-hour direct flight from New York) with no passport or visa required. Dollars were accepted alongside the local pesos and a dedicated Tourist Police, wearing armbands that read 'National Police – Speak English', patrolled the streets to keep Yankees out of trouble. Travel brochures marketed the island as a place for uninhibited fun deliciously distant from the usual American moral standards; the sleazier tabloids pointed visitors towards the Shanghai and Superman.

Not long after Matthews's piece appeared, an M26J activist approached the resident *New York Times* correspondent in Havana and offered up a scoop: Castro had survived the ambush. American media outlets had huge symbolic power in Cuba, a country where the locals had long rejected Spanish culture in favour of Hollywood films, dubbed television serials and baseball. The *New York Times* was the ideal place to announce the rebel leader's survival, but the plan immediately ran into trouble when correspondent Ruby Phillips refused to believe the story. The lifelong chain-smoker blew a plume of smoke in the activist's face and demanded proof. Two days later he returned with a rebel who'd been in the mountains with Castro. This time Phillips was convinced but decided, reluctantly, that a story this big needed a more experienced journalist.

She cabled head office in New York suggesting they send down the man who had written the paper's original piece about the rebel movement. On 9 February, Herbert Matthews and his wife flew in from Idlewild to find out if Castro was still alive.

• • •

The foothills of the Sierra Maestra were a foggy jungle of muddy paths and dripping foliage. Herbert Lionel Matthews had seen worse. Thin-haired and stooped, the 57-year-old foreign correspondent had reported from an invaded Ethiopia, a divided Spain and a London shattered by German bombs. He was experienced and respected enough a journalist not to be struggling up the slopes of Pico Turquino at midnight in search of a story, but Matthews had a feeling this Castro tale could turn into something big.

For many younger journalists, Matthews was the father of modern war reporting. He had made his name in Ethiopia when he rode a tank with the invading Italians and watched their machine guns mow down waves of native warriors armed only with swords and spears. His vivid prose pleased the *New York Times* readers back home, but some saw Fascist sympathies in the enthusiasm shown for Italian colonialism by this child of Jewish immigrants. He barely bothered to deny it.

'If you start from the premise that a lot of rascals are having a fight,' he said at the time, 'it is not unnatural to want to see the victory of the rascal you like, and I liked the Italians during that scrimmage more than I did the British or the Abyssinians.'⁴

His attitude changed in 1936 when the Spanish Civil War erupted. An initial enthusiasm for the right-wing Nationalists quickly faded when Nazi Germany intervened on the same side. Matthews switched allegiances and reinvented himself as a man of the left, a transformation helped along by some well-regarded Second World War reporting. In 1949, he joined the *New York Times* editorial board but elected to keep working as a reporter, which caused some controversy among colleagues but gave him the freedom to pick and choose his stories. When word came through that Castro might still be alive, Matthews snapped up the assignment and headed for Cuba.

He and his wife Nancie settled into the elegant Sevilla Biltmore hotel and went snooping around town. An American businessman from the United Fruit Company talked about working with Castro's father; the US embassy claimed rebel soldiers were already deserting the fight; a Cuban contact alleged Batista spent more money on snappy uniforms to keep vain generals happy than on anti-guerrilla training for his troops. Within a week, M26J activists made contact and took Matthews and his wife on a long night-time drive down to the eastern port city of Manzanillo with its filigree architecture and fish-canning factories. Nancie stayed at the home of two schoolteacher sympathisers while guides escorted her husband into the foothills of the Sierra Maestra. It took hours of uphill slogging through dark, damp woods to reach the rebel camp.

Matthews found makeshift huts and rebels in civilian clothes, with the whole scene illuminated by the light of flickering camp fires. The men crowded around him to give their stories: one had been a minor league baseball player, others had worked in America and wanted to practise their English. A young man with long hair wandered past and was introduced as Raúl Castro, younger brother of the rebel leader. It was near dawn when a tall man in a uniform strode into the clearing. Fidel Castro was still alive.

The journalist found Castro a physically impressive figure ('a powerful six-footer, olive-skinned, full-faced, with a straggly beard') who towered over the other rebels as he waved around a Swiss-made telescopic rifle and boasted about picking off government troops from 1,000 yards out.[5] Long weeks spent in the mountains had turned the lawyer into a muscled military man with a bushy beard, green combat fatigues and a cigar permanently bobbing in the corner of his mouth. The two men talked for three hours in Spanish. Castro convinced the American that he hated communism, respected democracy and had no interest in remaining a public figure once Batista had been removed. Matthews snapped a few photographs and asked Castro to sign and date his interview notes as proof of life. Fidel Castro, Sierra Maestra, Febrero 17 de 1957. Blue ink on a loose sheet of lined paper. Then the meeting was over.

Matthews and Nancie reunited in Manzanillo for a flight back to the capital. In Havana, they had time for an interview with the student leaders of another anti-government group, called Directorio Revolucionario Estudiantil, and dinner with the writer Ernest Hemingway, a friend from Spanish Civil War days who lived in a small fishing village just outside the city. As they headed for the airport and New York, Nancie smuggled the notes and film past

Cuban customs police in her girdle. Matthews began writing as the aeroplane climbed off the runway. Castro had urged him to get the story out as quickly as possible.

• • •

Matthews's first piece appeared on the *New York Times* front page for Sunday 24 February 1957 alongside dull local news ('Mediators Seek a New Tug Pact: Pier Men Return'), domestic stories ('Dulles Will See Senate Leaders Today on Israel') and international business involving a Spanish-speaking dictator ('Franco Shuffles Cabinet to Press Spanish Reforms'). Squeezed in between was a photograph of Castro posing with rifle above a reproduction of his signature taken from Matthews's notes. A column of prose to the left launched breathlessly into the facts: 'Fidel Castro, the rebel leader of Cuba's youth, is alive and fighting hard and successfully in the rugged, almost impenetrable fastness of the Sierra Maestra, at the southern tip of the island.'[6]

The rest of the story was buried deeper in the paper, on page 34. Matthews gave himself star billing as an intrepid reporter dodging Army patrols, trekking through jungle and playing undercover spy at official checkpoints. There was a lot of colourful prose, seasoned traveller observations and frequent use of the word 'youth' when referring to the rebels. Readers had to wait until the last paragraphs to find out the uprising's aims.

'Castro has strong ideas of liberty, democracy, social justice, the need to restore the constitution, to hold elections,' wrote Matthews, unaware – like everyone else except the rebel leader's closest companions – that those strong ideas were mostly negative.

A second story the next day analysed the Cuba situation and

predicted Batista would lose the struggle. A third and final piece on Wednesday reported on the anti-government student activists Matthews had met in Havana but downplayed the importance of their activities. Readers were left with the impression that Castro offered the only real opposition to the government. Matthews didn't seem to understand that the Movimiento 26 de Julio had many rivals in the fight against Batista, including the long-established Los Auténticos who remained loyal to former President Prío Socarrás; the remnants of the Partido Ortodoxo still carrying on the fight; the students of Directorio Revolucionario Estudiantil; the religious-minded crusaders of the Agrupación Católica who fought the regime beneath the sign of the cross; and many others. All had different, often competing, ideas and goals.

Despite the omissions and distortions, Matthews's work turned Castro into a minor celebrity, discussed in American radio programmes and dissected in editorials. In Havana, Batista's Minister of Defence claimed the whole interview was fake and challenged Matthews for proof that showed the reporter and rebel leader together. The *New York Times* quickly published the reporter's private photograph of the two men seated on a blanket companionably smoking cigars. A humiliated Batista sent for his generals and ordered an assault on Oriente province to wipe out the rebel forces.

Cuba had barely recovered from the story when another kind of US intervention took place. Three American teenagers from Guantánamo Bay naval base had run away from home to join the rebels. They were all over the newspapers, but they soon found guerrilla warfare was tougher and more dangerous than they expected.

3

TEENAGE REBELS

GUANTÁNAMO BAY NAVAL BASE/SIERRA MAESTRA, SPRING 1957

Guantánamo Bay was forty-five square miles of all-American military presence at the tip of eastern Cuba. It had fallen into the hands of the US Navy back in 1903 for the bargain price of $2,000 a year in gold coins as an expression of thanks for helping expel the Spanish during the independence struggle. By 1957, the base housed 4,000 American Navy personnel and their families in a miniature city of barracks and runways split either side of the bay. The brass supplied baseball fields and air conditioning and Budweiser flown in every Friday to make everything seem just like home, but no one was fooled, especially not the sailors who took a bus out of the base every evening to get stinking drunk in ramshackle brothels with dark-eyed señoritas.

As the adults did their part for Uncle Sam, their kids attended the base high school and sat stewing in boredom while the teachers droned through the syllabus. In February 1957, Chuck Ryan and two teenage friends escaped into the Sierra Maestra to find some adventure. Nineteen-year-old Ryan, the son of a Navy medic and the kind of young man who believed he had the answer for all the world's problems, had forged a friendship with Mike Garvey and Vic Buehlman at Sunday Mass. During the week, they sneaked into brothels alongside the sailors and drank themselves into a stupor while the music played loud and couples slipped away into curtained alcoves. The seventeen-year-old Buehlman was a dandy with a fetish for bow ties and well-shined shoes, while fifteen-year-old Garvey greased up his quiff like Elvis Presley. Both were happy to listen as the older Ryan lectured them about politics and culture and whatever else came to mind as they pounded down beers.

Ryan was obsessed with the recent Hungarian Revolution, when the people had risen against communism in the streets of Budapest and been crushed by Soviet tanks. He thought things would have turned out differently if some Americans had been there to help. It wasn't a big leap from Budapest to Havana and the rebels who'd gone up into the mountains a few months back to overthrow Batista. All three teens sympathised with the cause.

'I didn't like Batista's police standing on the street corners with guns,' said Garvey.[1] 'I didn't like what his cops did to young people. People were disappearing.'

One evening in January, a nearby group of Cubans who'd been eavesdropping on the teens' conversation introduced themselves as members of the M26J movement. After some heavy hints about guns being in short supply up in the Sierra Maestra but plentiful in the US naval base, a boozy Ryan told them he could help with that. When the hangover wore off the next day, it still seemed like a good idea. The trio started to hang around the beer parties on Windmill Beach where off-duty sailors drank too much and drooled over the base's contingent of high-school girls.

'We'd go out there and get drunk,' said Garvey.[2] 'The sailors thought we had access to teenage girls, and they'd say: "She's a fox. Hey buddy, what's her name? Can we buy you a six-pack?" We'd say sure. And guns too.'

By February, the teens were part of a smuggling operation based in a local bakery that trafficked guns out of Guantánamo and up into the mountains hidden in barrels of flour. When Ryan heard that a column of fifty-five Cuban volunteers from the area were setting out to fight with the rebels, he persuaded his friends to tag along. There didn't seem much point in telling their parents first.

• • •

Herbert Matthews had been receiving fan mail at the *New York Times* ever since the appearance of his first article about Castro. Some congratulated him on his bravery while others called him a commie spy who didn't appreciate Batista's position, but the majority of letters came from young American men who wanted to join the rebels. Typical was one from a student at Berkeley asking for advice about bluffing his way through the government lines around Pico Turquino. He and seven friends intended to buy some Army surplus jeeps and spend spring break with Castro's guerrillas.

'We are all honor students at the University of California,' the Berkeley man wrote.[3] 'We have all been student leaders. Some of us have spent a summer with the American Friends Service Committee [a Quaker charity] in Mexico. We consider ourselves liberals. Lastly, we are all adventurous.'

The letters horrified Matthews. During the Spanish Civil War, he'd seen enough idealistic Americans join the International Brigades to fight fascism overseas and end up in shallow graves outside

Madrid. When the letters about Cuba started arriving, he told his correspondents to leave the fighting to the professionals and limit their activities to propagandising for the rebel cause on campus. Then news came in about three American teenagers up in the Sierra Maestra and Matthews felt a pang of guilt that his writing might have encouraged them to risk their lives. It was a relief to find the trio had set out a week before his stories appeared in the newspaper.

Chuck Ryan and his two friends had walked off the base on 17 February and entered a safe house to find other volunteers chattering nervously as they posed for photographs in their new red-and-black M26J armbands. The group spent a week waiting for guides who could take them up into the mountains and had barely started the journey when the *New York Times* interview with Castro appeared. Suddenly, the Americans were being ecstatically slapped on the back by their fellow volunteers, heroes just for being the same nationality as the newspaper which had brought their cause to the attention of the world.

It took more safe houses and some creeping through government lines before they reached rebel headquarters up in foggy Pico Turquino and found that the famed rebels were a tiny group, ragged as shipwrecked sailors in disintegrating uniforms and shoes held together by electrical wire. An excited Castro strode forward, his prayers for a fresh propaganda coup answered by a God he didn't believe in, and pumped the Americans' hands in welcome. He immediately sat them down to write open letters to President Dwight Eisenhower and the American ambassador in Cuba. Ryan picked up a pen and got to work.

'We are trying to bring them some friendship from our country,' he wrote.[4] 'We feel that young men in the United States would help if they had the chance to. We trust that our government will make every effort to help us not hinder us. We are fighting side by side with the Cuban people. I personally will fight Batista until Cuba is free or I have not any life in my body.'

He signed the letter Charles Edward Ryan. Castro insisted on adding some barbed comments about the American government's support for Batista; the rebels were convinced the bombs being dropped on them by air had been supplied by Washington as a reward for the dictator breaking diplomatic relations with the Soviet bloc. The teens posed for more photographs against the jungle foliage with rifles before M26J couriers smuggled the film out to exile publications in the USA, which would run the pictures under headlines like 'Saving the Honor of the American People' (*La Batalla*) and 'Three Brave Men in the Mountains' (*Patria*). From there, American newspapers picked up the story, although they preferred to go with the distraught parents angle rather than anything political. Archbishop Pérez Serantes, a mediator used by the government but trusted by the rebels, was soon clambering around Pico Turquino hoping to persuade the boys to come home.

As the teens started a new life as guerrilla fighters, an older American was on his way to the Sierra Maestra. He arrived with one mission but left with another, and his life would never be the same.

• • •

Frank Fiorini figured he'd shown enough bravery in the war to earn a little cowardice in his private life and left Norfolk without telling his wife. It was easier to sneak out of the apartment early one morning in March 1957 while Juanita was asleep than sit down and explain the marriage was over. He slung a bag of clothes into the trunk of his car and set off for Miami.

Down south, Prío Socarrás briefed him on his assignment in Cuba: locate Fidel Castro, discover the strength of his movement and find out if the rebels still backed Prío for President once Batista had been overthrown. Fiorini bought a $26 car ferry ticket to Havana and arranged to meet some anti-government activists on arrival. Weeks later, he was waiting at a farm outside a tiny town called Santo Domingo on the banks of the Río Yara, halfway up a mountain in Oriente province. He sat around the farmhouse while locals assured him that Castro would arrive '*mañana, mañana*' but shrugged when asked for a more specific date. The days rolled on dull and humid without any sign of the rebel leader.

A week had passed before a gang of men in olive green fatigues escorted a tall, bearded figure onto the farm. Fiorini introduced himself as a representative of Prío come from Miami to check out the struggle and mentally noted how unimpressed Castro seemed by this information. Sleep-deprived and irritable, the rebel leader outlined the situation in the mountains: government troops now ringed Pico Turquino and aircraft bombed the slopes most days; the underground M26J organisation in nearby towns like Manzanillo and Santiago was enduring harsh repression and supporters had learned to fear the olive patrol cars of the local police cruising to a halt outside their homes; a private paramilitary unit called Los Tigres had been created by government lackey Rolando Masferrer, a heavyset man with a passing resemblance to a Hispanic Ernest Hemingway, and was leaving the corpses of anyone suspected of rebel sympathies by the sides of the road. Despite all the setbacks, Castro remained certain the revolution would prevail.

In other circumstances this list of reversals and disaster would have sounded as cheerful as a funeral dirge, but Castro's unwavering faith in victory was contagious. It helped that he and Fiorini had history, of a sort. The American had heard Castro speak during a 1955 fundraising tour of Miami and been so inspired by the talk of direct action and guerrilla warfare that he'd offered his services in any forthcoming revolution.

'He even subscribed to a Miami newspaper,' said his wife Juanita, 'and began putting together a Castro scrapbook.'⁵

Fiorini's offer got no response and he transferred his allegiance to Prío, but in the small farmhouse overrun by guerrillas smoking cigars and checking their rifles, he felt his loyalties shifting again. Castro sensed this and turned on the charisma with a long talk about politics in which he claimed to hate communism, despise Batista and love his country in a strictly democratic fashion. The same speech had already convinced a veteran reporter from the *New York Times* and Fiorini was no less susceptible. If he wanted to help, Castro suggested, the rebels were short on guns and ammunition. The M26J underground in Miami knew nothing about weapons and was smuggling in a mishmash of rifles and shotguns in various calibres that had a tendency to overheat after the first few shots.

Here was the new life Fiorini had been looking for, served up on a platter. All loyalty to Prío melted away like spring snow and he was reborn as a gunrunner for Castro's version of the revolution.

'You see, Prío is a politician,' Fiorini told friends later.⁶ 'What he does is four-fifths talk, one-fifth action. Fidel and his guys were all action.'

After a final handshake, rebel guides escorted Fiorini out of Santo Domingo. A sceptical Castro found it hard to believe an emissary of his rival would switch sides so easily and didn't expect to ever see the American again. He already had enough problems with the trio of teenagers from Guantánamo Bay.

• • •

Life in the Sierra Maestra was difficult for American teenagers used to hot showers and regular meals. They clambered around the mountains in sweat-stained uniforms and straw hats, with heavy ammunition belts chafing their shoulders and nothing but tomato juice and crackers to eat. Ryan and Buehlman grew straggling beards while Garvey carved the name of a girlfriend into the wooden butt of his rifle. The three were given posts in the rearguard, where the Argentinean medic Ernesto 'Che' Guevara, one of Castro's original companions, could barely hide his disdain for the soft Yankees. Castro jovially counselled Buehlman to stay away from Che.

'*Muy malo, muy malo*,' said the rebel leader.[7] '*Comunista!*' ('Very bad, very bad. A communist!')

Their days were spent climbing higher into the mountains to avoid government patrols, but on one occasion they joined the hunt for a supposed Batista spy creeping around the perimeter and crashed through the long grass until the man was cornered. Other guerrillas led him away to be executed as the teens tried not to look horrified. The irregular diet soon gave Garvey and Buehlman stomach disorders and Che sneered as they fell behind to relieve themselves in the jungle.

Ryan stayed healthy and was looking forward to his first firefight, but the only action seemed to be in Havana, where the Directorio Revolucionario Estudiantil student group tried to assassinate Batista with a suicidal attack up the sweeping steps of his presidential palace that left blood stains on the stone for days afterwards. A few students made it into Batista's office before getting shot down, unaware that he was chairing a conference on the floor above. The last thing they saw was an empty desk with a book about the assassination of Abraham Lincoln, the Cuban leader's favourite reading, splayed face down on the shiny wood. A simultaneous DRE attack overran the studio at Radio Reloj, a popular station broadcasting a mix of entertainment and speaking clock announcements, two blocks from the University of Havana. The gunmen managed to tell listeners that Batista was dead before a volume overload shut down the broadcast and they spent their last minutes shouting impotently into a dead mic before the police opened fire.

Publicly, Castro celebrated Directorio Revolucionario Estudiantil's martyrdom, but privately he complained that it had shifted support from M26J to other movements in the cities. News that the remnants of the DRE were considering establishing their own guerrilla group in the centrally located Escambray mountains also worried him. An M26J activist in New York contacted Herbert Matthews to arrange more publicity but was directed by the busy newsman to the CBS studios on Lexington Avenue instead. There he found a 38-year-old television reporter called Robert Taber who'd already spent a few fruitless weeks in Cuba failing to get access to the Sierra Maestra and was well aware what a scoop it would be to get footage of the rebel camp. A deal was arranged.

A few days later, Taber disembarked at Havana airport with a cameraman, both claiming to be Presbyterian missionaries making a documentary about church schools. The trusting customs officials let them through, unaware that CBS was about to turn Castro into a fully fledged media star.

4

THIS IS THE HARD CORE

SIERRA MAESTRA, SUMMER 1957

Robert Bruce Taber was a respected CBS television journalist with a big secret. During his teenage years in Chicago, he had fallen in with a bad crowd, turned to crime and been arrested for armed robbery. He got a long sentence from an unsympathetic judge and would have spent his best years in the Illinois prison system if the outbreak of the Second World War hadn't created a manpower shortage for the Merchant Marine. The authorities agreed to commute the term of any prisoner who volunteered for the duration. Taber joined up, served his country and firmly buried his criminal past after the war when he became a journalist. Only a taste for brutally short haircuts and a certain wariness around the eyes gave any hint that he hadn't sprung from the same bourgeois privilege as his contemporaries.

The opening shots of what would become *Rebels of the Sierra Maestra: The Story of Cuba's Jungle Fighters* were filmed soon after Taber and beefy CBS cameraman Wendell Hoffman arrived sweating at the guerrilla camp on Pico Turquino.[1] Hoffman got footage of rebels sitting around campfires, swinging in hammocks and cleaning their rifles, as well as some close-ups of Taber's blistered feet after the hard climb up Pico Turquino. Back in a New York editing suite, Taber would add flamenco music to liven up the grainy black-and-white footage, and overdub a narration in which his disembodied voice provided authoritative sound bites about the toughness of the rebels ('This is the hard core') and talked about being pursued by government forces through the jungle on the way to the camp. Their guide, Celia Sánchez Manduley, a whip-thin thirty-something doctor's daughter who worked undercover for the movement in nearby Manzanillo, didn't remember any pursuit, but massaging facts into something closer to a spy thriller was standard practice for journalists like Taber. His audience seemed to expect it.

The CBS pair spent two weeks soaking up life in the rebel camp. They bathed in a river, ate tinned sardines and milk, and flirted awkwardly with Sánchez and the handful of Cuban women among the guerrillas. After a few days, Taber persuaded Chuck Ryan, Vic Buehlman and Mike Garvey to give a joint interview. The teens perched on a log and smoked cigars as the sweat dripped through their patchy beards and the journalist crouched at their feet holding up a microphone. Ryan spoke about fighting for freedom and peace and democracy, and how the three had done their duty by joining the guerrillas. He hoped his parents weren't taking the experience too badly.

'They should be proud of their sons,' said Ryan.[2] 'I only hope that they can try to realise what their boys are doing ... Their boys are fighting for an ideal ... for their country and the world.'

He choked up a little towards the end and Fidel Castro unexpectedly appeared to sit beside the teens and announce he was proud of them. He sounded like a fatherly schoolmaster praising some gifted students.

What would become the climax of the film was recorded a little later at the peak of Pico Turquino, where a bronze head of national martyr José Martí stared out across Cuba. The writer had become a national hero after dying in a cavalry charge sixty years earlier during the battle for independence against the Spanish, and Castro milked the symbolism for all it was worth as he positioned himself below the statue and asked America to support his struggle against Batista. He didn't mention the activities of other opposition groups. Taber got the perfect final shots for *Rebels of the Sierra Maestra* when a group of rebels gathered at the peak to sing the Cuban national anthem.

With the film in the can, the CBS team set off on the long journey back to a Lexington Avenue editing suite where the footage would be cut, rearranged, trimmed down and rearranged some more. As they packed up their equipment, Castro approached Taber and asked him to take the American teens back to Guantánamo Bay. The rebels didn't need them any more.

• • •

Buehlman and Garvey were sick and getting sicker. The older boy could barely walk and fellow guerrillas had to carry his gun and equipment. Although a propaganda boon, he and Garvey were a drag on the military effectiveness of a group which depended on speed and agility to avoid government patrols. Neither boy complained much when Castro told them to accompany Taber and Hoffman off the mountain. Che Guevara carried Buehlman's pack down through the trees but could find no sympathy for the sick and emotionally exhausted Yankee.

'What he has', Guevara wrote sourly in his diary, 'is a mixture of cowardice and homesickness.'[3]

The two teens arrived back at Guantánamo on 9 May 1957 to hugs from their weeping parents and stern debriefings from uniformed men with crew cuts. They flew out the same week to another military base, another high school and another life. Only Chuck Ryan insisted on staying, still determined to experience his first firefight.

In New York, Taber edited *Rebels of the Sierra Maestra* quickly and the documentary was a sensation when it aired on 19 May in a prime-time slot. Hoffman's shooting style drew on the cinematic language of spy films and Hollywood adventure romps, while the narration owed a lot to Taber's idealised self-image as a tough foreign correspondent. The end result was romanticised, fairly artificial and a smash hit that spread Castro's message far wider than any previous report. The rebel leader became such a star of popular culture that his beard and cigar and forage cap would become instantly recognisable shorthand for anti-government rebellion in the work of newspaper cartoonists for years to come.

A little over a week after the programme went out, Castro's forces launched an attack on a military garrison in the coastal town of El Uvero. Chuck Ryan was there with a rifle in his hands, blasting away at barely glimpsed defenders in the building's windows. After three hours of intense fighting, the garrison surrendered; seven rebels and fourteen soldiers had died. Ryan was promoted to lieutenant for his bravery, but the adrenaline high soon faded and was replaced by a sickened feeling as he looked at the dying men in puddles of blood.

The victory showed the rebels could match their propaganda successes with military ones and donations flowed into overseas M26J offices in Mexico City, Miami and New York. Streams of journalists headed for Cuba hoping to interview Castro while a fresh wave of young Americans with time on their hands and a lust for adventure began thinking about joining the rebels of the Sierra Maestra. One of the first was a Jewish New Yorker and leftist activist called Daniel M. Friedenberg who travelled through Oriente province on holiday and claimed to have helped the M26J cause along the way. His low-key description of events left it to readers of Manhattan's *Dissent* magazine to fill in the narrative gaps.

'[I] sojourned in Cuba [in 1957] while Batista was at the apogee of power', he wrote, 'and became an avowed partisan of Fidel Castro. Traveling through the island, [I] became involved in a guerrilla uprising at Manzanillo and served as a contact with Fidelista forces at Santiago de Cuba. Partly through [my] aid, a young Canadian idealist imprisoned after fighting in the Sierra Maestra mountains succeeded in escaping the firing squad.'[4]

The Canadian was never identified and no one could remember a guerrilla uprising in Manzanillo that year. Friedenberg's friends expressed polite scepticism that a property manager and expert on medieval Jewish seals had spent his holiday as a Cuban guerrilla. Similar doubts were expressed about rumours suggesting a 'boy from Iowa' had joined the rebels around this time.[5]

At least one young American undeniably made it into Oriente province at this time: Donald Soldini was a street rat from Staten Island who found a cause in Castro's rebellion.

• • •

Havana was cockfights and cabarets, baseball and bars, the ocean detonating against the Malecón seaside boulevard and the beaches white as sugar. Tourists were everywhere, ogling the naked statue of Anita Ekberg at the Cuban Arts Center, betting on the horses at Oriental Park and touring the elaborate mausoleums at Colón Cemetery. The dancing girls jiggled, the bartenders flashed white smiles and American celebrities like singer Nat King Cole and actor George Raft could be seen pressing the flesh at nightclubs.

Donald Soldini walked around feeling stunned by the spectacle. He was a stocky eighteen-year-old blue-collar boy from Staten Island who wanted something more out of life than his father's world of manual labour. He dropped out of school at sixteen to work the shipyards but maintained a passion for adventure he blamed on his Italian and Irish roots. His mother was an Irish Republican Army supporter who liked to curse the British; his father had been involved with the radical trade unionists of the Industrial Workers of the World, known to all as the 'Wobblies', and had a relative deported back to the old country for agitation.

After a year in the shipyards, Soldini quit to hitchhike around the country. He got as far down south as Mexico, hung out with beatniks and their poetry and bongos and marijuana, and had his eyes opened by a universe very different to the working-class life of Staten Island. Back home and restless in October 1956, he saw a possible escape in a war boiling over halfway round the world.

'I was always the internationalist,' he said.[6] 'When Israel invaded Egypt, I was highly indignant and I went to the Syrian embassy and enlisted in their Army! I was looking for a cause, a good fight. If it was 1938, I would have been in the International Brigades.'

The Suez crisis was over in nine days and the Syrians never called on Soldini's services. A few months later, he was at the Staten Island

Ferry terminal chatting with a US Army recruitment sergeant who jokingly remarked that Soldini should have joined the Cuban rebels when he was in Mexico. Soldini had never heard of Castro and headed for the library to read up on the situation. The Cuban Revolution seemed to have everything he was looking for: rebellion, adventure, a dash of political radicalism. He was working as a pipe fitter with Bethlehem Steel when *Rebels of the Sierra Maestra* broadcast on CBS and crystallised his support for the rebel cause. The next month, he quit his job and used some of his $150-worth of savings to visit Havana.

Nothing he'd seen in Mexico could compare to the light and colour of the Cuban capital. Soldini was still wide-eyed when he left Havana and watched the rest of the island unfold before him: the turquoise water of Varadero Beach, the breezy cane fields, shady San Juan Hill and the men on horseback trotting through the countryside. In Santiago, he rented a hotel room and began searching for M26J activists. He got lucky and found some who were impressed by an American who had made such a long trip to join their struggle. Always a gun nut, Soldini could lie convincingly about having been in the Army ('I told them I had military experience, which was bullshit') and appealed for a place in the mountains.[7] They agreed but told him to wait.

Everything was going well until 30 June, when Soldini spontaneously joined a demonstration being held in town to protest the death of Frank País, a 22-year-old Sunday school teacher who had headed the M26J operation in Santiago until Batista's police shot him in the head. Mourning Santiago workers took to the city streets in their thousands and the police washed them all over the tarmac with fire hoses. A furious Soldini confronted the newly appointed American ambassador, E. T. Smith, who was in town on a poorly timed fact-finding tour of Oriente province, and gave him a fierce tirade about Washington's role in Batista's repression. The next day, a Cuban Army unit knocked on Soldini's hotel room door and told him to pack his suitcase. He was being deported.

Back in New York, Soldini joined up with the local M26J chapter, based at the El Prado restaurant. His colleagues were initially suspicious of the gringo, with his stories about Santiago and riots, but Soldini proved his loyalty by getting in the newspapers for flying the red-and-black M26J flag from the Statue of Liberty viewing deck. Later, he smuggled pro-Castro leaflets into the stands at Yankee Stadium during a game against the Milwaukee Braves and hurled them out into the wind. Bemused baseball players watched the leaflets settle across the field.

On days off from work at the shipyard, Soldini trained out in northern New Jersey with young Cuban émigrés who thought Castro would be marching on Havana any day now. They were itching to join the revolution and become heroes.

• • •

Chuck Ryan made it through three more months of scrappy low-intensity warfare in the mountains before contracting a stomach disorder of his own that made it impossible to continue. In October 1957, he left the base for a long journey back to Guantánamo Bay and America. Che Guevara helped him down the mountain but, with his usual lack of sympathy, preferred to believe Ryan was too scared to fight any more. The Argentinean Marxist took to his diary afterwards to record his views on the contribution of the three teenagers to the rebel cause.

'The boys were not ideologically prepared for a revolution,' he wrote.[8] 'All they did was give vent to their spirit of adventure while in our company. We felt a sort of affection for them, but we were glad to see them go.'

Ryan stayed loyal to the cause after his return. Following medical treatment, he visited New York on a fundraising tour wearing his rebel uniform with the sweat and blood dry-cleaned out. Herbert Matthews of the *New York Times* provided some free publicity and crowds paid to see Ryan give a good speech about the revolution's need for guns and money. He received regular standing ovations but soon became disillusioned after getting caught between two squabbling M26J factions who cared more about sabotaging each other than aiding the struggle. When a shipload of weapons was seized before it left the docks and FBI agents started tapping his hotel telephone, Ryan dropped out of the exile scene and got on with his life. He joined the US Army to become a career military man.

His friends Garvey and Buehlman were already studying at American high schools, where they kept quiet about what happened in Cuba. Their parents were glad to have the boys back but couldn't hide the damage that had been done to their naval careers.

'We never talked about it at home after I came back from the mountains,' said Buehlman.[9] 'My dad had a hard time with it.'

The Guantánamo Bay teens hadn't lasted long and Soldini had failed to make it into the mountains, but more volunteers were on their way. A soldier of fortune and jailbird from Ohio called William Alexander Morgan was heading into the Escambray mountains to join up with a new Cuban group that hated Batista but was equally suspicious about Castro. It was the first step on a long path that would lead him to the firing squad.

5

IN THE BELLY OF A SHARK

ESCAMBRAY MOUNTAINS, WINTER 1957–EARLY 1958

Late one night in December 1957, a Cuban medical student called Roger Rodríguez and his pudgy, boisterous, chain-smoking American friend were walking through Havana city centre discussing the rebel movement. The pair had originally met in Florida and bonded over drinks and a shared dislike of the Batista regime. Rodríguez boasted connections with the underground Directorio Revolucionario Estudiantil group and his new acquaintance Bill Morgan seemed to be involved in running guns to Castro's rebels, although the American kept close-mouthed about the extent of his activities. Together they'd drunk the bars of Miami dry and agreed to meet up again if Morgan ever visited Cuba.

Not long before Christmas, Rodríguez got a telephone call that his American friend was in town. The medical student was expecting a night of rum and laughter but found himself involved in something more serious when the 29-year-old Morgan confessed he'd slipped through Havana customs disguised as a tourist and was on a quest for revenge against the Cuban government.

'I was wearing a two hundred-fifty-dollar suit, white-on-white shirt, and thirty-seven-dollar shoes,' remembered Morgan months later.[1] 'I looked like a real fat-cat tourist – but I only had four dollars in my pocket.'

Morgan explained that a gunrunning American friend had been arrested by the Cuban police, beaten to death and thrown into the ocean. His remains were probably in the belly of a tiger shark cruising around the Gulf of Mexico. Now Morgan had come to join the rebellion against Batista and had already made contact with an M26J activist who promised to smuggle him into the Sierra Maestra. When he mentioned the activist's name, Rodríguez looked horrified. The man was a well-known police informer and was undoubtedly setting up Morgan for an arrest.

Rodríguez offered to put his friend in touch with another group of rebels operating closer to Havana. After the DRE's failed attack on the presidential palace, the group had turned to open warfare and established its own guerrilla group in the Escambray mountains. The medical student agreed to make an introduction but warned that new members would only be accepted if they had the stamina and skills to help the revolutionary struggle. Morgan didn't speak Spanish, smoked heavily and was badly out of shape, but he muttered something about fighting in the Pacific so Rodríguez called his contacts under the impression that his friend was a Second World War combat veteran. The truth was more complicated.

William Alexander Morgan came from a middle-class Catholic home in Toledo, Ohio. His father was an important man at the local utility company and his mother a housewife so religiously devout the neighbours dubbed her 'Miss Cathedral'. They tried to give Morgan a conventional upbringing in a Midwest town, but he was a misfit from the start. Smart and creative, his attention was

44

easily diverted away from schoolwork into the kind of comic books and adventure stories that over-stimulated an already vivid imagination. His parents once had to talk him down off the roof as he prepared to try out a homemade parachute.

No one was too surprised when Morgan ran away from home at fifteen years old. He joined a circus, worked a ranch, signed up with the Merchant Marine and sold tickets in a movie theatre. Along the way, he picked up some juvenile delinquent friends and accompanied them on night-time raids through the city streets to steal cars and rumble with other gangs. He got into fights serious enough to earn him a mess of knife scars across the chest. When the police stopped Morgan one evening, they found a gun tucked into his belt. There was talk of prison, but eventually the authorities settled for shipping him back to Toledo, where his parents lovingly but firmly suggested joining the Army as soon as he turned eighteen.

In August 1946, Morgan was a private in the 35th Infantry Division with orders to join the occupation forces in Japan. His parents hoped their son would acquire some discipline in the forces, but Morgan turned their world upside down before even leaving the country by impulsively marrying a woman sitting next to him on the train. The couple spent a two-day honeymoon in a California hotel before Morgan boarded his troopship.

The barracks near Kyoto were bitterly cold that winter, but Morgan stayed warm in a nearby nightclub with a Japanese-German hostess called Setsuko Takeda. She taught him the language and he ensured she didn't starve to death in the post-war wreckage of Imperial Japan. By the autumn, Takeda was pregnant and Morgan deserted to be with her but got arrested en route by the military police. In custody, he overpowered his guard, stole a gun and was waiting for Takeda at a house in Kyoto when she arrived, crying, accompanied by a phalanx of American soldiers. Morgan thought about shooting it out but handed over the gun instead. A court martial gave him five years to be served in a federal prison back home.

'I guess I got what was coming to me,' said Morgan.[2]

Back home, his mother prayed for him, his father shook his head ruefully and Morgan's wife demanded a divorce. He was nineteen years old.

• • •

After two years in a Michigan prison, Bill Morgan managed to convince the chaplain he was a reformed character and was granted an early release. Back in Toledo, his mother arranged a caretaking job at her Catholic church, but Morgan preferred to hang around with local thugs who worked for the thickset Cleveland godfather Dominick Bartone, a gangster with a criminal record stretching back to the days of Al Capone. When Morgan could take no more of respectable middle-class Toledo life, his new friends hooked him up with a job down in Florida on the fringes of Meyer Lansky's organisation.

Lansky was an important man in both Miami and Havana. Born Meier Suchowlański in Tsarist Belarus, he adopted a more American-sounding name at nine years old when his family migrated to the slums of New York. He was smart, tough, poor and amoral. Few were surprised when Lansky made a career in the world of organised crime. By the Prohibition years, Lansky was running a gang with his friend Benjamin 'Bugsy' Siegel which distributed bootleg alcohol, hijacked trucks and hired out hitmen. Siegel provided the muscle, but Lansky had the diplomatic skills to forge links with the Mafia and obtain access to a wider world of crime.

Lansky was smart enough to see the real money was in gambling. By the 1930s, he was running operations in Florida and New Orleans and in the next decade bought his way into Batista's Cuba with a suitcase of cash. In December 1946, he organised a conference at Havana's Hotel Nacional for his Mafia friends like Santo Trafficante and the Mannarino brothers to divide up the island's gambling and hotel businesses among themselves, a process which was accelerated by Batista's return six years later. Small and dapper with a permanent smirk, Lansky became an official in the Cuban government with responsibility for the gambling industry.

Morgan thought the Florida job would involve Lansky's gambling empire and was disappointed to discover the work was something embarrassingly legal in one of the mob boss's fruit vending front companies. Looking for more excitement, he quit to join a travelling carnival as its fire-eater and knife-thrower. His rugged looks caught the eye of the carnival snake charmer, a petite but emotional woman with black hair and green eyes called Ellen May Bethel. They got married and moved back to Morgan's home town of Toledo, where Bethel gave birth to two children and demanded her husband get a proper job. He took a course in electronics at a local college and got work at Mus-Ad Inc., a company in Dayton producing muzak for department stores. It looked enough like a regular nine-to-five job to please his wife, but Morgan never bothered to mention that the owners were a pair of small-time crooks who worked for Bartone. He played the law-abiding citizen for a few years until he could take no more and volunteered to help his bosses smuggle guns from Bartone to the rebels in Cuba.

Morgan assumed the Cleveland crime boss was gunrunning on behalf of Meyer Lansky, who had publicly declared his faith in the Batista regime but was rumoured to be hedging his bets in case the rebels won. Others thought Bartone was working with a different set of gangsters looking to shake up the situation in Havana and snatch a piece of the gambling action for themselves. Whatever the truth, Morgan proved to have a talent for gunrunning and the business of arranging routes, loading up lorries in dark warehouses and handing over the merchandise to fanatical-looking Cubans down south. It gave Morgan a taste of the adventure he'd been missing for the past few years and the more time he spent away from his family, the less he missed them. He was in Miami at the end of the year when a long talk with a group of Cuban exiles about their cause convinced him to visit the Sierra Maestra and join the rebels. There was no talk of any dead American gunrunner friends back then and a letter he produced later discussing his motives focused purely on political idealism.

'I belive [sic] that the most important thing for free men to do is to protect the freedom of others,' he wrote.[3] 'I cannot say I have always been a good citizen but ... over the years we as Americans have found that dictators, and communist [sic] are bad people with whom to do business yet here is a dictator who ... would fall from power tomorrow if it were not for the American aid.'

Morgan took the ferry from Miami to Havana and within a few days of meeting with Rodríguez was being driven through the countryside outside Havana towards the Escambray mountains. At police roadblocks he sat silent in the car while Rodríguez explained his American friend was a rich businessman come to check his plantations. The police always allowed them through. The last part of the journey was an uphill slog on foot through vines and banana palms up the mountain. Rebel guerrillas looked up from their food as the pink-faced foreigner with thinning blond hair and sharp blue eyes stumbled into camp gasping for breath. Commander Eloy Gutiérrez Menoyo could see his newest recruit was not in good shape.

• • •

The Segundo Frente Nacional del Escambray (Second National Front of the Escambray) was only a month old. Most of its members were middle-class twenty-somethings who had been students, lawyers or doctors before they abandoned their families to trek into the mountains. They had a handful of old rifles that barely shot straight and lived on a diet of plantains, beans and rice. On a good day, they might catch and roast a hutia, a bent-backed forest rodent that looked like a cat mated with a rat. Life was hard but they were dedicated enough to their cause not to care.

Eloy Gutiérrez Menoyo, known to all as Menoyo, led the Second Front. He had been born in Spain two years before civil war ripped the country apart and still spoke with the soft lisp of the old continent. His socialist father and elder brothers served with the besieged Republican forces but, after three years of hard fighting, found themselves on the losing side and discovered that Spain under the victorious General Francisco Franco was an unpleasant place for those who leaned to the left. Menoyo and his family moved to Havana for a new life in a country that still had some kind of democracy, but when Batista took power in 1952, it seemed like a repeat of the Spanish tragedy they thought had been left behind.

Menoyo's older brother Carlos joined the Directorio Revolucionario Estudiantil and died in the attack on the presidential palace along with the group's leaders. The scrambled remnants of the DRE went underground and begged Menoyo to take his brother's place. The thin-faced, long-necked 22-year-old in glasses had little interest in politics but agreed with the intention of getting vengeance on the men who had killed Carlos. A brief campaign of urban terrorism failed to achieve much so Menoyo took to the Escambray mountains in November 1957 with a small group of supporters. The founding members of this new guerrilla army signed an idealistic document: 'Each of us swears the following: First: Not to argue with orders but to comply with them. Second: To be honorable and loyal to my country and my comrades. Third: To maintain and guard all the war secrets of the II Front. Fourth: To never abandon a weapon under any circumstance, which are considered the property of the country and must not be deserted. Fifth: To denounce traitors and deserters.'[4]

The Segundo Frente Nacional del Escambray called itself a left-wing movement but hated communism. Menoyo had grown up listening to his father talk bitterly about how the Soviet-backed Spanish communists had undermined the Republic with political witch-hunts and the infiltration of rival groups. Menoyo's political seismograph started twitching the moment Bill Morgan walked into the camp sweating through the armpits of his suit.

The American was too exhausted to notice Menoyo's suspicion. By the time he was in a state to answer questions, Rodríguez was already on his way back to Havana and an English-speaker in the Second Front had to be recruited to translate Menoyo's questions. Morgan lied about fighting in the Second World War and offered up non-existent wartime experience as proof he could help the rebels.

'I can probably help train up some of your men in basic skills,' he said.[5] 'How to use a weapon, execute an ambush, approach a target, fight hand-to-hand combat, set up a rescue mission for a downed man. That sort of thing.'

Sensing resistance, Morgan asked for a knife and whipped it dead centre into a tree. An impressed Menoyo thought he was watching the fruit of a Special Forces programme rather than a few months working in a carnival. He allowed Morgan to stay with the Second Front but spent the first weeks running the new arrival ragged with endless chores, pushing him to give up and return to Havana. Morgan proved too tough to discourage. He dropped weight, learned Spanish and told everyone who would listen in the camp about wanting payback for his dead gunrunner friend, now described as an old Army buddy called Jack Turner. Roger Rodríguez wasn't around to hear how the story had changed into the friend dying when his car was forced off the dock and into Havana Harbour. Morgan was still worried the Second Front would kick him out if they discovered he was only there for adventure.

The American's knowledge of Cuba didn't stretch much further than having watched slick comedian Ricky Ricardo in the sitcom *I Love Lucy*, so Menoyo educated him about the corruption in the cities, the Mafia contacts behind every hotel and the sugar barons who ruled their plantations like medieval lords. Every day the rich got richer and the poor stayed poor, and it was all Batista's fault. Morgan saw the poverty for himself when the rebels took route marches through the Escambray region and passed families of six or more sleeping on the mud floors of thatched huts, living off coffee cut with black beans and a few eggs from a scrawny hen. The hardship disturbed him but, as a patriotic American, he was equally bothered by rumours circulating through the camp that rival rebel leader Fidel Castro was a secret communist.

'He's a son of a bitch,' said Menoyo confidently.[6] 'But he's no communist.'

Morgan believed him. As his Spanish improved, he taught the other guerrillas about weapons discipline, small unit tactics and old Army tricks like breathing through a reed underwater. The Second Front rebels grew to like his cheerfulness and enthusiastic swearing in two languages. Soon he was an accepted member in their world of wood-smoke campfires, hammocks slung between trees and nervy patrols zigzagging to avoid Batista troops because they couldn't spare the ammunition for a firefight. A shipment of weapons was due in February, but until then the Segundo Frente Nacional del Escambray had to pick its battles carefully.

As Morgan trained, other American volunteers were making their way to Cuba hoping to fight. In January, a sixteen-year-old boy from Omaha called Roger George Young somehow made it into the Sierra Maestra to join Castro's troops but left the next month. Few others got that far. A harassed staffer at the US consul in Santiago told a journalist that most of his work involved repatriating fellow countrymen who had been arrested trying to penetrate the Army checkpoints ringing the area.

'The Americans', reported the journalist, 'fall into three categories: (1) ex-World War II paratroopers who are intrigued with the idea of fighting; (2) professional adventurers who feel they will be awarded large sums of money when Castro takes over Cuba; (3) idealistic teenagers who want to fight dictatorship and establish democracy.'[7]

Few who made it into Oriente province managed to connect with the M26J activists they imagined were waiting to gratefully welcome greenhorn Yankees into their ranks. Those who did would often be turned away by paranoid rebels who suspected every

American was really a CIA agent reporting to the Cuban government. Some of Menoyo's men had similar suspicions about Morgan, but their mistrust faded away when the new recruit proved himself a good comrade up in the mountains, even though his first taste of battle would almost end in disaster.

In Havana, Batista had his own problems after Washington suspended arms sales that March under popular pressure, but he made up the shortfall by dealing with everyone from British government officials to Trinidadian arms dealer Hubert Julian, who had a monocle and upper-crust affectations and had once fought for Ethiopia's Haile Selassie against Fascist Italy. The Cuban government used its new equipment to pour troops into the Sierra Maestra and attack the rebels. As the battle raged, most Americans remained firmly on the side of the guerrillas until a mass kidnapping of US military personnel by Raúl Castro in the summer threatened to reverse the nation's sympathies and destroy the rebels' heroic image.

PART II

VICTORY OR DEATH

6

TIGERS OF THE JUNGLE

ESCAMBRAY MOUNTAINS/SIERRA MAESTRA, SPRING–SUMMER 1958

The sunlight slanted down through the trees onto six government soldiers ambling up the path in single file. They carried their rifles in the loose, casual manner of men who never expected to use them and were blind to a unit of Segundo Frente Nacional del Escambray guerrillas tensely observing them from further up the mountain. The rebels had strict instructions from Eloy Menoyo not to alert the government to the Second Front's presence and were waiting silently for the soldiers to pass without a confrontation.

The six men were almost directly below the rebel positions when Bill Morgan pushed a rifle butt into his shoulder and opened fire. The leading soldier fell, then a chaotic firefight broke out that killed another and sent the survivors scrambling away through the trees.

'Damn it, why did you fucking shoot?' shouted Menoyo.[1] 'I specifically said no shooting!'

'I thought you said to shoot to kill the first soldier,' replied a confused Morgan.

The American's grasp of Spanish was so poor he'd misunderstood the orders. Now he could barely comprehend the barrage of curses that flowed from Menoyo or the talk about government airstrikes and the need to move camp. His guerrilla career could have ended there, back in February 1958, but Menoyo couldn't afford to lose any men and grudgingly allowed Morgan to remain with the Second Front. The American looked shame-faced as everyone gathered their belongings and prepared to move higher into the mountains. Things looked bad, but within months Morgan would be a comandante confidently hunting down government patrols and on equal terms with Menoyo at the Second Front's permanent base on a coffee plantation. He was a fast learner.

In the aftermath of the firefight, Morgan earned back some of his comrades' respect when a large government patrol sweeping the area approached on a collision course. He organised an ambush in a small valley that caught the enemy in a fierce crossfire and killed thirty in a three-hour battle, with no casualties for the Second Front. It was a major victory for men who had only received their first arms shipment from Florida a week ago and barely knew how to use the mix of Italian carbines and Thompson sub-machine guns. The guns came with useful tents, lamps and backpacks, although no one knew what to do with the swastika-decorated Nazi helmet left over from the last war.

The Second Front marched higher into the Escambray mountains and set up a new headquarters near a peasant farm outside Guanayara. New volunteers arrived and swelled the numbers to a few hundred men. Morgan made a reputation as leader of a ten-man unit that tracked government troops like jungle cats, quiet and ferocious and leaving only corpses behind. Batista's men responded by burning down villages suspected of helping the rebels, raping local women and torturing the men.

In breaks from patrols, Morgan got himself a girlfriend, a Cuban peasant called Olga Rodríguez, who tucked her long black hair under a cap and acted as medic to the wounded. He teased her, tried out his improving Spanish and impressed her romantic heart with his love for Cuba. When Cuban Air Force aeroplanes droned overhead, they would lie in a ditch staring into each other's eyes and pray the bombs fell on someone else. Morgan wrote letters to his mother in Toledo regretting the pain he had caused his wife and children but confessing he felt happy and mature and fulfilled in Cuba. He wrote a letter to Herbert Matthews of the *New York Times*, titled 'Why Am I Here?', about fighting for freedom and democracy. Matthews liked it enough to run a story on 3 April about the Segundo Frente Nacional del Escambray and the 'tough, uneducated young American' who seemed, judging by his letter, to be running things.[2]

The story was on its way to print when Morgan heard that another American had joined the Second Front. He went to see the new arrival and was surprised to discover the brown-haired six-footer was a fellow Ohio native.

• • •

Richard A. Witzler had joined the Second Front in late March but didn't seem to be enjoying it much. The 31-year-old from Maumee, Ohio, had served in the Army after the war as a private and become a hairdresser on return to civilian life. Crew cuts and Brylcreem failed to satisfy Witzler's craving for a meaningful existence and, inspired by all the stories in the newspapers, he flew to Havana and joined the Escambray rebels under the impression they were Castro's soldiers.

One day he came off duty to find Bill Morgan looking for him. They chatted and Morgan gave him the usual lies about a friend being killed by Batista's forces and having fought in Korea. Witzler believed him but was left with the strong impression that his fellow American was more interested in financial reward than politics. He didn't have too long to think about the implications of that before Batista sent in a 1,000-strong column that forced the Second Front to flee up the mountain or risk annihilation. At a river crossing called Charco Azul, the guerrillas walked into a heavily armed Batista unit dug in on the opposite bank. The Second Front lost five men in a nine-hour firefight and took many more injured. By mid-afternoon, Morgan was arguing for a brute force attack to punch through enemy lines, while Menoyo preferred to slip away into the trees. Things escalated into a shouting match and then the angry American was jumping into the water and wading across with his Sten gun chattering. Government soldiers on the far bank were caught by surprise and fell back as more rebels followed Morgan into the river. The enemy line broke and the guerrillas clambered out on the other side to flee into the jungle, safe but exhausted.

'We were so tired after nine hours of fighting', said one, 'that we wanted to die.'[3]

Witzler was more exhausted than the rest. On 2 June, government troops found him walking along a remote road having deserted, although he claimed to have got lost on the way back to camp. The Cuban government held Witzler for three weeks in Santa Clara prison then deported him to Miami for a lengthy interview with the FBI. Most of it was taken up with the former rebel failing to convince bureau agents he had visited Cuba to collect information for newspaper articles and accidentally joined the Second Front. The only thing the FBI seemed to believe was Witzler's claim that Bill Morgan expected a substantial financial reward when the revolution was successful and that all the talk of fighting for democracy was a lie to cover his self-interest.

As Witzler slipped back into civilian life, another American arrived in the Escambray mountains. At the end of June 1958, Morgan was introduced to a man who called himself Johnny Spirito and claimed to be a war veteran of Sicilian ancestry. Neither his name nor military career was real.

The black-haired 34-year-old's real name was Juan Mepleece Espiritu and he had been born in San Pedro, Los Angeles, to a Mexican labourer father and an American mother of Mexican descent. His unusual middle name came from his mother's side of the family, although its origin and meaning were lost to time. During the 1920s, the family moved back and forth enough times between San Pedro and the Mexican city of Guaymas that Espiritu's four brothers and sisters were born both north and south of the border. Espiritu was proud of his Mexican heritage, but no one ever spelled his name correctly, so it made sense to call himself Johnny Spirito and explain away the thick accent and occasionally erratic English as the fruit of Sicilian ancestry. Italians usually got better treatment than Mexicans.

In 1943, the draft board registered him under his real name as a married nineteen-year-old doing menial restaurant jobs ('civilian occupation: Bus Boy') in New Mexico.[4] In March the next year, he joined the Army but was back in civilian life four months later without completing basic training after contracting a nasty case of non-gonococcal urethritis. After the war, Espiritu drifted through the poorly paid world of steamy kitchens, angry chefs and dishwasher jobs before ending up at a hotel in Havana. The life of a revolutionary appealed enough that Espiritu lied his way into the Second Front by pretending to be a war veteran. At least he spoke fluent Spanish, which was more than Bill Morgan could claim.

By the time Espiritu joined, the Segundo Frente Nacional del Escambray was 1,000 strong and had settled at a new base in a coffee plantation high up in the mountains. Menoyo started a radio station to broadcast propaganda about Second Front victories, built a factory to make uniforms and shoes and opened up a school for local peasant children. Morgan was promoted to comandante and was given control of a column called the 'Tigers of the Jungle', which ambushed any government soldiers brave enough to enter rebel territory. The American sewed a Stars and Stripes badge on his uniform sleeve and soon the men of the Second Front began treating him as joint leader along with Menoyo. Bill Morgan had come a long way in four months.

The Second Front's victories in the Escambray mountains had humbled Batista's soldiers. That summer, government troops turned their attention east to Oriente province hoping for an easier time against the rebels of Fidel Castro.

● ● ●

Batista and his cronies in Havana thought Operation Verano was a work of genius. Over 12,000 men had trekked into the mountains under the command of General Eulogio Cantillo with orders to surround the Sierra Maestra and tighten the noose until the rebels had nowhere to go except the plains north of Santiago. Out in the open, Castro's 300-strong guerrilla army would be exterminated like vermin under the farmer's gun.

Cantillo knew better than to criticise his superiors but was well aware that at least half his men were poorly trained, demoralised peasants who'd only enlisted for a regular salary and a hot meal. They remained ambivalent at best towards the government and had no intention of being heroes when the bullets started flying. The general requested more disciplined reinforcements but was told none could be spared from guarding the sugar mills owned by Batista's friends. Ordered to launch the operation with inadequate forces and believing Castro's army to be much larger than in reality, Cantillo quietly abandoned the encirclement plan in favour of a more cautious march into rebel territory.

At the end of June, two of his battalions set out from the Estrada Palma Sugar Mill but within four miles had walked into an ambush at the hands of guerrillas under the command of Che Guevara. Cantillo's armoured cars blew up in a minefield and the battalions fled back to the sugar mill as Guevara's men picked off stragglers. Cantillo lost eighty-six men and the Argentinean only three.

One of Guevara's officers was an American called Herman Frederick Marks who'd arrived in the mountains earlier in the year claiming to be an ex-Army veteran of the Korean War. The dark, moustached 36-year-old from Milwaukee knew his way around a sub-machine gun and had served as instructor before joining Guevara in the field. His new comrades found him brave, dictatorial and worryingly sadistic. Those characteristics would have made more sense if they'd known Marks was a jailbird with a long, grim criminal record.

'He was a real stinker,' said the warden of Wisconsin State Prison.[5]

The bad seed of four brothers born to a Jewish single mother, Marks had been arrested thirty-two times since his teens for everything from armed robbery to drunk driving. Most recently he'd done four years in Wisconsin for the rape of an underage girl ('How are you supposed to know a pick-up is jailbait?' he asked reporters, surprised to be found guilty), where his lack of repentance had the warden shaking his head.[6] The closest Marks had got to respectable employment had been a brief tour in the Merchant Marine during the war and a briefer period working as a hospital orderly afterwards. He had no military training and had once been arrested for dodging the draft, only escaping punishment when the judge agreed that his extensive criminal record made him an unsuitable soldier. Somewhere along the line, Marks had acquired the richly ironic tattoo of a snake and dagger entwined with a scroll that read 'Death Before Dishonor'. His mother loved Herman, but no one else did.

Working a shrimp boat in the Florida Keys brought him into contact with Cuban exiles and Marks liked their cause enough to smuggle himself into the Sierra Maestra. He grew a thick black beard, falsely claimed to be looking for vengeance over a friend killed by Batista's police and by March 1958 was an instructor in Las Minas del Frío. That summer, he joined Guevara's column to repel the government incursion. Guevara thought his new comrade brave in battle but too fond of executing unarmed prisoners when the shooting was over.

The victory at the Estrada Palma Sugar Mill was followed in July by a successful counter-attack against Cantillo's attempts to land troops near the mouth of the La Plata River that left the area littered with spent cartridges and the glassy-eyed dead. Things only started moving in the government's favour later that month. Cantillo still had a battalion in the mountains, stranded after the failure of a previous attack, and ordered it to stage a noisy but enticingly slow retreat in the hope Castro would be too eager for another victory to notice he was being lured into a trap.

The rebel leader took the bait. As Castro blundered forward, another potential disaster was unfolding further north in Oriente province, where his brother Raúl's kidnapping of US citizens threatened to reverse American sympathies and change everything.

7

PRIVATEERS AND PATRIOTS

NEW YORK/SIERRA CRISTAL/MIAMI, SUMMER–LATE SUMMER 1958

The well-spoken man sipping clam chowder in a New York fish restaurant claimed to have 300 soldiers of fortune ready to rescue the hostages. It was all legal, or so he claimed, under Article One, Section Eight, Paragraph Eleven of the Constitution of the United States of America. He just needed the politicians in Washington to agree.

Lyle H. Munson didn't look the type to lead a boatload of adventurers on a rescue mission. He was a forty-year-old publisher with a bow tie and sleek greying hair who had surprised everyone a few days back by petitioning Congress to grant him a 'letter of marque'. Reporters raided their encyclopaedias and discovered that letters of marque had last been issued during the golden age of sail to men who spliced mainbraces and fired cannon along the Spanish Main.

'The undersigned', wrote Munson in his petition, 'is prepared to demonstrate financial and moral responsibility to lease, equip, and staff a seaworthy man of war to liberate these pirate-held American citizens at personal and private expense and risk.'[1]

The strange story got even stranger when a United Press International (UPI) stringer in Manhattan tracked down Munson enjoying a bowl of chowder at a Third Avenue restaurant in July 1958 and got an interview. Munson complained about a man from Sydney who called him at 06:00 every day with the offer of fifty strapping Australian volunteers and wouldn't take no for an answer. Another telephone enthusiast closer to home thought the rescue mission would go smoother if Munson bought the decommissioned aircraft carrier *Enterprise* (wartime crew: 2,900 men) to show the kidnappers he meant business. The publisher didn't think he could afford it.

Journalists were happy to portray Munson as a clown loading himself into a circus cannon after first packing away the safety net, but no one doubted that the issue which had inspired his freebooting fantasies was serious. On 26 June, Raúl Castro's rebel column had kidnapped ten Americans and two Canadians from their jobs at the Moa Bay Mining Company. The next day, the rebels stopped a busload of Marines and Navy enlisted men on leave from Guantánamo Bay and marched them off into the Sierra Cristal on the northern coast of Oriente province.

The territory in Sierra Cristal had been carved out by Raúl that summer with the help of a guerrilla column that included Donald Soldini, who'd returned to Santiago the previous November to help out local activists. After seven months of ferrying messages, hiding guns and dodging the police, Soldini joined the guerrillas in the mountains. Raúl Castro gave him the rank of corporal and a lever-action .44-40 rifle left over from the Spanish–American War. At first the American was happy to be in a 'hardline nationalist unit' and looked forward to fighting the Batista forces, but things quickly soured when Soldini realised his fellow guerrillas only engaged the enemy when necessary and spent most of their time executing anyone who refused to accept Raúl's authority, usually tying them up first to ensure a sitting target.

'I was very uncomfortable with this,' he said.[2] 'That wasn't my idea of fighting.'

Soldini made his feelings known and a row broke out. Raúl leaned even further to the left than his brother and his communist sympathies didn't leave much room for debates about battlefield morality with an insubordinate American. After a shouting match, he threatened to hang Soldini as a traitor to the revolution. Other rebels calmed him down, but Soldini found it wise to leave the Sierra Cristal, using the excuse of needing medical treatment for a light neck wound picked up during a skirmish. Raúl only let him go after the American promised to fly in some guns, but a deal Soldini set up with IRA supporters and Algerian guerrillas at a bar on New York's Third Avenue fell through when the FBI moved in and he had to take off running, only escaping by sliding across the hoods of cars gridlocked in traffic.

By the summer, Raúl commanded a force over 1,000 strong and had carved out new roads by tractor, set up a factory to produce munitions and organised a makeshift airbase. When the government reacted with a programme of airstrikes that threatened to undo his empire-building, Raúl launched a wave of kidnappings under the name Operación Antiaerea (Operation Anti-Aircraft) that he hoped would halt the attacks. The plan worked but backfired in every other respect. Brother Fidel was furious and even the usually sympathetic New York Times described the kidnappings as 'juvenile escapades' and called for the hostages to be released.[3] Other newspapers preferred a more active solution and gave some publicity to an Indianapolis man who telegrammed President Eisenhower demanding 'our citizens back alive and well or Castro dead'.[4] The stories about Lyle H. Munson became less mocking by the day.

Eisenhower ignored the sabre-rattling and pressed for a peaceful solution. The American consul met Raúl Castro in a jungle clearing and listened while the baby-faced Cuban with a pencil moustache and black hair tied back in a bun harangued him about Batista's air raids. A CIA man posing as the vice-consul met less excitable rebel representatives elsewhere and opened negotiations over a bottle of Bacardi.

The story brought foreign correspondents to Guantánamo Bay like ants to a picnic. They sneaked into the mountains and quickly outperformed American military intelligence by locating the rebel headquarters and interviewing the hostages, all of whom claimed to be well treated but sick of the daily diet of boiled plantains. Raúl's men had spent the first days of captivity touring them around a carefully curated selection of local civilians maimed in air raids. Fragments of bomb casings with English-language markings were handed around: 'Bomb, Fire, External, 750lbs. Made by Bowser, Inc. Property of the US Air Force'.[5] No reporter could find a hostage willing to criticise his captors. The worst that 23-year-old Sergeant Gerald George Holthaus had to say was that the rebels clearly needed better training in the use of firearms.

A Navy airman called Thomas Mosness, from Iowa, became so close to his captors that he joined up and patrolled the camp with a .45 automatic pistol on his belt. None of his fellow Americans seemed to mind.

'We are all rebel sympathisers anyway,' said one hostage.[6]

• • •

On 30 June, the rebels kidnapped six more Americans. Four worked for a United Fruit Company sugar mill and two were employed at an American-owned nickel facility. Raúl Castro now had fifty prisoners and the American ambassador in Havana began talking about military action.

Back in New York, Lyle H. Munson's buccaneering pretensions started to look a lot more realistic, at least until Congress turned down his application for a letter of marque. Reporters doing a reaction piece found the publisher surprisingly calm and soon realised Munson had always been more interested in publicity than action. The mail-order publisher sold the kind of polemical books that rarely appeared in respectable bookshops and appealed to a market share most other publishers ignored: fanatical right-wingers who couldn't see a bed without checking underneath it for Reds. Munson was the man to see for a copy of rightist classics like *The Enemy at His Back* or *The Naked Communist*.

American anti-communism had a history almost as long as the ideology it opposed. In November 1917, the Bolsheviks seized power in Russia and triggered a civil war that spread mass murder from Helsinki to Vladivostok. Siberian Bolsheviks hammered nails into the shoulders of captured enemy officers, with one nail for each epaulette star, while the secret police in Moscow perfected the art of skinning prisoners alive. Their opponents weren't much better, but that didn't stop foreign powers, including an American expeditionary force, intervening in an effort to replace the Bolsheviks with a friendlier government. The intervention failed and the defeated foreigners returned home to tell stories of the horrors they'd witnessed. Soon the terms 'Bolshevik' and 'bloodthirsty savage' were synonymous for many Americans.

During the interwar years, anti-communism established itself as a respectable ideology shared by everyone from conservatives to moderate leftists, with Catholics strongly represented on all sides. A temporary alliance with the Soviets against the horrors of the Third Reich silenced many voices until a Moscow-run spy ring stole America's nuclear secrets and the world plunged into the Cold War. Anti-communism became fiercer than ever as Eastern Europe fell under Soviet control, China created its own version of Marxism–Leninism and parts of south-east Asia wobbled dangerously close to Moscow's orbit. The crusade only began to flag in the 1950s when Senator Eugene McCarthy's hunt for Soviet sympathisers in Hollywood, along with the outspoken extremism of rightist groups like the newly formed John Birch Society, alienated a growing number of influential liberals. Attitudes began slowly shifting, but anti-communism remained the default political position of most Americans, even if its more extreme enthusiasts like Munson were frowned on in polite society.

Journalists half-expected the publisher to give them a speech about Raúl Castro being an agent of the Red Menace, but not even Munson believed something so extreme. He described the kidnappers as patriots who'd made a serious mistake by involving ordinary Americans, then launched into a heartfelt rant about the government's inability to protect its own citizens. Munson had never intended to set sail for Cuba but hoped the letter of marque affair would encourage Washington to do something.

'Clearly there is public concern here,' Munson said.[7] 'I may not be commissioned, but if my effort serves to focus public concern on this subject, it may serve to awaken some Administration interest.'

With a growing feeling that the joke was on them, newspaper editors dropped the story and redirected their attention back to the US government negotiations with Raúl Castro. Nobody was aware that Raúl really was a communist who'd belonged to the Partido Socialista Popular youth branch, toured the Soviet bloc and become close friends with KGB agent Nikolai Leonov. He was Lyle H. Munson's worst nightmare and the publisher didn't even know it.

Raúl's demands for the release of the hostages were simple: he wanted America to officially recognise the rebel-controlled Territorio Libre de Cuba (Free Territory of Cuba) and stop supporting Batista. Washington's response was simpler. It refused the first demand and pointed out that America had already stopped supplying weapons to the Cuban government. An agreement was quickly reached for the rebels to release their hostages in small groups, with Raúl dragging out the process as long as possible to hold off government airstrikes while he reorganised his headquarters.

It was the middle of July when the first American helicopters descended, thundering onto a makeshift landing ground in the mountains. On site was the American consul in Santiago, Park Wollam, supervising the hostage evacuation. As he paced around the rebel camp, Wollam encountered a dark-haired and smooth-faced young American wearing a rebel uniform and carrying a rifle. Charles Bartlett Jr had deserted his ship a week earlier to fight for Castro.

• • •

Bartlett was a twenty-year-old machinist's mate on the USS *Diamond Head* who'd been sympathetic to the rebels even before his ship pulled into Guantánamo Bay for a routine stop during the early days of the hostage crisis. That sympathy turned into something deeper when the sailors got leave for 4 July and headed out beyond the base to the bars and brothels of the nearby town.

'I was on liberty in the city of Guantánamo when I saw some soldiers, for apparently no reason at all, beat up some civilians,' he said.[8] 'I couldn't stomach it and thought it an injustice. So I decided to join the rebels.'

He made contact with M26J activists in the area, asked to be taken up into the mountains, and a few days later was on guard duty in the Sierra Maestra with a rifle in his hands. Park Wollam tried to persuade the deserter to return to Guantánamo Bay but had no more luck than Bartlett's parents, who were asking journalists to pass on messages begging their son to come back to the Navy and 'someday to all of us'.[9] The sailor refused. He had been given the same guided tour of crippled civilians as the hostages and was convinced American weapons were being used by Batista against his own people. It was hard also to ignore the prospect of a military prison if he surrendered.

By the end of July, the last American hostages had been released and their return home sent the needle of domestic public opinion flicking back towards support for the rebels. It helped when *Life* magazine ran a photospread of 27-year-old Raúl Castro looking appealingly fresh-faced in uniform with his long hair spilling out from under a Stetson. In the next panel his girlfriend and political adviser Vilma Espin managed to look both stern and sultry as she rested a sub-machine gun on her hip. The kidnappers looked more like a gang of youthful Robin Hoods who'd taken a detour through the beatnik district than ruthless revolutionaries prepared to kill for their cause.

One of the last Americans to leave was Thomas Mosness. He gave up his pistol and morphed back into a skinny 22-year-old airman in glasses worried about what his wife would say when he got home. Raúl Castro suggested Mosness return to the rebel ranks later.

'I couldn't do that,' said a shocked Mosness.[10] 'That would be deserting.'

Americans might have forgiven the guerrillas, but their law enforcement officials still held a grudge. As revenge for the kidnappings, customs agents swooped on M26J's most dependable gunrunning pipeline after Frank Fiorini was betrayed by someone he trusted.

•　•　•

Fiorini's operation was raided after one of his associates got himself a girlfriend who disapproved of the smuggling life and convinced her new love to talk with the authorities. US customs officers kicked in Fiorini's door to find a pile of prima facie evidence in the form of pistols, rifles and fake travel documents for names like Frank Campbell and Fred Attila. They quickly rounded up the other members of the team, which seemed to consist mostly of friends from the Norfolk area like Marine veteran Jay Allen Kilgore and a 22-year-old former Marine sergeant called Richard 'Rex' Sanderlin who was dedicated to the rebel cause but had confused ideas about Cuban politics.

'[Sanderlin] stated that he was helping to overthrow the communism of Batista and would continue to do so no matter what happened to him,' noted an informant.[11]

Fiorini only escaped arrest because he was already behind bars in El Morro castle at the mouth of Havana harbour. The turncoat who betrayed the operation to the US authorities had stopped at the Cuban consulate first and let them know a Cadillac loaded with weapons was on its way to their country. He got $500 for his information and Fiorini got beaten senseless by the Havana police when he was found behind the wheel. It was the dramatic end of a long, successful arms smuggling operation that had begun a year earlier when Fiorini bought his first shipment of weapons from the International Armament Corporation, a business located conveniently close to his hometown of Norfolk that was happy to sell military surplus to hunters, collectors and men from Miami with murkier motives.

His initial smuggling run used a light aircraft, hired under the pretext of a pleasure flight around the Caribbean, which descended out of the clouds over the Sierra Maestra towards a thin landing strip cut by rebels into the side of a mountain. Watching from below was a chunky Hungarian émigré called Andre Szentgyorgyi, better known as *Look* magazine photojournalist Andrew St George, who had trekked into the mountains to interview Castro then hung around to watch the first air delivery into rebel territory. Unlike fellow journalists Matthews or Taber, the Hungarian had no tolerance for leftism. As a twenty-year-old, he had barely escaped his homeland ahead of the post-war Soviet takeover and his first question to Castro had been whether M26J tolerated communist elements. The rebel leader gave his standard answer.

'This is absolutely false,' said Castro.[12] 'Every American newsman who has come here at great personal peril – Herbert Matthews of the *New York Times*, two CBS reporters and yourself – has said this is false. Our Cuban support comes from all classes of society. The middle class is strongly united in its support of our movement. We even have many wealthy sympathisers.'

St George accepted the reply, being no more immune to the romanticism of a guerrilla band in the mountains than anyone else, but noted sceptically how Castro's personal telescopic rifle was handed to anyone being photographed to give the impression of a well-equipped army. The rebels shrugged off the deception and told him Frank Fiorini's arms delivery would provide plenty of rifles for everyone. Soon he was standing among them watching the aeroplane widen from a dot to a silhouette as the engine grew louder and the wings wobbled in the turbulence. The plane circled the landing strip, dropped suddenly and bounced off the packed soil before rolling to a halt. Rebel soldiers rushed forward cheering.

'Frank Fiorini had done the impossible,' wrote St George later.[13] 'He had landed a supply plane at the jungle hideout of Fidel Castro's rebel army, the passenger seats buried under piles of Garand rifles and Mendoza machine guns, belted ammo and cans of three-in-one oil, other goods the guerrillas needed more than gold and, as Frank clambered out onto the wing, khaki shirt sweat-stained but the Italian-American grin flashing white-on-white, Fidel Castro shouted in exploding admiration "*Eso si es un yanqui bárbaro!*" ("This is one helluva Yankee!").'

Fiorini fished out a plastic envelope containing receipts and went through the cost of the guns with Castro. The rebel leader seemed surprised that Fiorini had skimmed so little off the top for himself.

The guerrillas were unfamiliar with the ex-Army M1 Garand rifles and Fiorini remained in the mountains for a few days to train them. He met Che Guevara, who seemed cool and distant, but became friendly with Pedro Díaz Lanz, a tense-looking airline pilot in his early thirties with a bouffant hairstyle, who had recently come over to the rebel cause. When it came time to leave, Fiorini announced that he couldn't fly in again: the aircraft had damaged a propeller on landing and the hiring company would be asking awkward questions. His new idea was to hide weapons inside the door panels of second-hand cars, take the ferry to Havana and park the vehicles in town to be retrieved by M26J activists.

Fiorini's car operation worked smoothly until one of his team turned informer and US customs made its raid. Other gunrunners stepped in to fill the gap, ranging from émigré Cubans glowing with idealism to Mafia wise guys motivated only by money. Samuel and Gabriel Mannarino, the Mafia bosses of New Kensington in Pennsylvania, supplied what they claimed was over a million dollars' worth of guns to the rebels in the hope of wrestling control of Havana's casinos from Meyer Lansky. Their point men Norman 'Roughhouse' Rothman and Joseph 'Sad Joe' Raymond Merola buzzed between Miami and Havana, pleading loyalty to Batista even as they arranged guns for his enemies.

The guns were more necessary than ever that August as the rebels pursued Cantillo's battalion as far as Las Mercedes, thinking they were on the verge of a great victory only for the trap to snap shut. Castro lost seventy men in three days and the death toll would have been much higher if Cantillo had been a less cautious commander. Fidel turned politician and asked for a ceasefire.

'It is necessary to open a dialogue so that we can put an end to the conflict,' he wrote to the general.[14]

Cantillo believed him and persuaded a suspicious Batista to send a negotiator from Havana to discuss surrender terms with the rebel representative. On 8 August, the rebel failed to appear and government troops discovered Castro had used the previous week to evacuate his men in small groups through their lines. The rebels reformed in the mountains and Operation Verano collapsed as Cantillo's demoralised soldiers returned to their barracks convinced their own leaders were either moronic incompetents or secret rebel sympathisers.

Castro capitalised on the problems of his enemies by expanding rebel operations across the island, even snaking a tentacle as far east as Pinar del Río province, where the guerrillas included an American with a South Carolina drawl and an easy familiarity with weapons. Unlike Marks or Espiritu, this volunteer wasn't lying about his military experience. Neill Macaulay had served in Korea and come to Cuba to put his skills at the service of the revolution.

8

TRAINING UP THE FIRING SQUAD

NEW YORK/PINAR DEL RÍO, WINTER 1958

The exile headquarters in Manhattan was an old brownstone building on Amsterdam Avenue with a black-and-red banner draped under the first-floor windows. Neill Macaulay paused outside to read the banner's Spanish text – '26th of July Movement, Militants and Sympathisers' – then entered to find the place full of clean-cut young Cubans in shirtsleeves and ties, their faces shining with devotion to the cause.

Macaulay was a tall, dark 23-year-old Army veteran from South Carolina who liked guns but was liberal enough to oppose racial segregation. Soldiering had been in the family since a grandfather fought on the losing side of the Civil War, and Macaulay got his history degree from the Citadel, a prominent military college, before joining the infantry in Korea. By the time he got overseas, the shooting had stopped and Macaulay spent fifteen months managing a PX store that kept soldiers supplied with all the comforts of home. During his off-duty hours, he read about the Cuban Revolution in *Time* magazine, wrote to his girl Nancy back home and daydreamed about exploring lost cities in Peru when he left the service.

He got back in the summer of 1958 to find Nancy thinking about marriage, and a rejection letter from the university that would have sponsored his Peruvian trip. Macaulay briefly considered law school but couldn't face three years of dusty textbooks. Instead, he came up with a plan that might have seemed overly optimistic to anyone lacking his tough-minded self-confidence: he would marry Nancy, visit the Sierra Maestra alone and offer his military skills to the rebel cause.

'She would return to her parents and to school at the University of Michigan,' he rationalised, 'while I would go to Cuba and rise to power with the revolutionary forces. I assumed that the war would be over by the end of the semester, and by then I should have acquired a home and a livelihood.'[1]

Macaulay picked his way through the bustle of the M26J's New York office, with its cardboard boxes overflowing with leaflets and a huge portrait of Castro leaning against a wall, to introduce himself to the movement leaders. One assured him that Raúl Castro's recent kidnapping of American soldiers was a misunderstood gesture; another handed over a pamphlet that claimed Batista was really a far-left extremist. When Macaulay announced he was here to fight in Cuba, the movement treasurer regretfully told him no foreigners were being accepted but suggested having a talk with Donald Soldini, who had just swaggered in through the front door with his fedora at a rakish angle.

Since his return from the Sierra Maestra, Soldini had been active in the New York exile scene raising money, running guns and getting himself into local newspapers with various publicity stunts. He was currently trying to convince the M26J activists to allow him to put together a column of American volunteers and, over ten-cent beers in a local bar, offered Macaulay a place in the unit. The Korea veteran preferred to go solo but agreed to buy Soldini a bus ticket to Miami in exchange for an introduction to his contacts in the Havana underground. They drank another beer to seal the deal among the cigarette smoke and barroom chatter. After a few more glasses, Soldini confided that he didn't really care about politics but was just 'a guy who likes a good fire fight'.[2] Another beer and he was loudly denouncing Raúl Castro.

'All Raúl did is sit around on his ass and send patrols out after the *chivatos*,' he said.[3] '*Chivatos* are people who are for Batista; they give information to the army. Raúl's patrols would take these guys from their houses and bring them to Raúl's camp and Raúl would string 'em up.'

Macaulay was tough enough not to be put off by the talk of exe-cutions, or by having to rescue Soldini from a fight on the subway when his new friend spent too long leering at a Puerto Rican girl and her date threw a punch. The South Carolina native was just happy to have a path into the mountains.

By September, he was in Havana sleeping on the kitchen floor of a wheelchair-bound waiter who did underground work for the guerrillas. After three days of questioning, the waiter trusted him enough to give the address of a safe house outside the city. There, a peasant on horseback guided him through sugar cane fields and along forest trails to the Sierra del Rosario of Pinar del Río province, in the far west of the island. Macaulay walked into a clearing to find twenty young men swatting mosquitoes as they played cards and cleaned their weapons. Music drifted softly from a transistor radio. Most of the local rebels were urban working-class Cubans drawn from the ranks of bus drivers, gardeners and hospital orderlies, with about a quarter being Afro-Cuban. Their camp was little more than a few hammocks slung between saplings.

A black-bearded 21-year-old who called himself Captain Claudio welcomed Macaulay into the group, assumed he was a Korean War veteran and gave him an M1 carbine. The son of a foreman at a local sugar mill, Claudio had been in the mountains for five months after killing some Batista soldiers riding a jeep and taking their weapons. Now he was temporary commander of the group but told Macaulay that a senior commander from M26J would soon return to officially make the men, semi-independent until now, into an arm of the Sierra Maestra forces. Fidel Castro's territory was expanding.

• • •

The Cubans loved their cigars, which probably explained why cancer was the second largest cause of death on the island. Rebels and government ministers alike welcomed a good box of Romeo y Julieta *puros* and it was widely suspected that the fighting had stayed out of Pinar del Río, the country's westernmost province and main tobacco producer, to ensure nothing disrupted both sides' mutual enjoyment of a relaxing smoke. The first major unrest had only occurred in the spring of 1958 when a disorganised group of rebel sympathisers unified under a 27-year-old American called Howard Kenneth Davis. The Army veteran had served in Korea as an Airborne Ranger and came back with a pilot's licence and a deep cynicism towards the men who gave the orders.

'They would tell us to take a hill,' Davis said.[4] 'We would take the hill. Then they would tell us to withdraw from the hill. Then they would tell us to take the hill again. Each time we took the hill, men would die.'

He settled in Miami to work as an airline pilot and married a Cuban woman with connections to the guerrilla underground. After months of fundraising and gunrunning, Davis smuggled himself into Pinar del Río province, where a small group of rebels was looking for anyone with military experience to help them fight the government. He tried to organise a guerrilla column, but his barely trained men were so short of supplies and ammunition that Batista's forces scattered them almost immediately. Davis escaped back to Havana at the end of April and, posing as a tourist, boarded a plane back to America determined to limit his future rebel support to fundraising.

The next serious rebel activity in Pinar del Río didn't occur until late that summer. By then, Fidel and brother Raúl had recovered from the setback at Las Mercedes to conquer most of Oriente province with a combined force of 2,000 men, leaving the besieged capital of Santiago as the only major town in government hands. In August, Castro sent a 150-strong column under Che Guevara marching west across the island to the central province of Las Villas, with a second column of sixty men under Camilo Cienfuegos making its own way into the province, and a third of fifty men under Dermidio Escalona leapfrogging past them both into Pinar del Río at the western end of the island.

All three columns needed to cross Camagüey province with its flat agricultural land and unsympathetic locals. An attempt to bribe the Army commander in the area was rebuffed and the rebels had to push their way through heavy air and ground attacks. Herman Marks fought alongside Guevara for a while, showing his Cuban comrades how to detonate bombs with a car battery, a skill picked up from robbing armoured cars, until a foot wound sent him back to base in October. Guevara was glad to get rid of the American, whose relish for killing prisoners had started to disturb the other guerrillas. Eventually, Guevara and Cienfuegos reached Las Villas to find the Second Front had at least 1,000 men up in the Escambray mountains who were unwilling to subordinate themselves to the new arrivals. Bill Morgan fell out with Guevara immediately and loudly complained that the Argentinean was a communist who stole weapons intended for other groups; Guevara retorted that the American was a fake guerrilla whose men did nothing except exploit local peasants. After some tense confrontations, an operational pact united both groups in a drive to capture the provincial capital of Santa Clara, which would cut Cuba in half.

Escalona's column pushed past the infighting to enter Pinar del Río and unite the province's existing small guerrilla bands into a miniature M26J army. The process was only partly completed when Escalona was badly injured and evacuated to a sympathetic doctor in Havana; he was still there when Neill Macaulay began his career as a guerrilla with Captain Claudio's unit. The American's early days were spent on long marches that tore the heels off his boots and sent him crashing into exhausted sleep at every rest stop. A few attempts at ideological debate didn't get far, as his comrades were dedicated to overthrowing the government but had no real idea what should replace it.

'The level of political discourse in the guerrilla camp was considerably below that in the movement office in New York,' remembered Macaulay.[5] 'Claudio's band was composed of working people who simply wanted what Fidel said he wanted: land for the landless, jobs for the unemployed, no more corruption or police brutality.'

After a few weeks, Dermidio Escalona returned from Havana with a fresh column of rebels to take control. He was a hard, unlikeable man in his late twenties who combined fanatical loyalty to

Castro with a martinet severity that ignored all complaints about lack of food and sleep. When two high-school boys got sick of the new regime and deserted, they were hunted down and hanged. Revolutionary discipline had arrived in Pinar del Río.

•　•　•

As 1958 moved into its winter months, other Americans could be found in the rebel ranks. John 'Jack' Nordeen was a long-nosed, curly haired twenty-year-old from Green Bay in Wisconsin with a withered leg from childhood polio and a blank expression that hid a lot of emotional pain. Two years earlier he had been cleaning a hunting rifle at his family's expansive house in an upscale part of town when the gun went off. The bullet killed his sixteen-year-old brother.

The death seemed to be an accident, but the Nordeen family inspired malicious gossip among the locals when they closed ranks and refused to help the police investigation. Officers discovered the boys had been arguing earlier in the day and noted Nordeen was 'a highly strung boy who was easily upset' but couldn't find any evidence of foul play.[6] Eventually, a judge handed down two years' probation for negligent homicide. Trying to outrun the rumours, the family moved to Chicago, where Nordeen got a job with an advertising agency and began attending local Cuban refugee meetings after work.

All the talk of revolution in the mountains lit a fire within him and by September 1958, Nordeen was in Havana looking to join the rebels, despite not being able to speak Spanish. He took a bus down to the east of the island and avoided any difficult questions at roadblocks by sitting next to a Batista sergeant eager to learn English.

They spent the rest of the journey talking, with his new friend waving away any soldiers who climbed on board to check papers. In Bayamo, Nordeen slipped away into the Sierra Maestra and was accepted into Castro's guerrillas.

'He helped by writing news articles for Castro and helped them with the mule trains which were carrying food etc.,' noted an FBI report.[7] 'Nordeen stated he did not do any fighting as he has a bad leg which was crippled from polio.'

The following month, a plump 37-year-old from North Carolina called James 'Jimmy' Linwood Gentry turned up at Raúl Castro's side, acting as an adviser. Gentry had served in the US Army during the war then gone into the aeroplane parts business. In early 1958, some M26J representatives looking to build up a rebel air force in the mountains had got in touch and Gentry began selling them spare parts before being persuaded to visit Cuba and serve as an aviation expert, intelligence officer and explosives expert. Even some of Raúl's subordinates were surprised at the enthusiasm with which Gentry embraced the rebel leader's communist beliefs.

Gentry replaced another American aviation expert who'd spent a few months in Raúl's territory over the summer. Walter 'Jack' Youngblood was a self-styled soldier of fortune who had turned a stint in the Army into a life as a womanising pilot for hire. He liked to tell journalists about his time running a short-lived airline in Cuba, hanging out in casinos in Guatemala and Mexico City and Nevada, and flying guns around Central America. Youngblood was less keen on discussing a charge of assault and reckless driving in Nevada, the rape allegation that got him expelled from the University of Arkansas and the accusations of fraud that followed a donor-funded but fruitless 1956 search for a downed aeroplane in the Mexican jungle rumoured to contain an American gangster's cargo of gold bullion.

'He's a conman, a swindler, a fraud,' said journalist Andrew St George.[8] 'But women loved him – a handsome, clean-cut, persuasive, all-American fake.'

In May 1958, Youngblood had got involved in a gambling scam that got him deported from Cuba. Two months later, a Batista agent with a poor judgement of character hired Youngblood to collect weapons from Guatemala for government forces. To no one's surprise but the agent's, the pilot instead flew the guns into Raúl Castro's territory and stayed on to train guerrillas for a month or two. Back in Florida, Youngblood told exaggerated versions of his adventures to anyone who would listen but quickly clammed up when American authorities began cracking down on gunrunners that autumn after discovering that Mannarino Mafia associate Joseph Merola had stolen hundreds of sub-machine guns from a National Guard armoury and shipped them to the rebels.

A criminal investigation into Merola couldn't stop American newspapers running enthusiastic coverage of Castro's cause alongside maps that showed arrows stabbing out of the mountains and inching ever closer towards Havana. Men like Nordeen, Gentry and Youngblood had become heroes to many readers – the latest in a long line of Americans who went overseas to fight for democracy, justice and liberty.

• • •

In Pinar del Río, the rebels spent much of their time hanging peasants suspected of being informers. None of it seemed to bother Macaulay much, not even when a mentally challenged peasant who didn't seem to understand the seriousness of the situation or the questions being asked was lynched from a tree.

'The hapless little man danced on toes that barely touched the ground and tugged at the noose that was choking him to death,' Macaulay remembered.[9] 'Three guerrillas jerked him a foot higher and there he died, his face frozen in a grotesque popeyed stare.'

It seemed like the only time an execution truly affected him was when a prisoner tried to escape beforehand and Macaulay brought the man down with a shot to the leg. As the hanging took place, the American lay in his hammock feeling a strange mix of disgust and elation. Later, he got the job of instructing guerrillas at a makeshift rifle range and Escalona jokingly began to call him 'the American who is training the firing squad'.[10]

Macaulay was glad to see some real action when he joined a team assaulting the Army barracks in the town of Las Pozas. The hand grenades he rolled up to the door failed to explode and most shots went wild, while from inside the barracks came rapid bursts of sub-machine-gun fire and the sound of someone frantically cranking a field telephone. After twenty minutes, the rebels retreated, carrying a comrade semi-conscious from a chest wound. Macaulay jogged alongside them, full of adrenaline from dodging bullets and with a throat raw from screaming obscenities at the defenders. Back at the forest camp, Escalona gave a speech and singled out Macaulay as 'un Americano con cojones' ('an American with balls').[11]

In the Sierra del Rosario, they shot up a two-car patrol on the highway and killed seven military police, one of them machine-gunned in the stomach after he surrendered. The next day, Batista's men hanged fourteen peasants in retaliation. Soon light aircraft were flying low over the tree tops trying to locate the rebel base, so Claudio's group pulled back up the mountains and settled into a regular routine of hot chocolate, cigars and avoiding enemy patrols. They were still there in November when Batista held elections and promised to step down in favour of the winner. Castro retaliated with a nationwide boycott and ordered his guerrillas to burn ballot boxes and shoot any candidates who registered, whatever their politics. No one was especially surprised by the victory of the government's favoured successor Andrés Rivero Agüero, a former Prime Minister and senior figure in Batista's Partido de Acción Progresista (Progressive Action Party). He was scheduled to take power in February 1959.

In late November, Macaulay posed as a tourist to fly out of Havana and visit some friends in Charlotte, North Carolina, who had offered to sell guns to the rebels. He spent time in endless suburban basements photographing merchandise and haggling over a price list. The next month, Macaulay returned to find the sun-drenched streets of Havana full of Santa Clauses collecting for charity among imported Nordic pine trees. He left the surreal scene to head up into the Pinar del Río mountains with the good news that the American government had withdrawn official recognition of Batista's regime.

Clambering uphill through a sudden rainstorm, he wondered if the fighting really would be over by the New Year. Despite all the military and diplomatic reversals, Batista seemed determined to hang on in the hope America would renew its support and legitimise his successor. Macaulay wasn't sure he had the stomach for a fight that dragged on into the next year.

9

THE LAST DAYS OF OLD CUBA

HAVANA, NEW YEAR'S EVE 1958

Cuba's President sat defeated but uncomprehending in the back of a car speeding through the streets of his capital. The nightclubs and restaurants that scrolled past the car's bulletproof windows on the drive to an Army base outside the city were brightly lit and half empty. Castro's rebels had ordered locals not to celebrate tonight and most had obeyed, happy to welcome 1959 from behind closed doors in a show of support for the guerrillas who now controlled most of the country. Everything Rubén Fulgencio Batista y Zaldívar had built was running through his fingers like sand and he couldn't understand how it had happened.

Back in the interwar years, Batista had been a young revolutionary loved by the Cuban people for overthrowing a regime that was little more than a pawn of America and introducing democratic elections. Now he was a 57-year-old tyrant, corrupt and money-hungry, who blamed Cuba's descent into civil war on a poisonous stew of snobbery and racism cooked up by an elite which had never accepted him.

Batista had been born in a dirt-floored two-room shack in Oriente province to a family so steeped in indigenous, African and Spanish heritage that later opponents would call him 'El Negro' and portray his face in racist caricature. He found it bitterly ironic that Fidel Castro, son of a rich white Spaniard, could pose as a champion of the poor while he was dismissed as a man of privilege. In reality, it had been Batista who struggled in his younger days, cutting cane on sugar plantations as a teen after his mother died, then living rough and nearly being killed in a railroad accident. At twenty years old, he found a path out of poverty by joining the Army, a brutal institution proud of its role as kingmaker in Cuban politics, and spent the next decade working his way up to sergeant. As he climbed the ranks, Batista grew to hate the superior, incompetent officer class with a fury that only deepened when a lieutenant delayed him seeing his dying father until it was too late.

In the 1930s, Cuba was ruled by President Gerardo Machado y Morales, a silver-haired patriot who'd started off a reformer but ended as a dictator propped up by American interests who found his regime useful. Batista despised him and joined an underground group called the ABC, made up of students and soldiers with a taste for the matching shirts of European fascism and the revolutionary rhetoric of the Russian Bolsheviks. The ABC's bombs and bullets sent Machado fleeing for the Bahamas in August 1933, his hydroplane taking off into a Havana sky glowing red from the burning houses of his supporters, but couldn't stop the Americans ushering in an equally dictatorial successor in the form of Carlos Manuel de Céspedes. The violence continued for weeks until Batista came out of nowhere as the brains behind a 'sergeants' revolt' that united the lower ranks of the Army with workers and ABC terrorists to overthrow the government. The officers were too out of touch and the politicians too weak to stop him.

In the aftermath, Batista purged the armed forces and promoted his supporters, then defeated a counter-revolutionary uprising to introduce democratic elections, of a sort. Now anyone could be President, as long as they had his blessing, but those who challenged the military or lost popular support found themselves ruthlessly removed.

In 1940, Batista emerged from the shadows to become President with the help of an unlikely coalition forged between conservative and far-left parties. He repaired relations with America by supporting its war effort, although Washington never much trusted him ('scheming, self-confident, and unscrupulous', in the words of an American general)[1] and remained deeply suspicious of Batista's relationship with both senior Cuban communists and Mafia figures like Meyer Lansky. As President, he promoted reforms to help the poor, but opposition to any real change was too deeply entrenched and his enthusiasm more sentimental than practical. He seemed more interested in trying to worm his way into the upper classes with the help of an etiquette teacher and a young, pretty mistress he soon promoted to second wife.

In 1944, Batista left office and retired to the sleepy Florida town of Daytona Beach, floating all the way there on a wave of goodwill from the Cuban people. If he'd stayed in Daytona, the former President might have been remembered as a hero who'd liberated his country and nudged it in the direction of modern democracy. But Batista couldn't keep away from his homeland. He had become accustomed to a certain lifestyle as President and it was hard to ignore the huge sums of money flooding into his homeland through gambling and tourism; hard also to ignore the Mafia bagmen who whispered in his ear that a ruler who granted them even more autonomy could turn that flood into a tsunami. By 1948, Batista had a seat in the Cuban Senate and four years later was running for President to succeed the notoriously corrupt but strangely well-liked Prío Socarrás. When it became obvious Batista could not win, he gathered together some old Army buddies and made himself President at gunpoint.

The shrewd ditching of his communist friends brought Washington onside, but no amount of hotel building or infrastructure investment could win back the respect of the Cuban people. Batista persuaded himself they would change their minds and devoted his days to cheating at cards and dozing off in front of American horror films starring Boris Karloff, reassuring his cronies that the good times would never stop.

Now, after two years of violence, the government was tottering and decisions had to be made. That New Year's Eve, Batista was being driven towards the military base of Camp Columbia to meet the few high-ranking officers and Cabinet ministers who remained loyal. There would be only one subject of discussion: how long before the President had to flee for his life.

• • •

Radio Rebelde broadcast news of guerrilla victories, upbeat music programmes and endless speeches by Fidel Castro across the island from a wooden hut hidden among the trees of the Sierra Maestra. On 31 December, listeners tuned in to hear an excited announcer tell them that Che Guevara's forces had taken Santa Clara, the capital of Las Villas province and last major obstacle on the road to

Havana. After a bitter siege that had lasted most of December, the town's garrison surrendered that afternoon when the derailment of a vital supply train finally broke their morale. The announcer went on to boast about advances in Pinar del Río and mopping-up operations in Oriente province. Radio Rebelde pushed a strong patriotic line, with plenty of references to José Martí and rebuilding the nation, so it wasn't much of a surprise to anyone that the triumphalist bulletins didn't mention the part played by American volunteers in helping along the victory.

One of them was Frank Fiorini, then training guerrillas in the Sierra Maestra. He'd helped set up a camp there during a spring visit but only decided on a permanent move after Batista's police arrested him in August with a Cadillac full of weapons. He was imprisoned in El Morro castle at the mouth of Havana harbour and tortured.

'They beat the hell out of me with bullwhips,' he said.[2]

Fiorini was eventually deported to face gunrunning charges from the American authorities back in Florida. The case would collapse, thanks in part to Fiorini horrifying the judge by pulling up his shirt to display a back beaten all the colours of the rainbow, but by that time his fellow gunrunner Rex Sanderlin had already fled to Cuba to avoid jail. Sanderlin came from a dysfunctional but wealthy Norfolk family with a forty-acre estate on the banks of the Lynnhaven River, and grew up an artistic, gentle young man without the willpower to resist the military career his parents so clearly expected. He joined the Marines at seventeen years old and by 1956 was stationed at a naval air station in Korea, keeping a watchful eye on the armistice between North and South. A year later, he was out of the Marines looking for something interesting to do. He found it in Norfolk native and fellow former Marine Frank Fiorini, who had just got into the gunrunning business for Castro's rebels.

Sanderlin jumped bail after the American authorities swooped on the operation that summer and headed for Cuba to make contact with rebel forces in Oriente province. He was soon training the guerrillas in martial arts, weapon handling and combat techniques. In the autumn, he moved on to Raúl Castro's forces and briefly met another American volunteer when ex-Marine Ed Bethune appeared in the mountains. Like Sanderlin, the new arrival was restless after serving in Korea but, unlike Sanderlin, he didn't last long. Bethune only stayed a few days at the training camp before leaving for Havana and then Miami, complaining of toothache and not trusting the dentists at the camp.

In the last months of the year, Sanderlin helped set up a new column under a Nicaraguan called Carlos Iglesias Fonseca then volunteered to fight with it, feeling he would lose the respect of the men by staying at the base. He took part in a series of ambushes, including an attack on a railroad line at Sampera Bridge, but Sanderlin's luck ran out on 19 December when he was shot in the throat, chest and left arm charging a machine-gun nest. His men rushed him off to a field hospital in a sugar mill where a barely qualified doctor had to be restrained from amputating his arm. The mangled limb would never heal properly.

'This arm is just bad luck,' he later told a journalist.[3] 'I broke it twice before when I was sixteen, and this left hand got it in Korea. Now this.'

As Sanderlin writhed in a hospital bed, his friend Fiorini was with rebels in the Sierra Maestra. The collapse of the court case had stiffened his resolve to see the fight up close and he smuggled himself into Cuba to help pilot Pedro Díaz Lanz create a primitive rebel air force from a B-25 bomber and C-46D transport plane bought cheap in America. Once the planes were airborne and moving guerrillas across the battlefield, Fiorini shifted into under-cover work around Santiago, the last big Oriente province city still in government hands. One Friday night in December, he was at the Casa Grande Hotel posing as a tourist and playing bingo when an American who called himself Patterson sidled up and began to chat.[4] The new arrival claimed to be a vice-consul, although Fiorini assumed his new friend was CIA when the conversation turned towards rebel troop strengths and Castro's contacts with foreign powers. Whatever his true role, Patterson had arrived at the right time. Fiorini and Díaz Lanz had both become concerned about Castro's indulgence of communist activists in the rebel ranks and were worried what kind of democracy would follow the revolution. A sympathetic ear was exactly what the American needed.

By the end of the evening, Fiorini had agreed to pass along any information he thought might be useful to his country, as long as it would not hurt the rebel cause. Patterson shook his hand and called him a true patriot. The next day, Fiorini headed back into the Sierra Maestra, wondering if he'd done the right thing and aware that some of his fellow countrymen elsewhere in the rebel ranks would think him a traitor for his actions. Some had been forced to cut all ties with home and put themselves in legal jeopardy just to join Castro's forces.

• • •

The American sailors who spent their leaves in the brothels and bars of Caimanera before the revolution began would barely have recognised the port on New Year's Eve. Buildings had been wrecked by shellfire or blackened by smoke, and those which escaped damage were squatted by the rebel guerrillas who'd taken the town ten days earlier. Among them was a 22-year-old American Marine deserter called Gerald George Holthaus. He'd been one of those US soldiers kidnapped by Raúl Castro in the summer of 1958 and had become impressed enough by the rebel cause to sneak off the base a few months later to join the revolution.

The cheerful, big-chinned man from Illinois had joined the Marines the day after his eighteenth birthday. Holthaus wanted a career and found it as a military policeman, serving first in Hawaii and then at Guantánamo Bay. He'd been in Cuba less than three months when Raúl Castro's men hijacked his bus and politely escorted him up into the mountains with the other hostages. Released after a month, he returned to work at the naval base eager to find out more about the guerrilla fighters and what motivated them. The Cuban employees at Guantánamo were reluctant to discuss the revolution, but prostitutes who worked outside the perimeter fence proved more eager to talk and Holthaus was impressed by what he heard.

One August night, as he served as sergeant of the guard at a base gate, a Cuban man approached and discreetly asked for advice about a malfunctioning mortar. Holthaus climbed up into the mountain foothills after his shift and showed the rebel group how to remove the safety rings from mortar shells, a detail the untrained guerrillas had overlooked. The next month, he took another trip into the mountains to teach them how to operate a bazooka and a recoilless rifle. An impressed Raúl Castro asked Holthaus to join the revolution full-time and on the evening of 25 November the American drove a truck full of equipment off base and disappeared. Gerald Holthaus was now a deserter.

He joined the rebel ranks at the same moment another American deserter left. That November, Charles Bartlett Jr finally wandered out of the mountains back to the base at Guantánamo Bay looking exhausted and undernourished. His parents in Sebastopol, California, sobbed with relief that he was still alive. The Navy remained dry-eyed, put Bartlett in hospital to recover, then court-martialled him.

By then Holthaus was in action with the recoilless rifle near La Maya, where he impressed the rebels with his coolness under fire. Two days later, while preparing an ambush, he met another American fighting with the rebels called Anthony Mozinsky. The young man barely looked eighteen and declared his only reason for joining Raúl Castro's forces was to discover what it was like to kill somebody; he wouldn't get a chance to find out before the rebels, disturbed by his psychotic stare, sent him back behind the lines. Holthaus went on to the unsuccessful siege of a government fort at Río Frío then returned to La Maya, where he found himself desperately firing faulty shell after faulty shell from a bazooka during an attack. Afterwards came an ambush against 600 Batista soldiers marching down a road near La Guada before, exhausted from battle, he was sent to a rebel base at Filipinas.

There he ran into Mozinsky, still complaining he hadn't been able to kill anyone. The young man had become a sloppier soldier under the influence of an American volunteer called Thomas Eugene Spychala, a moody 29-year-old blond from Chicago who constantly moaned about the food and refused to visit the front lines. Spychala claimed to be a former Marine officer, but Holthaus thought this unlikely and believed the rebels only tolerated him because the Chicago native had taken part in some earlier fighting. Mozinsky and Spychala constantly caused trouble over their reluctance to accept that the comforts of home weren't available in the Sierra Maestra. Holthaus was glad to leave them behind in

December to join the fighting around Caimanera. Using a heavy machine gun salvaged from a crashed aeroplane and rigged up to car batteries and a compressed air tank, he helped beat back waves of charging government soldiers and secure the town. He was still in Caimanera with his rebel column on New Year's Eve, all of them sure that final victory was close.

Other Americans felt the same. Over in the Escambray mountains, Bill Morgan and Juan Espiritu were pushing north-west towards the capital with the Second Front. They seized town after town before reaching Topes de Collantes, 160 miles south-east of Havana. Elsewhere, Jack Nordeen was on guard at Castro's headquarters, Jimmy Gentry was advising Raúl Castro, Herman Marks was still recovering from his wounds, Neill Macaulay was in Pinar del Río and an American called John Francis Michael Shea, known to all as 'Jack', was somewhere else with the rebel forces, although little was known about him. Only the 26-year-old José Abrantes, born in Florida to Cuban parents, had been accepted into the rebel forces as an equal rather than a curiosity and was serving as respected aide to a senior commander.

Across the Caribbean Sea in Miami, former rebel Donald Soldini was preparing to lead a foreign legion of Americans to join the revolution. After meeting Neill Macaulay, he had visited Mexico, where M26J activists asked him to courier documents into the country posing as a tourist. The police arrested him near Havana and Soldini was beaten and tortured, while prisoners were executed outside his cell. On three occasions he was dragged out to dig his own grave.

'You take control of yourself,' he said.[5] 'You rationalise they are going to kill you. Then fear takes control – a horrific feeling.'

He refused to break and wriggled out of custody by insisting his parents owned a restaurant in New York popular with Batista's family. Expelled from Cuba and back in New York, local M26J activists had finally agreed to his foreign legion idea and given him a bundle of applications from American would-be volunteers. Soldini organised seventy men into a column, although the overall quality wasn't high in his opinion, and worked out a plan to lead them into the Cuban mountains. He hoped the manpower would allow him to muscle into the higher reaches of the rebel command. By the end of December, his foreign legion was stashed in cheap motels around Miami while Soldini waited for clearance from the rebels to come join them. He wanted to get there before the fighting was over.

• • •

As the clocks chimed midnight to welcome in the New Year, dancers were waving Cuban and American flags at the Tropicana floorshow while the band played the theme to *The Bridge on the River Kwai* over a cha-cha beat. The spectacle earned a round of applause from American tourists in the audience and distracted them from wondering why so many seats in the nightclub remained empty. No one had told them about rebel orders to stay indoors tonight.

Similar spectacles were taking place in half-full venues across the island when Fulgencio Batista arrived at his quarters in Camp Columbia to find the upstairs living room full of friends, cronies and family all celebrating the New Year. He pasted on a smile and circulated through the throng, turning down a cocktail but accepting a cup of coffee laced with brandy. When everyone had been greeted, he herded his senior officers into a nearby office and asked for an honest assessment of the situation, as General José Pedraza sat in the corner listening to broadcasts coming out of the surrounding areas on a shortwave radio.

'Calling Cuban Red Cross, Cuban Red Cross...'[6]

'Listen here, Chico, we have six comrades badly wounded at kilometre sixteen...'

'OK! OK! We shall try and send a truck out for them. In the name of God, tell your people not to shoot at us...'

'Calling Comandante William Morgan! Comandante William Morgan!'

'Hear me! Hear me! Send us reinforcements. We need help – ammunition! If we stay here, they will wipe us out. We are going to move north.'

As the radio crackled, other officers laid out the cost of the civil war so far: perhaps 2,000 government troops dead against 1,000 rebels, with many thousands of civilians murdered by police or by guerrillas for supporting the wrong side; the economy was contracting, with its only growing sectors being prostitution and pornography; the Americans had disengaged and made it clear they expected to be dealing with a new regime soon; and rumours suggested cabals of Army officers were conspiring to overthrow Batista and replace him with someone more attractive to Washington or the Sierra Maestra, depending on their political leanings. The outlook was bleak.

Party guests began departing, unaware of anything historically important happening upstairs. Batista asked the few politicians who had remained loyal to stay and moved everyone into a cramped dining room to discuss his options. Some urged him to fight on, others to flee. Batista searched his soul and felt only disgust at the thought of more bloodshed in defence of a lost cause.

'After the disloyalties, surrenders and treacheries, with only a scrap of the Army left,' he remembered later, 'there was only the prospect of a mountain of bodies and the Red Horsemen of the Apocalypse seizing the remains of the Republic.'[7]

He agreed to step down as President and leave Cuba. It took an hour to work out a suitable constitutional method for transferring power to a junta run by Oriente military chief General Eulogio Cantillo, with a figurehead President. No one in the room seemed to understand they were forming a new administration whose orders would never be obeyed. As Batista was signing his resignation letter, his wife Marta appeared in the doorway of the dining room with a reminder that they were expected to make an appearance some time tonight at El Colony on the Isle of Pines, a recently opened luxury hotel run by the Mafia, where guests included Robert Kennedy's brother-in-law. Batista shook his head and told her to pack a bag instead.

Soon the Cuban elite were carrying sleepy, pyjama-clad children into bulletproof limousines for the short drive to the airfield. DC-4 propellers began to turn as wives wearing fur coat over fur coat waddled on board, aides stowed away suitcases stuffed with money and half-mutinous soldiers shouted insults from the darkness of the perimeter. Batista and his family climbed into their private aeroplane and took off for Florida, with everyone on board mourning the loss of something.

'In the Palacio,' remembered Batista, 'we left the suits, the dresses, the children's toys, the trophies won by the eldest at horse shows, the expensive gifts made to the children on their birthdays, pictures and works of art, jewels and ornaments of the First Lady, my personal possessions, acquired or presented to me from the 1930s on.'[8]

Halfway to Florida, the DC-4 received instructions from the American authorities that Batista had been refused permission to enter the country. After a panicky discussion, the aeroplane diverted south-west to the Dominican Republic, where ruler Rafael Leónidas Trujillo welcomed his fellow despot with a chilly smile and demanded a large slice of Batista's $300 million fortune in exchange for a suite in his capital's Jaragua Hotel. The former Cuban President's cronies were already landing in Miami Beach to gather at the Biltmore Terrace Hotel, secretly owned by Batista, and make plans to take back their country.

On the Isle of Pines, the guests at El Colony awoke to find the hotel in rebel hands and prisoners from the nearby camp wandering around with sub-machine guns. The sugar cane millionaires and rich Americans pulled on M26J armbands and tried to look as if they welcomed the revolution. Against the odds, Fidel Castro and his rebels had become the new rulers of Cuba.

10

THIS WAY FOR THE FESTIVITIES, LADIES AND GENTLEMEN

REVOLUTIONARY HAVANA, SPRING 1959

Four months after the revolution, a tall American was drinking a cocktail in the garden of the Floridita bar and listening politely as a dark-haired man in a linen shirt invited him to observe a firing squad. Havana was full of strange people that spring, and even stranger offers. The American was 31-year-old Harvard-educated George Plimpton, a journalist who enjoyed a small, refined audience for his work on the highbrow *Paris Review* and a more boisterous readership for his mainstream reporting in which he challenged serious athletes on the field, the joke being that the gawky beanpole wouldn't last a minute against real professionals. He dubbed the idea 'participatory journalism', but in Havana that April the only participation on hand was the chance to watch the latest in the wave of executions that had been rolling across Cuba since the revolution. Plimpton wasn't sure he could stomach it.

The blood had started flowing soon after Batista and his cronies fled the island before dawn on New Year's Day. The Directorio

Revolucionario Estudiantil took over the University of Havana campus and got into a firefight with the hardcore remnants of Rolando Masferrer's Tigers, who were making a last stand in a building on Manzana de Gómez street. Bullets sang through balconies and windows, and neither side was in the mood to take prisoners.

Elsewhere, mobs roamed the city decapitating parking meters with baseball bats and battering slot machines in casinos. By the time the sun rose over the capital, contemptuous farmers had let loose a truckload of pigs in the lobby of Meyer Lansky's $8 million Riviera hotel and were laughing as the livestock tracked filth across the expensive carpet. With Batista gone and his government collapsed, there was no one around to stop them.

A group of Second Front guerrillas were the first rebels into the city, closely followed by the rebel columns of Che Guevara and Camilo Cienfuegos. All were greeted by locals weeping with joy. Former President Carlos Prío arrived later that day in an aeroplane piloted by Jack Youngblood to be surrounded on the airfield by cheering supporters who thought he was here to guide Cuba back to democracy. On the other side of the island, Fidel Castro was making his own way towards Havana in a jeep convoy full of men in sun-faded uniforms and wild beards, their progress slow because the rebel leader stopped at every town to make a speech. Neill Macaulay had already reached the capital with Escalona to scout the DRE positions at the University of Havana and assess how much resistance they would pose to an M26J assault. It was the first indication that Castro's men had no intention of sharing power with anyone. After their reconnaissance, Macaulay and Escalona reported to Guevara at his headquarters in La Cabaña and found him besieged by admirers.

'It was a balmy winter afternoon,' Macaulay said, 'and hordes of giddy adolescents in long skirts and saddle oxfords and pullover sweaters jammed the hall and lined the sidewalk outside Che's office. They could have been American girls anticipating a glimpse of Elvis Presley.'[1]

Guevara was already listing categories of Batista supporters to be shot in order to minimise the risk of counter-revolution: policemen, Army officers, intelligence agents, informants. Approval for any killings would have to wait until Castro arrived, but the rebel leader was still taking his time. On 6 January, he diverted the convoy to Cienfuegos, where Bill Morgan of the Second Front was in charge, for a public show of unity neatly undercut by a two-hour speech from Castro that made it clear M26J wasn't looking for a coalition. Despite the political games, he seemed to enjoy Morgan's company and the pair joked in Spanish for a while before Castro manoeuvred Menoyo away for a private chat.

'How much do we have to pay this American adventurer to go home?' Castro asked.[2]

'He's not an adventurer,' said Menoyo. 'He's a revolutionary. He's like us.'

'Even worse,' said Castro darkly.

The rebel leader finally arrived in Havana two days later to be greeted by ecstatic crowds throwing flowers into his jeep and the news that the US government had officially recognised his new regime. He requisitioned the penthouse suite at the Havana Hilton Hotel for a base and formed a Cabinet from M26J loyalists and members of the Communist Party, with Manuel Urrutia Lleó as a figurehead President. Menoyo's Second Front got only a handful of minor posts elsewhere in the government, but that concession proved enough to persuade DRE militants to give up their positions at the University of Havana and go home without any shooting. All other political parties were banned and a furious Carlos Prío was ordered back into ineffectual American exile at gunpoint before he could establish a powerbase.

American television crews raced to Cuba for an interview with the country's new masters. First on the scene was Ed Sullivan, the bulldog-faced compère of a popular television variety show with ambitions to be a serious journalist, who peppered Castro with questions about the future political direction of his government. The rebel leader reassured him that democratic elections were on their way, asked American tourists to return and waved away any idea that he intended to keep power for himself.

'You can be sure that Batista will be the last dictator of Cuba,' Castro said.[3]

A few days later, Coca-Cola took out a full-page advertisement in the magazine *Bohemia* to praise the new regime in the name of carbonated beverages: 'The Coca-Cola Bottling Company rejoices with the people of Cuba for the resurgence of democratic liberties in our country.'[4] Coke's example was immediately followed by Shell Oil, Cristal beers, Canada Dry soda and thirty-seven banks. On the streets, Havana was full of armed rebels with a surprisingly prudish streak who were closing down every casino and strip club, leaving the city looking like a Las Vegas forcibly occupied by the Amish. The puritanism extended to the leadership as Castro ordered his men to marry their battlefield girlfriends, pushing both Guevara and his own brother into marriages about which both felt less than enthusiastic.

Casino owners got desperate as their bills mounted with no income to pay them. In America, a sharply dressed man who claimed to represent a consortium of Italian-American business-men visited the home of former rebel Mike Garvey and offered the teenager $50,000 for a personal introduction to Castro. Garvey and his shocked parents agreed to think the matter over and the man drove off in a Cadillac promising to return but never did. In February, the mobsters in Havana found a different way to re-open the casinos by organising a noisy protest march of unemployed croupiers, waiters, entertainers and prostitutes. The government was persuaded to change its mind but insisted on stricter surveillance of the tables, a job that got delegated to Frank Fiorini, and ordered prostitutes to wear more modest clothing when propositioning clients.

The return of gambling did little to encourage traditional tourism, but that spring Havana found itself welcoming a new kind of American visitor: some looking for work, some trying to make money and others like George Plimpton just soaking up the ongoing fiesta of revolution and firing squads.

• • •

In 1959, a lot of people thought Ernest Hemingway was a punchy, alcohol-sodden wreck whose days of Nobel Prize-winning glory were far behind him. His minimalist, modernist prose had changed American literature for ever and made him a celebrity in the process, but New York literary circles judged the new work flabby, the macho posturing outdated and the obsession with bullfighting embarrassing. George Plimpton strongly disagreed with those assessments. The patrician editor of the *Paris Review* had hero-worshipped Hemingway ever since interviewing him five years back and grabbed any opportunity that came along to spend time with the great man of American letters. When Hemingway extended an invitation to visit post-revolutionary Cuba, Plimpton was on the next flight. They spent days talking about revolution and bull-fighting and courage over endless pitchers of mojitos until Hemingway shambled off back to his writing room and left Plimpton to wander Havana with a crowd of fellow foreigners who'd flown in to see the revolution up close.

One of his companions was Kenneth Tynan, a sex-obsessed British theatre critic determined to uncover traces of old Batista filth beneath the new revolutionary puritanism. There wasn't much to find: the nude floorshow at the Tropicana was still going, but the Shanghai was temporarily shuttered and Superman had retired. For a while Tynan was on the trail of another sexual athlete who called himself Superboy, until rebel militia raided a club which hosted live sex shows and put the performer out of work. When a guide managed to track down a hardcore porn film of the type once shown at the Shanghai, the British critic and Plimpton visited a cramped, pet-infested apartment where a nervous Cuban man projected the flickering image on a wall and the light splashed grainy acts of penetration onto the shell of a sleeping tortoise.

One afternoon in the early days of April, Plimpton, along with Tynan and his wife Elaine, the American playwright Tennessee Williams and an heiress to the United Fruit Company fortune were at table on the Floridita's sunlit patio drinking cocktails so cold they brought on a pain behind the eyes. They group were exchanging literary gossip when a dark-haired man in a linen shirt sat down and introduced himself as an American soldier of fortune who had fought with Castro in the mountains.

'After a while he said that Castro had given him an interesting job over in the Morro Castle, on the other side of the harbour,' said Plimpton.[5] 'He was in charge of the execution squads. He was being kept very busy, especially in the evenings, and sometimes his squads didn't get through with their work until one or two in the morning. We all stared at him.'

It was Herman Marks, who'd exchanged the front line for command of a teenage firing squad which was enthusiastically eliminating enemies of the state. According to official figures, only 300 people had been executed by the new government, although most believed the real figure to be much higher. Some of the dead were guilty of horrific war crimes while others had done little more than wear the wrong uniform, but none of that bothered the Cuban crowds who gathered at execution sites to chant '*Paredón!*' ('Up against the wall!') and applaud as the corpses were bulldozed into trenches.[6] The whole country tuned in when the stocky figure of Colonel Cornelio Rojas Fernández, commander of the garrison at Santa Clara, was executed on live television, his fedora flying into the air as bullets clipped the top off his skull.

Castro's government proudly supplied American media outlets with graphic photographs of the score-settling, not understanding that foreign stomachs might be turned by the images. Some Americans even felt queasy over milder shots, like that of an avuncular priest with his arm around the shoulders of a bitter-looking young man getting the last rites as the firing squad reloaded. The bodies of seventy other Tiger paramilitaries could be seen on the roadside behind the pair. When pilots and ground crew from Batista's air force were tried in February for genocide and found not guilty, Castro reversed the decision and ordered another tribunal to give the accused thirty years in prison. The head of the original tribunal was found dead in his car afterwards, apparently a suicide.

'We are not executing innocent people or political opponents,' Fidel Castro told foreign journalists.[7] 'We are executing murderers and they deserve it.'

Marks wasn't the only American who took part in the bloodletting. In Pinar del Río, Lieutenant Neill Macaulay dispassionately conscripted a firing squad from the men who performed best on the rifle range, trained them against a man-sized paper target, then joined the squad himself in case nerves buckled on the day. The firing squad shot their first eleven men with unwavering aim and Macaulay reduced his role to barking orders and putting a bullet in the head of anyone still quivering on the ground after the smoke had cleared. He rationalised his actions as the meting out of justice to a defeated enemy, but Herman Marks just seemed to enjoy killing people.

On the Floridita patio, Marks cheerfully asked if Plimpton and his friends would like to join 'the festivities'. As a special treat, a young German mercenary, one of the few foreigners who had served with the Batista forces, was being shot that evening. Marks offered to arrange transport in his own vehicle.

'Let's see … five of you … quite easy … we'll drive over by car … tight squeeze … I'll pick you up at eight.'[8]

Plimpton was turning the offer over in his mind, thinking about courage and cowardice and a writer's obligation to the truth, when Kenneth Tynan reared up from the table in a stuttering fury at the execution being turned into a social event. He called Marks 'loathsome', 'frightful', 'sickening' and yelled that he would only attend in order to throw himself in front of the guns and stop the execution. He then yanked his wife out of her chair and stormed out of the bar.

'What the hell was that?' said Marks, puzzled that anyone would take offence at being invited to watch men die.[9]

Plimpton's friends might have been even less enthusiastic about accepting the invitation if they'd known a fellow American would be facing the death penalty on 12 April for trying to assassinate Castro. His defence wasn't looking strong.

• • •

La Cabaña was a white stone fortress perched on the mouth of Havana harbour. Late one Saturday night, a trial was held deep within its walls in what had been the ballroom of an officers' club before the revolution. The dance floor once glided over by generations of slick-haired captains and their wives was now crammed with wooden chairs for lawyers, reporters and any spectators curious to see the gangly 31-year-old American accused of plotting to kill Fidel Castro. Alan Robert Nye was blond and emaciated, having spent the past three months in a prison cell where the daily meal was a plate of beans mashed together with dead insects and coils of human hair.

'The food is so bad,' he said, 'you have to eat it with your eyes closed.'[10]

Nye was used to better things. His earliest years had been spent in the Dominican Republic, where his father worked for Standard Oil, but the idyll had ended when Nye Sr died and his wife took their baby boy back home to Whiting, an Indiana town little more than a dot on the map near Chicago. Nye flourished in his new home and grew up to be one of those all-American straight-A high-school students with a crew cut and a place on the swim team. He did two years at a liberal arts college, two more working for the post office, then decided he wanted something more out of life and joined the Navy with a deal that let him study engineering at college when not landing fighters on the deck of an aircraft carrier. Nye saw action in the Korean War and left the service as a restless 27-year-old pilot with a passion for aeroplanes and adrenaline.

In the mid-1950s, he impulsively married a French girl met overseas after only a few days of knowing her. He didn't speak French, she didn't speak English and no one was surprised when the marriage failed and a heartbroken Nye relocated to Florida for a new life. He worked as a crop duster, spraying carcinogenic trails of insecticide over farmers' fields from a light aircraft. Weekends were spent selling aircraft parts for extra cash or acting as lieutenant in the Naval Reserve.

Sometime during the autumn of 1958, Nye got chatting to a fellow Miami pilot called Daniel Vasquez. His new friend was a Cuban who had arrived in America six years earlier with Carlos Prío Socarrás but had soon been expelled from the former President's entourage as an informer for the Havana government. Vasquez protested loudly, but the accusations were right: he had made his peace with the Batista regime and did occasional undercover work for it. By late 1958, his controllers in Havana had become convinced the only way to stop the revolt was to assassinate Fidel Castro and decapitate the rebel movement. No Cuban could be trusted with the job so they asked Vasquez to locate an American with a love of adventure, some financial problems and a moral compass that didn't always point true north. Alan Robert Nye was ideal.

The two pilots talked about flying, war and the damage that would be done to Cuba if Castro won. Soon they understood each other well enough for Vasquez to suggest a test mission. At the start of November, Nye sneaked onto an airfield in Fort Lauderdale with a can of petrol and set fire to three P-51 Mustangs destined for Castro's forces. Vasquez was pleased enough to offer a follow-up mission in Cuba without explaining exactly what it involved and Nye liked the idea of some well-paid spy versus spy action enough not to ask any questions. On 12 November 1958, he touched down in Havana posing as a tourist.

Nye spent his first few days hanging around the bar of the Hotel

Comodoro, a building like a sleek modernist ocean liner beached in the streets of the capital, and waited for his contact. The bulky man who eventually sat down and bought him a drink had a lot of oiled hair piled high on his head and a moustache like two black slugs trying hard to escape his nose. He gave a fake name, but Nye knew enough about Cuban politics to recognise Colonel Orlando Piedra Negueruela, the head of Batista's secret police. The colonel bluntly asked Nye to infiltrate the rebel army and kill Castro, offering to supply a rifle and pistol, pay all bills at the Comodoro until the mission began and hand over $100,000 if the assassination succeeded. The colonel explained that Castro had good security but might turn his back on a trusted new recruit, especially an American who claimed to be inspired by the writing of Herbert Matthews.

Nye did some light wrestling with his conscience, then accepted the mission and spent the next few weeks at the hotel running up a bill of $694 under a fake name. His clumsy attempt to keep a low profile earned him the nickname 'El Misterioso' (the Mystery Man) from staff. In December, a Cuban Air Force plane landed Nye in Oriente province and pointed him in the direction of the nearest rebel camp.

The guerrillas accepted him without much questioning but never gave the American a chance to get close to Castro. Nye did little except grow a moustache and march around with a rifle on his shoulder until rebel soldiers arrested him near Santa Rita on 26 December 1958 after one of their informers revealed the assassination plan. Nye spent the next three and a half months sharing a prison cell with twelve other men at La Cabaña and trying to persuade his mother not to visit him: 'I can straighten this out within an hour,' he wrote home.[11] Nye was either deluded or putting on a brave face. In court, he had no defence beyond claiming he'd only gone along with the murder plot in order to reach enemy territory and join the revolution.

'Nye was a poor witness on his own behalf,' observed an American diplomat.[12]

The pilot's case got some inadvertent help from the other side when the Cuban prosecutor overreached himself by claiming Nye had been caught leaning out a Havana hotel window with a rifle as Castro passed underneath. No one in the courtroom believed that version of events, but it made no difference to the verdict. The panel of judges took nine minutes to find Nye guilty of arson, collaboration and unaccomplished assassination and sentenced him to death by firing squad. Nye sagged at the knees when he heard the verdict, then looked astonished when the chief judge announced the sentence would be suspended if the American left Cuba within forty-eight hours and never returned. Castro was making a goodwill trip to the US in the following month and didn't want to fall out with his hosts.

A day after the trial, Nye was back in Whiting posing hollow-cheeked with his mother and stepfather for local newspaper photographers. He refused to discuss his experiences but managed some bitter words about Cuban justice.

'I had as much chance of a fair trial in Havana', he said, 'as a snowball in that place made famous by Dante.'[13]

Nye's misadventures didn't stop his fellow countrymen visiting Cuba in search of work. In the streets of Havana could be found men like a 6ft 6in. former Marine called Gerald Hemming, about to join the newly formed Parachute Regiment; private detective Vincent J. Hanard, who seemed to be on Raúl Castro's payroll; pilot Paul Joseph Hughes and Army veteran Loran Hall, who'd got themselves mixed up with some exiled Nicaraguans; former actor

Ignatius Paul Alvick, trying to get a job but keeping quiet about having been kicked out of the Air Force back home for 'alleged homosexuality';[14] and the Canadian airman Douglas Lethbridge. Others were in Cuba as entrepreneurs: Bill Morgan's gangster friend Dominick Bartone had an aeroplane he wanted to sell, while Jewish nightclub manager Jack Ruby from Dallas was working on a plan to offload surplus Army jeeps onto the new regime.

As spring turned into summer, the Americans started to notice an increasing chill towards them from formerly friendly Cuban colleagues. They soon discovered the reason. Over in Miami, local soldiers of fortune were being paid by Batista's associates to slip undercover into Havana and help members of the old regime escape the firing squads. The Cubans didn't know who to trust and, even worse, suspicions were growing that some of the men who had fought up in the mountains with Castro had turned traitor and were plotting a revolution of their own. The name Frank Fiorini kept appearing in secret police reports.

11

THREE FERRARIS ON YOUR TAIL

By the summer of 1959, the Biltmore Terrace Hotel in Miami Beach was swarming with dark-haired men from Havana who carried huge wads of cash and held secretive conversations in quiet corners. Cronies of Fulgencio Batista, they had fled their homeland one step ahead of the firing squad and found themselves marooned in an alien world of Kwik Chek supermarkets, square White Castle hamburgers (seven for a dollar) and something called *The Mouseketeers* on television. The well-established 10,000-strong Cuban community in neighbouring Miami wanted nothing to do with them, so these new arrivals hunkered down inside the Biltmore Terrace's ten storeys of white-and-orange concrete to plot the overthrow of Fidel Castro.

Their new home of Miami Beach was an island carved from landfill three miles off the coast, where tourists broiled themselves in the sun then went home to bore their neighbours with artless photographs of the shiny dolphins at Key Biscayne zoo. Most of the island was covered in hotels, among them the Biltmore which sat on the seafront and had a reputation as a louche place with prostitutes in the cocktail lounge and shows full of scantily clad dancers cocking a hip alongside a leering compère. Its sudden transformation into the heart of the anti-Castro resistance movement only made sense to those who knew that Batista had quietly bought the hotel a few years back and had been planning on moving into the penthouse suite right up until his aeroplane diverted to the Dominican Republic.

In his absence, brother-in-law Roberto Fernández Miranda took over and channelled Batista's money into a two-pronged assault on the new Cuban government: boatloads of guns were smuggled in to loyal soldiers organising in Pinar del Río province, and old friends hunted by the new regime were flown out from obscure parts of the interior. Most of the pilots touching down on deserted highways at night were Cuban exiles, but the Biltmore had recruited local daredevils like Bill Johnson and Richard B. Jaffe to fly rescue missions into Havana disguised as tourist charters. This group already had a martyr, of sorts, in 38-year-old Austin Frank Young, who'd been in a Cuban prison since late February.

Young was the son of a wealthy General Motors executive and had enough British in his family tree to have flown for the RAF during the war. There was a marriage overseas that didn't last long, then a few years flying for the China National Aviation Corporation until communist sympathisers defected with most of the aircraft. Young headed to the Caribbean for a short stint with a Haitian company and then made a failed attempt to run his own airline. Other business ventures came and went, and another marriage collapsed, but none of the setbacks curtailed Young's love of adventure and adrenaline. In his spare time, he raced Ferraris semi-professionally for a team overseen by Swiss motoring journalist Hans Tanner.

By late 1958, he was partner in a failing Miami garage and free-lancing as a private pilot around Cuba for the gangster Norman Rothman, the black-haired and Bronx-born son of Romanian Jewish immigrants who ran Havana's slot machines for the Mannarino brothers. Young enjoyed the Caribbean sun, a humming engine and the chance to escape the loving but increasingly suffocating domesticity supplied by his third wife, Corinne, and three children. After the Batista regime collapsed, Mafia associate Rothman joined the crowd at the Biltmore Terrace, bitter that his efforts to smuggle guns to Castro's rebels had not bought the expected influence with the new regime. He asked his pilot to help loyalist friends escape Havana and Young didn't hesitate.

'You know how you'd feel when you're going around a turn with three Ferraris on your tail?' he told a journalist.[1] 'It's like that in Cuba. Excitement.'

Young posed as a charter pilot and all went well for the first few trips until he raised suspicions trying to exchange $1,500 for pesos at a Havana bank and the local police swooped. A photographer caught the American looking sullen and sharp-jawed in a black polo shirt at the police station. He would serve six months in prison for counter-revolutionary activities. Back home, Corinne was crying on the shoulder of the FBI agent who came to interview her and claiming she thought her husband had been in New York on business. Corinne's mother did her best to get Young into even more trouble.

'Mrs Huber advised that she dislikes her son-in-law, Austin Young, intensely for neglecting his wife and their children,' noted an agent, 'and for that reason would not put anything past him.'[2]

The Biltmore plan took another hit when Richard Jaffe and two companions were arrested the next month and barely managed to wriggle out of the charges by insisting they were innocent sight-seers. Cuban officials began looking suspiciously at any Americans in town, even former rebels wearing the revolutionary uniform. Rumours were already spreading about a circle of conspirators in the Air Force with plans to overthrow the new regime.

• • •

When Batista was in power, the mobsters in Cuba liked to claim their casinos had no need of cheap tricks like rigged roulette wheels and weighted dice to part gamblers from their money. It was sim-pler to introduce drunken visitors to honest games and wait pa-tiently while nature took its course. When the casinos reopened in February, Castro refused to believe the Mafia boasts about their un-impeachable integrity and ordered strict surveillance of the tables to prevent any cheating. The job got delegated to Frank Fiorini as the closest the new government had to an expert on the subject, although Havana's gambling fraternity remained unimpressed.

'I used to go to the casinos and go up to the crap table and I'd grab, if somebody would roll the dice, I would grab the dice,' Fiorini said.[3] 'I would look at the dice and I would say excuse me, I'm just checking the dice and so forth. These are things I would do. They would be very angry at me for doing it.'

His interventions reminded the gangsters who was in charge but only reinforced how little Fiorini really knew about tampered dice and other techniques to rig the odds. He soon gave up on the cheating angle and went to work untangling the complicated webs of shell companies and front men which hid the real owners of each establishment. The job would have been tougher without the help of an American casino owner called 'Stretch' Rubin who'd been a grateful friend ever since Fiorini rescued him from a gang of hostile rebels in Santiago after the revolution. Following that moment of charity, Rubin kept turning up like a bad penny, loudly telling everyone within earshot that his new pal was a stand-up guy who'd saved his life. When Fiorini was transferred to a base in Havana as director of security by the new Air Force commander Pedro Díaz Lanz, it wasn't much of a surprise when Rubin appeared at the main gate offering to buy lunch.

The gangster's limpet-like attachment owed more to the benefits of having a friend in the government than any genuine gratitude, but the exploitation went both ways. Fiorini pressured Rubin into identifying which Mafia bosses actually owned the casinos and was soon meeting men like Santo Trafficante, owl-faced proprietor of the Sans Souci, to explain Castro's intentions for the gambling industry. Rumours went round Havana that Fiorini and the mobsters got a little too close, but he always denied any money changed hands.

'I never made any deals whatsoever with anyone,' Fiorini protested, years later and a lot poorer.[4] 'None whatsoever ... I would not be in this situation today, the way I am, if I did ... If I had mob connections, believe me, I would be all right.'

None of this encouraged the tourists to return, although Castro remained popular enough in America for *Time* magazine to put him on the cover and a New Jersey toy manufacturer to produce 'El Liberator' outfits so kids could run around in fake beards and Army caps pretending to be rebels. Hotel profits plunged and the Riviera alone had lost $750,000 by the end of April. The government blamed the losses on mismanagement by mobster owners and a new round of recriminations started up.

By then, Fiorini had put together an all-Cuban team to check the casinos and returned to his work at the Air Force base. Outwardly the American seemed a loyal servant of the revolution, cheerfully posing for photographs with fellow revolutionaries and praising Castro, but beneath the surface lay a man trying to square the circle of working for the new Cuba while simultaneously alerting the CIA to anything that might affect his own country. The mental gymnastics became simpler when the cloven hoof of communism made an appearance and Fiorini found himself fighting daily battles to keep Soviet sympathisers out of senior Air Force positions. Most were sent over by Raúl Castro, who was making no secret of his desire to bring brother Fidel over to Marxism–Leninism now power had been consolidated. Fiorini had lost a cousin in Korea and seen the Soviet machine up close in Berlin. He hadn't fought for Castro's revolution to see Cuba turn into a Russian outpost.

He made no secret of these views when Raúl's comrade Jimmy Gentry arrived at the air base and insulted Pedro Díaz Lanz for being 'counter-revolutionary'. A row began, got physical and escalated to Gentry pulling a gun on Fiorini.

'I in turn took his .45 away from him,' said Fiorini laconically, 'and marched him to the Air Force office of Pedro.'[5]

Fidel Castro stepped in to smooth things over, but his obvious favouritism towards the communist side provided a moment of clarity for Díaz Lanz and Fiorini. They began sounding out others who shared their concerns about Cuba's new government.

• • •

Ilona Marita Lorenz was emotionally fragile, darkly pretty and hungry for affection. She had been born in 1939 to a German luxury liner captain and his young American bride. The war had been spent starving behind the barbed wire fence of a concentration camp and when Allied occupation came, she was raped by an American soldier at a children's party. Traumatised and abused, Lorenz watched her parents divorce during the tough post-war years then moved to America with her mother in 1950 for a new life. She loved the country but hated school and quit at fourteen years old to join her father on his liner, the *Berlin*, gaining a command of several languages and an erratic education.

Lorenz was acting as a hostess when the *Berlin* docked at Havana in late February 1959 and Castro came on board as a guest. Electricity arced between them and a relationship began that turned serious enough for her to stay behind in Havana with a job as the rebel leader's secretary. Castro's romantic interest quickly burned itself out. By April, the nineteen-year-old Marita was in the arms of the handsome, married, Captain Jesus Yanes Pelletier but still nursing a passion for the rebel leader. In April, she fell pregnant to Yanes, who looked horrified when he heard the news and openly wondered how he could tell his wife. Lovesick and confused, it was hard to resist when Fiorini sidled up in the spring of 1959 to talk about patriotism and suggest she copy some important looking papers in Castro's office.

Fiorini had joined a network led by Pedro Díaz Lanz whose members all believed the revolution had been betrayed. Formed not long after the Jimmy Gentry incident, the network's first act was to have Fiorini recruit some expats living in Havana with access to the higher reaches of the Castro regime. Lorenz, the former girlfriend of Fidel Castro, became their star spy.

With a pipeline to the inner workings of the Cuban government, Pedro Díaz Lanz was able to pass important information to the American embassy in the hope of getting overseas backing for his group. Things looked promising with the appearance of local CIA freelancer Bernard Leon 'Macho' Barker, a Cuban of American descent who'd fought for Uncle Sam in the war and spent a year in a Nazi prison camp after his Flying Fortress went down over Brunswick. Barker had worked for Batista's secret police while serving undercover for the rebels, and now earned a third pay cheque running informants for the CIA. Díaz Lanz hoped Barker would introduce him to potential backers in American Intelligence, but it soon became apparent the agency cared only about collecting information and had no interest in rocking the Cuban boat.

As spring turned into summer, the Díaz Lanz circle realised that no one from the outside world was going to help them, even as Cuban politics turned further left every day. In May, the country's President, Manuel Urrutia Lleó, futilely protested about communist influence in government but was ignored and forced to rubberstamp an agrarian reform law which limited land ownership to 1,000 acres and confiscated the rest for minimal compensation. Communists infiltrated further into ministries, the courts and the armed forces every day with no pushback from senior M26J figures. The Díaz Lanz circle debated and argued, then finally concluded the only way forward was to assassinate Castro and seize control of the country. Frank Fiorini had no objection to killing his former hero.

'So I suggested, you know, like hey, Fidel comes to the Air Force base,' he recalled.[6] 'If he goes someplace in the country he flies in with a helicopter. He comes over, he sees, he hugs me, you know, and he has meetings on the second floor of the headquarters, Air Force Headquarters. Hey, supply me with plastic explosives. I'll kill him right there, you know, on the second floor. Or if you want me to stop him outside the gate I'll stop him outside the gate.'

He did a dry run with his team, timing everything as Castro's jeep convoy rolled up to the air base gate while men with guns on nearby rooftops squeezed imaginary triggers. The operation was workable. Fiorini's only condition for going ahead was that the American embassy give its approval to the forthcoming regime change. A horrified answer came back: abort the assassination immediately. The Americans still saw Castro as a potential ally in the Cold War and were appalled by the prospect of Cuba being plunged into its second civil war in a matter of months. Pedro Díaz Lanz wanted to push ahead with the operation anyway, but Fiorini convinced him to listen to the men in Washington, a decision everyone involved would come to regret.

'Because I was an American,' Fiorini said, 'my decision was more towards the Americans than my own friends, [when] I should have went along with my friends. I would have killed that dirty bastard.'[7]

The assassination plot died off, but its planning had sent enough ripples out into the wider world that the existence of the Díaz Lanz circle was no longer a secret. It was only a matter of time before the information reached Castro.

• • •

By the summer, Cuban secret police had picked up the scent of betrayal but couldn't track its source. Rumours circulated about Bill Morgan doing deals with Mafia friends in the Dominican Republic, while others told stories about the Biltmore Terrace Hotel gang plotting cane-burning runs over the Cuban countryside to destabilise the economy. A thick fog of paranoia was spreading everywhere and sometimes the wrong people got suspected.

They arrested Donald Soldini on 13 June along with his friend

David Bales, a 25-year-old from New Jersey who was in town to represent a sugar firm. Soldini had returned to Cuba after the revolution and been made a lieutenant in the Army with his own room at the presidential palace. His main job seemed to be making sure American journalists got access to government officials and local prostitutes, not necessarily in that order, in exchange for newspapers back home carrying overblown stories about his role in the revolution 'mostly in sabotage around Havana'.[8] Soldini was chirpy and personable and everyone seemed to like him, until the police arrived with handcuffs.

The charges centred on Bales having used official presidential stationery to intervene in an ongoing court case involving his firm, and Soldini helping him trespass in government offices after working hours. The pair spent a month in prison and were deported. Back in New York, a betrayed-sounding Soldini gave a lengthy interview to the FBI in which he claimed Castro was humanist not communist, but then said he couldn't see much difference between the two. Soon he'd head to the University of Mexico for a degree in business studies and a long life as an unrepentant capitalist.

Soldini's arrest was an overreaction by a nervy Cuban intelligence apparatus, but later that month a genuine threat to the state declared itself when Pedro Díaz Lanz fell out with Raúl Castro for the last time and went into hiding. As the spies scurried around Havana trying to establish who shared the Air Force chief's views, a still unsuspected Frank Fiorini was begging the American embassy to offer his friend sanctuary. The diplomats turned him away with a bland excuse. A few days later, Fiorini met with his well-connected Cuban colleague Sergio Sanjenís in the dark corner table of a restaurant opposite the Havana Hilton.

'Frank, Raúl Castro suspects you're working for American

Intelligence,' Sanjenís said.[9] 'Do me a favour. When you leave here, pretend you don't know me. That's it. Get your ass out of Cuba tonight, now. Because if he picks you up, he's going to kill you.'

Fiorini returned to the base, packed a duffle bag, then crept onto the airfield, where the C-46D and B-25 aeroplanes bought in the dying days of the revolution were still registered in his name. The sun was coming up when he and a sympathetic Cuban pilot took off for Opa-locka airport in Florida. Shortly after, the CIA somewhat reluctantly smuggled Pedro Díaz Lanz and a handful of his circle out of Cuba by boat. A new life was waiting for them all among the suburban tract houses and humid heat of Miami.

Eight hundred miles away across the Caribbean Sea, a very different kind of exile was trying to adapt to his environment. After fleeing Cuba on New Year's Eve, Fulgencio Batista had settled into a luxury suite at the Jaragua Hotel in Ciudad Trujillo, the capital of the Dominican Republic, bringing with him a phalanx of bodyguards and a nervous disposition. He refused to stand by open windows, fearing snipers, and the unexpected metallic click of a purse snapping shut in the hotel lobby could send him ducking towards the carpet. Dominican strongman Rafael Leónidas Trujillo Molina would have preferred his uninvited guest to leave, and for the first few months government newspapers like *El Caribe* openly suggested it, but no country was willing to take the former Cuban President. The icy relationship between the two men only thawed when Trujillo discovered that Fidel Castro had donated to a $300,000 fund organised by leftist Venezuelan students hoping to invade the Dominican Republic.

'Everywhere I hear the chant "Trujillo next! Trujillo next!"' Castro told the students during a trip to Caracas.[10]

A furious Trujillo invited Batista up to his rock-walled white palace to discuss eliminating their mutual enemy. Together they created the Legión Extranjera Anticomunista del Caribe (the Caribbean Anti-Communist Foreign Legion), a paramilitary army of several thousand Dominicans and exiled Cubans, with its officers hired out of a bar in Paris popular with Greek and Croatian right-wingers. Officially a self-defence force, Trujillo intended to use the legión in the overthrow of Castro later in the summer. Batista provided $20 million in funding.

The plan didn't stay secret for long. By August 1959, Cuban exiles in Miami and across the Caribbean had heard about the coming invasion and were counting down the days until the legión went into action and they could all return home. Only the really well informed knew that Trujillo had an inside man in the heart of Havana. Another of Castro's Americans had switched sides.

PART III

COUNTER-
REVOLUTION

12

THE DOMINICAN
REPUBLIC AFFAIR

REVOLUTIONARY HAVANA/NEW YORK/CIUDAD TRUJILLO, LATE SUMMER 1959

During the night of 13 August 1959, a private aeroplane motored to a halt at an airstrip near the town of Trinidad, on the southern coast of central Cuba. Aboard were nine Cuban exiles who had been living in the Dominican Republic since the revolution and knew they were risking execution by returning to their homeland. They'd been lured back by the success of a counter-revolutionary uprising sweeping through central Cuba that looked set to overthrow the government and return Batista to power. The exiles grinned as they climbed down the plane's disembarkation ladder and heard a chant go up from soldiers waiting among the mango trees at the airstrip perimeter.

'Down with communism! Death to Fidel Castro!'[1]

The leader of the soldiers stepped out of the shadows and walked across the packed dirt of the runway to greet the new arrivals. It was William Morgan.

Not many people in Cuba would have suspected Morgan had the capacity or inclination to become a turncoat. His loyalty to the revolution had recently extended to spreading it around Central America. Early in the year, Morgan had quit his post as military governor of Cienfuegos to help out some Panamanian exiles who'd fled their country's ruthless oligarchs and were looking to hustle sponsorship for an invasion. He and Juan Espiritu got approval from senior rebels, who liked the idea of remaking other countries in their own image, and were arranging a training programme for the exiles when a random bullet derailed their plans. At a political rally, Espiritu grappled with a fellow rebel who was shooting a gun in the air and accidentally killed him. Morgan would eventually get his friend's sentence reduced to a year's probation, but the Panama adventure fell apart while he was trying to rescue Espiritu from being chewed up by the Cuban legal system. He asked Frank Fiorini to step in and help save the invasion.

'I told him I thought he was crazy,' said Fiorini.[2]

Despite the refusal, the two men stayed in touch. Fiorini soon discovered that after a couple of drinks Morgan would talk bitterly about the Marxist–Leninists sinking their claws into the revolution and ruining everything he had fought for in the Escambray mountains. The American embassy subsequently became interested in recruiting the Second Front leader but, after doing its due diligence, concluded Morgan remained too supportive of the regime to risk an approach.

The Panamanian coup went ahead in May 1959 without the involvement of either Morgan or Fiorini, and failed. An expedition led by Cuban volunteers spent most of its time in the mountains seducing the local girls while a gunrunning operation intended to arm the urban underground collapsed when police raided the yacht of organiser Roberto Arias and his wife, the British prima ballerina Margot Fonteyn. The government in Havana publicly claimed to know nothing of the plan but quietly ordered the Cubans involved to return home. A similar uprising in Nicaragua, also approved by Castro, collapsed the same month.

As Cuba failed to spread revolution around Central America, rumours about Morgan's dissatisfaction with the new regime reached the Dominican Republic. Trujillo was intrigued enough to send over a minor American expat mobster called Francis John Nelson to find out more. The line went into the water without much expectation of hooking a fish and no one was more surprised than Trujillo when word came back that Morgan and his friend Menoyo were prepared to cooperate in exchange for a million dollars, with a cash advance.

Things started moving fast. Morgan offered up a simple plan: Second Front soldiers would seize central Cuba and hold on until the arrival of the Legión Extranjera Anticomunista del Caribe troops, then launch a joint attack on Havana. Trujillo liked the idea and paid the advance. A squad of Dominican agents smuggled themselves into Havana, introduced Morgan to leaders of the Batista underground and installed a hidden radio so he could request airdrops for his men in the Escambray mountains. In Miami, Morgan's gangster friend Dominick Bartone earned good money buying weapons for the legión and managed to get briefly arrested for it by the American authorities before wriggling free.

Security around the plotting was tight, but Bartone's evasive replies under questioning intrigued the FBI enough to interrogate Morgan when he visited Miami Beach that August with a pregnant Olga Rodríguez. He gave them vague answers and defended Fidel Castro against accusations of communism, while denying involvement in any counter-revolutionary movement. Bureau agents were unable to clarify the situation before Morgan slipped out of his room at the Eden Roc Hotel, dodged their surveillance and returned to Havana aboard a fishing boat loaded with $500,000-worth of Bartone's guns.

He arrived in the Cuban capital on 8 August and was told an American called Alex Rorke was in town asking awkward questions about a forthcoming uprising. Morgan vaguely knew the name from a scandal about a wedding seven years ago and was horrified to discover Rorke was now a journalist looking for a scoop.

• • •

Back in September 1952, the church organ was groaning out hymns and the bride looked virginal in white, but there was no sign of Alex Rorke's future father-in-law. Sherman Billingsley had vowed to boycott the union between his beloved daughter Jacqueline and the unsuitable love of her life, and the guests waiting at the Church of the Holy Trinity on New York's West 82nd Street were eventually forced to admit he was a man of his word. Billingsley had made a fortune bootlegging during Prohibition and invested it all in the Stork Club, a ritzy nightspot with the best cocktails in town. The jet-setters who dined there were happy to overlook the owner's criminal past in exchange for a good table, and in turn Billingsley hoped to join the social register by marrying his eldest daughter into the upper echelons of New York society. Then Alexander Irwin Rorke Jr came along.

Rorke was black-haired, blue-eyed, Catholic and right-wing. Born in 1926 to a well-off Manhattan lawyer with a Boston-Irish background and a much younger wife, Rorke grew up steeped in religion and its application to earthly politics. His father had been a district attorney during the Red Scare just after the First World War and had prosecuted home-grown Bolsheviks ('long-haired cranks who spout socialism, free-verse and free-love in their drawing rooms,' in his opinion) with such vigour that the left tried to assassinate him.[3] The plot failed, but Rorke Sr found it best to move into private practice and pray for the souls of his would-be killers.

His son was taught by the priests at Loyola School and spent the summers at a Catholic camp overlooking the dark blue water of Lake Spofford. By 1943, Rorke was studying at St John's University and so anxious to join the war effort that he squeezed underage into a local National Guard unit. He was accepted into the real thing two years later when the fighting was over, first serving in the 508th Parachute Division and then becoming an intelligence specialist with the 1st Constabulary Regiment, helping round up Soviet spies and fugitive Nazis.

Two years later, Rorke was enrolled at the Georgetown University School of Foreign Service. As a track star, undefeated intercollegiate debate champion and senior official in the National Federation of Catholic College Students, he seemed primed for a glittering career in politics or law. The first hint that Rorke had other priorities came with his resignation from a student job as an FBI file clerk after only a few months, bored by paperwork and routine. After graduation, he surprised everyone by starting up a vending machine business and pouring his spare time into freelance journalism. Rorke loved his parents and respected their hopes for him but wanted the freedom to live life on his own terms. To friends, he played up the image of a successful young businessman turned dashing photojournalist; only close family knew Rorke did shifts at his father's law firm to support himself when times were hard.

As his career wobbled uncertainly off the launch pad, Rorke could be seen dining and dancing around New York with a young actress called Jacqueline Billingsley. Best known for playing a nurse on the radio soap *Young Widder Brown*, she had wavy blonde hair and painted eyebrows and a face just the right side of hard. It was love, even if Jackie's overprotective father thought Rorke nothing more than a handsome charmer looking to snare an heiress and refused to attend the wedding.

'Oh, go ahead if you must,' Sherman Billingsley told his daughter when the engagement was announced, 'but I don't want to hear any more about it.'[4]

By 1959, the couple had two children and Rorke was still running his vending machines while doing occasional reporter work abroad for stories that carried his photographs but rarely his byline. In May, while covering an uprising in Nicaragua, a story came along that changed his life for ever. The former Spanish colony had lurched through a century of conflict-filled independence and was now in the iron grip of Luis Somoza Debayle, whose National Guard crushed the challenge to his rule within a fortnight. Picking his way through the aftermath, Rorke was surprised to hear defeated insurgents claim they'd been backed by the Cuban government. That contradicted the stories coming out of Havana, where the media had already denied responsibility and laid the blame on a thirty-year-old American Army veteran from Wichita, Kansas, called Loran Hall.

Hall was a scapegoat. He'd come to Cuba after the revolution looking for work and been steered towards the Nicaraguan exiles by militia officers. As a married father of four with a criminal record for drinking and burglary, Hall was just glad to be somewhere with regular pay where no one enquired too closely into his background. He trained the Nicaraguans and a few Cuban volunteers at a farm outside Havana but within a month had alienated some important exile figures who got their revenge by spreading rumours he worked for the FBI. Hall was arrested, questioned by both Raúl Castro and Che Guevara ('What do you think of the agrarian reform programme in Cuba?' they repeatedly asked the baffled American) and kept behind bars until July.[5] He shared an exercise yard with others who'd fallen out with the regime, from gangster Santo Trafficante to some disillusioned Panamanian revolutionaries, and got out to find himself smeared as an agent provocateur who had organised the invasions of both Nicaragua and Panama without Havana's permission. Deported back home, the FBI agents who interviewed him found a bitter, angry man with nothing good to say about Cuba.

Rorke knew little about Hall's ordeal but had independently come to doubt the Cuban media narrative. While looking for more answers in Panama, he met a Batista supporter who boasted about a projected summer invasion of Cuba but wouldn't give any more details. In Florida, Rorke tracked down Francis John Nelson, a fifty-something American crook and errand boy for the powerful, who admitted the invasion would soon be launched from the Dominican Republic and suggested contacting a man by the name of Dominick Bartone.

In the coffee shop of Miami Beach's Moulin Rouge Hotel, Bartone revealed that he and Bill Morgan were business partners in an arms concern called the International Trading Company and were jointly backing the overthrow of the Cuban government for a fee of $1 million. The invasion was planned for July. Rorke agreed to keep the story quiet in exchange for exclusive access and hung around Miami waiting for the action to begin, but the only thing that happened that month was an unexpected, unsuccessful raid on the Dominican Republic by Cuban forces. He was back in New York with his vending machines when a gravelly voice on the phone claimed the invasion had been rescheduled and suggested visiting Bill Morgan's home in Havana for more information. Rorke flew in to the Cuban capital on 8 August, asked around and was directed the next day to a mansion in the upscale Miramar district.

He was barely inside the door when a tense-looking Eloy Gutiér-rez Menoyo placed him under arrest. Rorke spent four days there at gunpoint as everyone who came to the house, including fellow American journalist Jean Secon and the neighbourhood egg seller, was pulled inside and held prisoner. When Rorke protested about 'moral law', a Second Front soldier sneered at him: 'Moral law? You speak of moral law and you bombed Hiroshima!'[6]

Rorke didn't like the crack about his country and couldn't un-derstand why he'd been arrested. The American didn't realise he had walked straight into the middle of the biggest double-cross in Cuban history. Bill Morgan had been working for Castro all along.

• • •

Morgan's house was a luxurious mansion in tiled marble where the dining table seated twenty and the courtyard had a swimming pool and bar. The day before Rorke's visit, a cabal of counter-revolutionaries loyal to Batista had gathered in the main room to finalise their plans. Morgan was absent in Florida buying guns, so delegated his friend Menoyo to lead everyone through the complex dance of urban uprising, Second Front guerrilla action and Legión Extranjera Anticomunista del Caribe invasion necessary to overthrow Fidel Castro. At the end of his talk, Menoyo excused himself and went outside. He came back in with a sub-machine gun.

'Don't move or I'll fry you all,' he barked.[7]

Cigars were already drooping from astonished mouths when Castro appeared behind Menoyo in the doorway with a broad smile on his face. One man tried to run upstairs and was shot in the hand. As he bled over the floor tiles, Castro told the counter-revolutionaries that their networks were being rolled up, their guerrilla camps surrounded, their spies and inside men arrested. It was all over.

Despite his complaints about Cuba's political direction, Morgan had never seriously considered aligning himself with the revolution's enemies. He held the view, common among Second Front militants, that Castro had only allowed communists into government under pressure from extremists like Raúl and Guevara and was waiting for the opportunity to push back and establish a democracy. After the Dominican Republic's approach, Morgan went straight to Castro and the two men came up with a plan to string along Trujillo, squeeze him for money and uncover any pro-Batista forces still active in Cuba. The intrigue would climax with the Legión Extranjera Anticomunista del Caribe troops being lured to some remote airstrip and exterminated the moment they stepped off the plane.

Part of the plan involved a half-hearted invasion of the Dominican Republic in July by a force of exiles, Cuban volunteers and Puerto Rican mercenaries recruited from New York's Upper West Side. The reasoning behind the attack remained murky even to those involved, but some close to Morgan assumed it was intended to delay Trujillo's own invasion, planned for the same month, until all the Batista-friendly underground networks in Cuba had been exposed. Trujillo took the bait.

'If aggressors want to see their beards and brains flying like butterflies, let them approach the shores of the Dominican Republic,' he thundered as the invaders sailed closer.[8]

The incursion was easily beaten back. Morgan informed Ciudad Trujillo by radio that his men had taken advantage of the confusion to occupy central Cuba and urged the arrival of the legión. Trujillo remained cautious and sent only an alcoholic Cuban priest to stumble around Morgan's carefully arranged panorama of turncoat Second Front troops and gunshots cracking in the distance. The priest returned and advised Trujillo to launch the invasion, but the dictator still hesitated.

It was becoming harder to maintain the deception. In early August, Morgan dodged the FBI and returned to Havana aboard a boat loaded with weapons but had to arrest the crew at gunpoint when they became suspicious. As the plan threatened to unravel, he had Menoyo swoop on the conspirators gathering in his Miramar mansion and then headed for Trinidad to radio the Dominican Republic again, hoping for a last chance to snare the legión. A cautious Trujillo preferred to send nine prominent Cuban exiles to check on the progress of the counter-revolution instead. They landed at Trinidad airstrip and, delighted by the spotlights and Morgan's troops chanting 'Death to Castro!', allowed themselves to be led into the airport building, where the trap was sprung. Most were too astonished to resist, with only the pilot putting up enough of a fight to take down two Second Front soldiers before being shot dead. Trujillo's dreams of invading Cuba died with him.

Fulgencio Batista immediately distanced himself from the whole affair, describing the Legión Extranjera Anticomunista del Caribe as 'murderers, vermin and riff-raff', and announced his permanent retirement from counter-revolutionary activities.[9] He moved to Portugal, a sun-drenched but austere Catholic dictatorship, and began working on memoirs that would blame everyone but himself for Cuba's misfortunes. His cronies at the Biltmore Terrace Hotel were shocked by their leader's defection but determined to fight on, while Trujillo put a $500,000 bounty on Morgan's head and asked Norman Rothman at the Biltmore to find a hit man who'd take the contract. The government in Havana immediately surrounded the American's house with armed guards.

'How does it feel to have a half-million-dollar price on your head?' asked a reporter.[10]

'Well, it isn't too bad,' said Morgan. 'They are going to have to collect it. And that's going to be hard.'

Other armed men were already escorting Alex Rorke and Jean Secon through the Cuban prison system. The reporters were moved into a military base for what Rorke called 'brainwashing activities', before ending up in a disused theatre crammed with 200 political prisoners. There they met 32-year-old Paul Joseph Hughes, an American pilot who'd arrived in the spring of 1959 and joined some Nicaraguan exiles for what turned out to be a repeat of Loran Hall's experience. The Nicaraguans had boasted about high-level government contacts they didn't possess and Hughes found himself under arrest after paranoid police mistook them all for Dominican agents.

The three Americans shared a decaying toothbrush, slept in the same cot and jumped every time the guards fired into the floor to deter anyone wandering too close to the theatre telephone. After a few days, they were deported. Hughes drifted off into the orbit of the Biltmore Terrace crowd, while Secon continued with her journalist career, and Rorke made a television film for NBC about his imprisonment that prompted death threats from M26J activists in New York. Later, both FBI and CIA agents met with him to discuss events in Havana but regretted their decision when Rorke ('somewhat garrulous,' noted a CIA report drily) began to ring them every few weeks with increasingly irrelevant information.[11]

Alex Rorke had not been a fan of Castro before he visited Cuba. After arrest, prison and deportation, he had become a fervent enemy. Other Americans felt the same way and were ready to take the fight to Havana.

13

THIRTY SECONDS OVER HAVANA

REVOLUTIONARY HAVANA/MIAMI/NEW YORK, WINTER 1959–SUMMER 1960

At cocktail hour on 21 October, representatives of the American Society of Travel Agents were gathered at the Havana Hilton to watch a girl in a grass skirt doing a floorshow. The junket had been arranged by Fidel Castro in the hope of enticing Yankee tourists and their desperately needed dollars back to his country. None of the travel agents present really believed it was possible to resurrect the Cuban tourist industry, but the drinks were free, so they politely flattered their hosts with optimistic talk about the future. As everyone sank cocktails and watched the girl wiggle her hips, the dull whine of an aeroplane engine broke through the chatter and suddenly the sky was booming with anti-aircraft guns. Overhead, a B-25 zigzagged low across the city with leaflets spilling from a rear hatch.

Despite the tourist-friendly image presented to the travel agents, Cuba had been on high alert for the past two months. In the aftermath of Bill Morgan's double-cross, Batista's cronies at the Biltmore had tried to keep the counter-revolution going by persuading Austin Frank Young, released from prison in August, to lead two dozen former regime soldiers and a young American called Lamb across to Pinar del Río province. They were barely off the boat when the militia captured them all. Young managed a daring escape and hid out in a Havana hotel room for a few days before being caught and sentenced to thirty years in prison.

When the B-25 appeared over Havana, many locals thought the exiles had returned on a revenge bombing mission. They were wrong: at the controls were former Castro loyalist Pedro Díaz Lanz, his brother Marcos and Frank Fiorini. The Díaz Lanz brothers had spent the previous few months trying to warn American officials about the danger posed by Fidel Castro, but they got no further than a few polite meetings with Washington figures who had trouble finding Cuba on a map. Now they were taking the message direct to their homeland by scattering leaflets that warned Cubans they were sleepwalking into a communist dictatorship. The Spanish-language text urged revolt before it was too late.

The original plan had been to leaflet Camagüey later that month, but things changed when the Cuban militia arrested Huber Matos, a senior rebel commander, for protesting the creep of communism into the government. He would get twenty years in prison. Díaz Lanz immediately moved his raid forward and changed the target to Havana. He and Fiorini swerved the B-25 through the sky over the capital as shrapnel burst all around them and the leaflets fell, then turned and headed for home. They made it back to Florida in one piece, but their mission was overshadowed by the poor aim of the Cuban anti-aircraft gunners, who missed the plane but managed to kill thirty civilians on the ground. Castro's newspapers blamed the deaths on the B-25 and called the raid 'Havana's Pearl Harbor'.

In the aftermath, Fiorini and the Díaz Lanz brothers were investigated by the FBI for a possible prosecution. Agents interviewed, researched and compiled a file but were unsurprised that no charges were ever brought. A steady stream of disillusioned Cubans had been arriving in Miami since the summer and the stories they told about executions and repression in their homeland had discredited the regime in the eyes of many Americans. In January 1959, the widely read *Life* magazine had described Castro as 'a bearded rebel scholar'; by November, it was calling him 'just another tinhorn tyrant'.[1] After the FBI had dispersed, Pedro Díaz Lanz was contacted by Bernard Barker, now in Miami as a full-time CIA agent working for a mysterious boss called 'Eduardo', who advised the pilot to consider a more political approach to getting rid of Castro. No one in Washington was yet talking openly about removing the Cuban leader, but wheels were starting to turn and Barker thought Díaz Lanz might prove useful in the future.

Frank Fiorini preferred direct action: leaflet raids, building up commando groups in the mountains, perhaps a bomb or two dropped directly on a military installation. Díaz Lanz told him to be patient, but the American was already watching enviously as the Biltmore Terrace crowd launched their own wave of attacks against the Cuban economy.

●　　●　　●

In the first months of 1960, sugar cane plantations began to burn across northern Cuba. Light aircraft would appear out of the morning sky, swoop in low, drop blazing marine flares among the acres of spiky green vegetation, then fly off towards the horizon. Plantation workers fought half the day to bring the fire under control only to see another plane appear that afternoon. The Biltmore Terrace exiles were using their freelance American pilots to bring death from above to Cuba's main export.

The pilots were housed at Great Exuma Island in the Bahamas in a hotel that lacked everything from electricity to running water but was located conveniently near an isolated airstrip operated by a sympathetic employee. Men like Paul Hughes and Richard B. Jaffe took off into the Caribbean sun with a Cuban co-pilot who would clamber back into the cabin to drop the flares once the target was in sight. The cane-burning flights had a significant impact on the Cuban economy in the early part of the year, but the operation began to unravel when a bomb exploded prematurely and blew Robert Ellis Frost's plane apart in mid-air.

Frost was a short, slight man from Oregon in his early thirties with a moustache and a criminal record. He had turned up in Miami that January at the invitation of a pilot already involved in the cane-burning operation and was rooming in the town of Hialeah with a landlady who thought him 'a nice young man', even though he could barely pay the rent.[2] The money situation got better in early February when Frost wrote excitedly to his stepmother in Oregon that he'd been made a captain in the 'Cuban National Air Force' and 'expected to be paid $1,000 per flight'.[3]

'I guess I will be starting pretty soon as my Spanish is getting real good,' he wrote.[4] 'I will give you a list of the people I have met since I have been here and you can watch the papers as their names keep coming up.'

On 18 February, Frost hired a light aircraft from Tamiami airport in the early morning and flew it ten miles to a deserted highway, where two Cubans waited in a car. Together they loaded three bombs made from Army surplus replicas, purchased from a local policeman at $300 each and packed full of dynamite in a Miami garage. A Cuban named Santana boarded the aeroplane, but his friend begged off the mission in favour of an early start at his job selling wholesale coffee. He was lucky. Frost touched down briefly at Great Exuma Island and was guiding the aeroplane towards Matanzas province when a bomb detonated and scattered pieces of plane, pilot and passenger over the Cuban countryside.

Things got worse for the Biltmore Terrace exiles when Frost's landlady began claiming the pilot had been working undercover for the US Border Patrol and had made regular phone calls to its offices with information about his Cuban colleagues. The exiles launched a panicky and unsuccessful witch-hunt to find out who else was spying on them, while an FBI investigation revealed that Frost's main reason for turning informer had been to cover himself from any legal consequences of the bombing raids. He hadn't been much of an inside man, at least according to the unimpressed border patrol agent who took his phone calls: '[He] said he considered Frost to be a "screwball" of questionable judgment and a very poor risk as an informant,' noted the FBI.[5] '[He] said that he rejected Frost's offer to engage in any undercover work on behalf of the Border Control.'

Things got worse on 21 March when a thirty-something pilot called Shergalis, who usually flew charter flights for Sunny South aircraft rental in Fort Lauderdale, was shot down as he flew low over the Cuban countryside. He ended up in a Havana prison, which surprised no one except the pilot who was secretly working for Cuban intelligence and had expected only to be photographed passing overhead to provide Fidel Castro with some propaganda material. The Biltmore Terrace crowd went half crazy wondering who else among their pilots was a double agent and found out the next month when a group led by Robert Duat tried to kidnap Batista paramilitary leader Rolando Masferrer on behalf of Cuban intelligence. A plan was set in motion and Duat's men, including Jack Youngblood and a pair of Miami policemen, headed to Masferrer's Miami house on the pretext of a strategy meeting. En route, Youngblood decided this was a crime too far and slipped away to call the local precinct, leading to the collapse of the kidnapping mission and some arrests.

The final nail in the coffin for the counter-revolutionary air war came on 12 May when 45-year-old Matthew Duke was shot dead landing on a Cuban highway. The former Navy man was famous locally for having married Melody Thompson, a well-known model and heiress to a $3 million tobacco fortune. They lived in luxury for a while, but the marriage fell apart after a 1957 move to Florida and Duke started up an aviation supplies business. His financial problems mounted, leading to an arrest for passing bad cheques, until an offer from the Biltmore Terrace Hotel promised to solve his problems. Duke was touching down on a lone highway in a two-engine Piper Apache to pick up some fugitive Batista loyalists when a militia patrol materialised from the roadside ditches and opened fire. He tried to wrestle the plane back into the air as bullets ripped through the cockpit but was barely off the ground when he slumped over the controls and the Apache bounced onto the asphalt and rolled to a halt.

'I told him! I warned him not to take trips to Cuba,' said a Miami friend to journalists.[6] 'Now look. He's dead.'

It was the end of bombing raids on Cuban cane fields. The demoralised Biltmore Terrace crowd retired from the battlefield to raise their children in huge Florida mansions and do occasional charity work for fellow exiles. Norman Rothman was sacked from the hotel and would soon go to jail alongside Joseph Merola for the burglary of a National Guard armoury back when Castro had been the good guy. Only Rolando Masferrer seemed willing to carry on fighting and his sole motivation was getting back the luxurious lifestyle he'd enjoyed under Batista by overthrowing the current regime and putting himself in charge. No one rated his chances very highly, especially not Frank Fiorini, who was now teaming up with Alex Rorke.

• • •

Since his return to New York from a Havana prison, Alexander Rorke had been milking his status as a minor celebrity by appearing on any radio show that would give him air time. Back in October 1959, he'd been a guest on *Celebrity Table*, a show broadcast nightly from Leone's restaurant where deep-voiced host Ray Heatherton interviewed anyone vaguely famous in the city. After the broadcast, a woman rang the station and asked Rorke to visit her daughter if he wanted a damning story about Fidel Castro. In an apartment filled with family and friends talking in a babble of languages, Rorke sat and listened while Marita Lorenz tearfully described forced abortions and stolen babies.

Lorenz had never been emotionally stable, but recent events had pushed her over the edge into a world where truth and fantasy intermixed like watercolours in the rain. She had returned to New York after losing her baby in Cuba but seemed unable to give a coherent account of the event. One moment she claimed to have been pregnant by Captain Jesus Yanes Pelletier, then the next insisted Fidel Castro was the father; she had lost the baby in a miscarriage or an abortion which was either voluntary or forced on her by the

Cuban authorities; later she would claim the baby had been ripped from her womb by Castro's doctors and grew up unaware of his real mother; Yanes had recently arrived in New York to kidnap her, but she voluntarily went dancing and drinking with him; she wanted no one to know her story but had already spoken to the FBI and now Rorke; she wanted to see Castro overthrown even though she was an activist at a local M26J branch; her ovaries had been removed after complications caused by the abortion, but she would go on to have children years later.

Like everyone else, Rorke was never quite sure if Lorenz was entirely sane but saw her value as the centrepiece for some anti-Castro propaganda. He wrote an article for scandal rag *Confidential* that claimed Lorenz had been raped by Castro. She agreed to play along with the deception but only after Rorke impersonated an FBI agent to scare off some former friends, a serious enough criminal offence that the bureau considered a prosecution but reluctantly dropped the case through lack of evidence.

'It is the opinion of the FBI that Rorke, being a freelance newspaperman and photographer,' noted an agent, 'will use any method in order to get a story or meet individuals and would even go to the extent of representing himself as being associated with the FBI.'[7]

Not long after their meeting, Lorenz was sent to live with her father's family in Germany to regain some emotional equilibrium. Rorke remained in New York and exploited his association with her to report on the city's Cuban exiles, becoming trusted enough to share a microphone with Pedro Díaz Lanz on a summer 1960 radio show. Afterwards, he was introduced to Frank Fiorini and the two men became friends.

Rorke's college-boy looks and enthusiasm formed a yin to Fiorini's aggressive blue-collar yang, helped along by both being

Catholic military veterans with experience of post-war Germany. Fiorini confided that, despite Díaz Lanz advising him to take the political high road, he intended to form a paramilitary group down in Florida. Rorke offered to introduce him to a Manhattan-based group called the Anti-Communist International that was run by Haviv Schieber, a fifty-something Israeli who had been kicked out of his own country for hard-right political activism. Staffed by retired Catholic generals, repentant former communists and worried businessmen, the Anti-Communist International was ahead of the curve in believing Castro to be a communist and had protested the Cuban leader's visit to America the previous year. Rorke thought they might provide funding for Fiorini's plans.[8]

The former Marine liked what he heard. He and the Díaz Lanz brothers had started off their anti-Castro crusade in relative comfort after selling the C-46D aircraft, with Fiorini getting enough from his share to rent a nice house with a swimming pool. The cash drained away after months of maintaining the other aeroplane, launching occasional leafleting missions over Cuba and opening a salvage business as cover for their activities. Now the trio were fighting for scraps of patronage from rich exiles and had to compete with other counter-revolutionary groups that had been formed in Miami by followers of Carlos Prío, young Catholics influenced by the Jesuits of the Agrupación Católica Universitaria and more recent arrivals holding a rainbow of different political opinions.

Pedro Díaz Lanz was still hoping to transition into a political figure funded by Washington, but Fiorini remained committed enough to a military path that he even tried to lure the Biltmore Terrace crowd out of retirement for a joint venture. Little came of it except a friendship with Bill Johnson, a mercenary pilot involved with Rolando Masferrer who ran a collections agency out of his

Florida home. After all those failures, Alex Rorke and his connections to the apparently well-heeled Anti-Communist International seemed to be the answer to Fiorini's prayers.

Neither man realised that things were about to change dramatically in the anti-Castro struggle. Clean-cut CIA agents would soon receive orders to overthrow the Cuban government and, out in the Everglades, the former Oriente province death squad leader Rolando Masferrer was about to launch a parallel war to take back his country.

14

NO CHILDREN, NO PETS, NO CUBANS

MIAMI/NO NAME KEY, LATE SUMMER 1960

A lot of people had tried to kill Rolando Arcadio Masferrer Rojas over the years. Spanish fascists had bombed him out of trenches, Cuban secret police had machine-gunned his windows and former President Carlos Prío Socarrás once offered $50,000 to anyone who could put him in the ground. They all failed. The heavyset and moustached Masferrer was tough as granite and those who challenged him rarely lived to regret their decision.

He grew up among the sugar mills and green parks of Holguín in Oriente province and cared enough about class injustice as a teenager to become a communist activist. On his eighteenth birthday, some right-wing Spanish Army officers an ocean away tried to overthrow their government and Masferrer became one of 35,000 foreigners who joined the International Brigades to stop them. He fought in the defence of Madrid then became a political commissar at the Ebro and came home limping with a bullet in his right heel when the Republican government lost the war. The feelings of rage and defeat never quite went away. Masferrer rejoined civilian life by studying law at the University of Havana, where he dressed like a cowboy from the American movies with a Stetson and boots and a revolver in his belt.

'He never came out unarmed,' said a fellow leftist.[1] 'He always had one or two pistols on him, and in his car he kept a few more, because back then he wanted to solve all problems with shooting.'

Masferrer fought the authorities at every opportunity, but his freebooting approach appalled fellow communists, who finally expelled him after his political fundraising crossed the line into extortion. He joined the Caribbean Legion but dropped all talk of proletarian revolution after its collapse and became a landowner in Oriente province, where he earned a nasty reputation for forcing local peasants to sell their property at a steep discount. Some of the old fire returned in 1952 when Batista staged his coup and Masferrer barricaded himself into the University of Havana with a gang of armed followers for a heroic last stand against the usurper. After negotiations, he left without firing a shot and three months later a photograph appeared in the newspapers of Masferrer hugging the new President at a ceremonial dinner. The one-time communist was elected senator for Oriente province two years later.

'It is said that although Batista does not particularly like Masferrer,' noted a CIA report at the time, 'he accepts his support because he prefers to have his gangster following with him rather than against him.'[2]

Masferrer's political compromise with the new regime made him wealthy and powerful. He established the national magazine *Tiempo en Cuba*, modelled on the American *Time*, and received a professorship of English at the University of Havana that paid well without requiring much attendance or work. He had a wife and sometimes other men's wives, in the macho Cuban way that delighted in cuckolding someone but would kill if the situation was reversed. The strutting rooster side of his personality was balanced by a private love of painting and writing poetry, although nothing in that artistic streak diluted his essential brutality. One day a passing police car found Masferrer forcing a political opponent to dig his own grave at gunpoint.

He still considered himself a 'Marxian socialist', but when the Movimiento 26 de Julio went up into the mountains, Masferrer stayed loyal to the government and formed his own paramilitary group called Los Tigres. Gunslinger friends from the 1940s and members of the Havana underworld put on uniforms and earned a reputation for midnight arrests, summary executions and torture.

'Hey, somebody had to fight the Castroites,' said Masferrer.[3] 'Batista's Army sure wasn't.'

When the regime fell and Batista's cronies fled abroad, Masferrer got less warning than most and arrived with his family in America nearly penniless. The authorities reluctantly granted him political asylum and Masferrer settled in Miami to spend long months plotting counter-revolution at the Biltmore Terrace Hotel. Batista's cronies gave up the armed struggle after the failure of the Dominican invasion and subsequent air campaign, but Masferrer couldn't afford to join them. His wife was already selling her furs to pay the rent.

By late summer 1960, he had recruited his own counter-revolutionary army from fellow exiles and a few American locals with a taste for adventure. Miami was already buzzing with rumours that the American President had authorised a forthcoming invasion of Cuba and Masferrer knew the only way to get a piece of the pie after Castro was overthrown was to have his own armed presence on the ground when it happened.

• • •

The 34th President of the United States of America was a career military man who regarded communism as a global infection and himself as the scalpel. Dwight David Eisenhower had capitalised on his impressive performance as a five-star general during the Second World War to win the 1952 presidential election in a landslide victory. Once in power, he pushed for the use of nuclear weapons to end the Korean War, supported French efforts against communist guerrillas in Indochina and authorised a rightist coup in Guatemala. His domestic policies were more moderate, but Eisenhower made it clear his primary concern was winning the Cold War against communism by using any means necessary.

By the spring of 1960, he had become convinced that Fidel Castro was a mentally unstable Marxist who needed to be removed from power. Cuba had few defenders left in America and the days when even the mass executions of political enemies could be excused were long gone, replaced by alarm over the freezing of foreign residents' bank accounts, the nationalisation of some American businesses and Havana's increasingly strong links with the Soviet Union. Newspaper cartoonists depicted the island as a shark cruising the waters off the southern coast with its fin sprouting a hammer and sickle, or Fidel Castro as a petulant child plucking feathers from the tail of an unamused American eagle.

Some support for Castro could still be found in the Fair Play for Cuba Committee, an organisation formed that April by CBS reporter Robert Taber and friends to combat what they saw as misleading reporting by the mainstream media. The committee's membership never got past a few thousand big-city intellectuals and had slipped into political irrelevance by June 1960 when American-owned refineries in Cuba were expropriated for refusing to process Soviet oil. The resulting boycott of Cuban sugar led to escalating retaliations on both sides. In the aftermath, a Gallup poll found 81 per cent of Americans hostile to Castro while only 2 per cent remained positive.[4]

Eisenhower had given the green light to the CIA for regime change a few months earlier while those problems were still in their infancy. His only conditions were that America should have plausible deniability and Castro be replaced by a junta which would call democratic elections within six months. The spies at Langley, Virginia, started planning. An early idea to parachute small groups of guerrillas into the mountains was soon abandoned in favour of a brute force amphibious assault by a few thousand exile volunteers. The only Americans present would be a handful of CIA observers and some Merchant Marine sailors paid a $500 bonus each for guiding the landing craft up to the beach.

White House mandarins approved the invasion plan under the name Operation JMARC and discreet recruiting began in Miami through an agency-controlled umbrella group called the Frente Revolucionario Democrático (Revolutionary Democratic Front), formed from representatives of the biggest exile organisations. The recruits went off to a secret training camp overseas while the CIA paid other exiles to launch regular attacks on their homeland, hoping to destabilise Cuba ahead of the invasion. Soon it seemed almost every Cuban with a presence in Miami had a boat, a sub-machine gun and a telephone number that rang somewhere in Langley.

Senior agency men toyed with the idea of assassinating Castro in the run up to the invasion and a small cabal, less wedded to the rule of law than some, approached the Mafia for advice. In August, Chicago mob boss Salvatore 'Sam' Giancana and Johnny Roselli, an illegal migrant from Italy who worked for Giancana in Las Vegas, offered to do the hit for free in exchange for some goodwill from law enforcement. They asked for poison, which the spies supplied as a vial of botulin tablets, and smuggled it to a Cuban contact with access to Castro's office. By the time the pills arrived, the contact had already lost his job and the assassination attempt fizzled out. The agency went back to spreading money around Miami's exile scene and was soon handing out up to $90,000 a month in subsidies.

In the chaotic, mutating world of exile politics, CIA agents often had no idea who was spending their money or why, but none of that seemed to matter with the invasion planned for next spring and everyone convinced success was inevitable. By autumn 1960, so many cabin cruisers with poorly concealed machine guns were moored under the Flagler Street Bridge that sightseeing boats were pointing them out to tourists as landmarks. In less public areas, exiles practised with agency-supplied hardware, most of it illegal.

'The array of outlawed weapons with which we were familiarised,' said one Cuban, 'included bullets that explode on impact, silencer-equipped machine guns, homemade explosives and self-made napalm for stickier and hotter Molotov cocktails.'[5]

Not everyone in Miami was happy to see their previously quiet city transform into an armed camp. Rental adverts for local properties began to include the words: 'No Children, No Pets, No Cubans'.[6] The exiles ignored the insults and prepared for a triumphant return to a post-communist Cuba.

• • •

Rolando Masferrer opened an office at 972 West Flagler Street and called his new organisation, with typical lack of subtlety, Cubana

Unete a la Batalla Anticomunista (Cuban, Join the Anti-Communist Struggle – CUBA). He filled the ranks with fifty or so former Tigers and secret policemen, then applied to the CIA for financial backing. A cool-mannered agent with a sharp haircut pointed out he wasn't permitted to fund anyone on the extreme left or right and, from his point of view, Masferrer was both.

The former senator for Oriente province was forced to finance his organisation with a patchwork of private loans and handouts that paid the bills but left little for luxuries like guns and ammunition. One of the few advantages that came from the lack of agency support was the recruitment of American citizens, who were generally banned from exile groups by the CIA to maintain the illusion that the anti-Castro struggle was a purely Cuban affair. Pilot Paul Joseph Hughes signed on with CUBA, as did a crew-cut and horse-faced 36-year-old Korean War veteran called Allen Dale Thompson. 'A down on his luck fisherman' originally from Texas, according to local journalists, Thompson didn't talk much about his past, but something about his behaviour convinced others he'd done time in prison.[7]

Also on the payroll were 25-year-old Robert Otis Fuller and 28-year-old Anthony Zarba. Short, handsome Bob Fuller had been born in Cuba to an American cattle-ranching family who held on to their citizenship but not their land when the revolution came. He served as a Marine in post-ceasefire Korea and decided to use his military skills in the fight against Castro when he got home. His friend Tony Zarba was a Miami carpenter, originally from Boston, whose asthma kept him out of the armed forces and sparked an adolescent hero-worship towards men like Fuller who'd served. The connection with Masferrer came via Fuller's father, who was providing some of CUBA's funding in the hope of recovering his property, but both Fuller and Zarba had been involved in the counter-revolution since the start. The previous year, they'd been caught loading guns and ammunition into a light aircraft at Key Largo, intending to parachute the supplies into Pinar del Río. Customs decided not to press charges but warned the pair against getting involved in Caribbean intrigue. They didn't listen.

In September 1960, CUBA rebranded itself as the Ejército Nacional Cubana (Cuban National Army – ENC) and rented a boarding house near its office to serve as barracks. The recruits received minimal training under their commander Armentino Feria Perez, a barely literate fifty-year-old veteran of the Spanish Civil War known as 'El Indio', who had the reputation of a stone-cold killer. The plan was for two waves of ENC volunteers to land at Oriente province over the next few weeks and join up with surviving groups of Batista loyalists in the mountains. Money was so short the group could only afford handguns and would have to capture anything more advanced from the enemy, an issue no one in the ENC seemed to think would be a problem.

On 3 October, twenty-four Cubans along with Thompson, Fuller and Zarba set off on a seaborne infiltration of the south-eastern coast of Cuba near Holguín. Paul Hughes helped captain the boat on a nightmarish journey of broken engines, half-mutinous passengers and dwindling supplies. They reached the Cuban coast with barely enough fuel to get back to the Bahamas. Hughes's last view of the group was watching them wade onto the beach to be greeted by a crowd of smiling locals who turned noticeably sour when Masferrer's name was mentioned, and then the American was gunning the engine towards international waters.

Back on dry land, the landing party commandeered a dump truck and stormed a garrison at Cayo Mambí, where they killed nine militiamen and captured thirty-seven. It should have been a triumph, but El Indio took a bullet in the head during the attack and the group's plans fell apart with his death. Their new commander decided against the projected march towards Guantánamo in favour of establishing a camp up in the Sierra del Cristal, an idea that could have worked if some prisoners hadn't escaped and warned the militia. As the ENC hacked their way uphill through dense foliage, Tony Zarba decided modern warfare was not for him and deserted back to the beach looking for a boat to sail back home. He was captured by Castro's men before finding one.

Within a few more days, the militia had caught another twenty-two ENC volunteers with only four, including Thompson and Fuller, managing to get away. On 12 October, the prisoners went on trial. Zarba unconvincingly claimed the aim of the mission had not been to wage war while the Cuban next to him in the dock loudly announced he would rather be a prisoner in revolutionary Havana than a hairdresser in reactionary Miami, then begged for mercy. The government was in no mood to agree. 'Death Penalties for Collaborators and Mercenaries' demanded the headline in regime newspaper *El Mundo* and the judges obliged for Zarba and eight others, with the rest receiving thirty years in prison.[8] Locals accused of helping them got twenty years. Tony Zarba was executed by firing squad at 05:00 the next day. A letter written before he left Miami, expressing his hatred of the 'diabolic communists' in Cuba, did the rounds of the exile community and moved many with its note of prescient self-sacrifice: 'I have confidence that God would give me the necessary strength and courage to die with honour and pride if this was necessary in the hills or in front of a Red firing squad.'[9]

Then it was discovered that Rolando Masferrer had written the letter himself after Zarba's execution to drum up support for his cause and the Cuban's reputation sank even further into the gutter. Masferrer's pilot Richard Jaffe quit in disgust and told the FBI his boss was 'a cold-blooded killer who sent men to their deaths' and more an extortionist than a counter-revolutionary.[10] Jaffe couldn't believe Masferrer still planned to dispatch a second ENC group and was currently recruiting from Americans who'd come to Miami looking for revenge after hearing about Zarba's execution.

While the controversy raged in Miami, the remaining four ENC men were captured on 16 October, exhausted and starving, and executed a few hours later at a rifle range outside Santiago de Cuba. Robert Fuller's father, who had helped to fund the mission, sank into a lifetime of guilt and mourning while Paul Joseph Hughes dealt with his feelings by carefully pouring liquid gelignite into some thick-skinned balloons and flying a stolen light aircraft towards Havana to settle the score. He disappeared without a trace somewhere over the Florida Straits before reaching his target.

Throwing more men into the meat grinder after what had happened would require an almost inhuman ruthlessness. Masferrer barely hesitated. It would take an FBI raid and a possible murder to stop him.

● ● ●

No Name Key was a flyspeck of wetlands out in the Everglades with little to offer except coconut trees and mosquitoes. The owners, a wealthy family of Cuban descent, had never been able to find a good use for the place and let it grow wild while they spent their days somewhere more civilised. In November 1960, the key finally found a purpose when a mutual acquaintance suggested it would be a suitably discreet training ground for Rolando Masferrer and the ENC. A short discussion with the owners secured the site and Masferrer's men began erecting makeshift shelters around the key's solitary building, a tumbledown wooden hut.

Word soon got out and FBI agents turned up to investigate the truth behind Jaffe's claims of a second invasion. They found sixteen Cuban and American volunteers doing survival training, trapping raccoons with wire snares and complaining about the local insect life. The men remained tight-lipped about their future plans, although balding 42-year-old tugboat captain and naval veteran Welburn 'Wilbur' Gee of New York State was happy to babble about his past. He'd been living in Venezuela after getting married and starting a family, but lack of work had brought him back to Miami in June for a dredging contract. Along the way he met some ENC men and would have joined the first invasion if a hurricane hadn't stranded him somewhere distant when the boats departed. He moved into the West Flagler Street barracks when the winds eventually died down, determined to join the next mission. Gee admitted he'd been an M26J member back in Venezuela but now saw the error of his ways.

'I got out of work and I am going to Cuba to fight communism,' he said, 'so it won't spread to the rest of the Latin American countries.'[11]

The agents wrote it all down in their notebooks and warned the men to call off their invasion and stay home. Everyone pretended to agree. A few nights later, the volunteers were back in Miami, drinking at a bar and talking about Cuba. Army veteran Russell Freeman Masker Jr, who'd worked with M26J activists before the revolution and been deported from Havana for trying to join the rebels, was having a beer in the corner with a Portuguese volunteer called Juan (known as 'El Musico' for his musical talents) and a former Batista secret policeman who preferred not to use his real name. After too many drinks, one of the trio quietly suggested that after landing in Cuba, they break away from the Masferrer group and link up with more competent guerrillas. Wilbur Gee overheard the remark and reported it to the ENC leadership who immediately expelled the policeman, cleared El Musico of blame and remained deeply suspicious about Masker.

Back in No Name Key for more training, the suspicions intensified when Masker found the physical fitness sessions too intense and dropped out, preferring to spend his time hunting rabbits with a .22 rifle. Words were exchanged, insults escalated and the Cuban camp leader threatened to execute Masker as a traitor.

Everything had calmed down by the time Rolando Masferrer visited the camp a few days later for a brief pep talk. He left behind an M1 Garand rifle which was immediately grabbed by Rolando Martínez Campanería, a former soldier in Batista's Army who claimed to have killed 200 rebels during the revolution. Early in the morning of 18 November, Masker followed his usual routine of getting up early to hunt rabbits. Around breakfast time, the rest of the group heard a loud shot and rushed towards the sound to find Martínez calmly walking back to camp cradling the M1. He claimed to have accidentally shot Masker while hunting. Gee and the others found Masker lying naked halfway out of a small natural pool where he'd been bathing.

'His side had been blown open,' Gee said later, 'and small fish in the pool were nibbling at his intestines.'[12]

A medical evacuation helicopter got Masker to the mainland, but he died in an ambulance after deliriously telling police he had shot himself, then blaming Martínez. An official investigation declared the shooting had been a hunting accident with no one at fault, and a demoralised ENC returned to Miami for some heavy drinking and recrimination. Plans for a second landing in Cuba collapsed.

As Christmas approached, the closest the American volunteers got to seeing any action came when 28-year-old male nurse Kenneth Proctor, who had a gold earring and a tattoo around his neck that read 'cut on dotted line', accepted $10 to beat up a Cuban exile newspaper editor who'd written something that annoyed Masferrer. The man and his wife were hospitalised. Shortly after, a drunk Proctor attacked another recruit called Weary, a blond neo-Nazi type with a moustache who annoyed everyone by obsessing over sinking Russian freighters with torpedoes.

The ENC was disintegrating and Frank Fiorini was happy to take advantage. He'd been trying to build up his own paramilitary group ever since drifting away from the Díaz Lanz brothers but hadn't got much further than shooting practice with a few friends. Then ENC member Jerry Buchanan, the scapegrace younger brother of well-known *Sun-Sentinel* journalist James, defected from Rolando Masferrer and brought a pack of Americans with him.

Fiorini named his new unit the International Brigade, apparently unaware of the Soviet-run Spanish Civil War units with the same name, and poached more men from the ENC while simultaneously having the nerve to suggest a merger with Masferrer. That failed to happen but stirred up enough gossip in the exile community to attract a visit from the FBI. Under interrogation, most International Brigade members claimed the unit was a social club that liked to keep fit, but recent arrival Paul Henri was more outspoken about his desire for death or glory.

'Henri stated he was aware of the fact that if he was successful in getting to Cuba his chances of remaining alive were very slim,' noted an agent.[13] 'However, if he died, he would go down in history.'

Paul Henri would have to work fast if he wanted to be remembered through the ages. As 1960 came to an end, President Eisenhower was preparing to hand over Operation JMARC to the incoming John Fitzgerald Kennedy, a boyish Democrat who'd run on a platform of liberalism at home and anti-communism abroad. An invasion of Cuba was scheduled for April. Miami's exiles wouldn't have long to build up a presence in their homeland if they wanted to take advantage of the political vacuum that would follow the inevitable defeat of Fidel Castro.

15

NOW DIG! WE'RE FIGHTING CASTRO!

REVOLUTIONARY HAVANA/MIAMI, LATE WINTER–SPRING 1960

Hans Tanner was sitting in the fifth row of the Teatro Shanghai in Havana watching the naked girls dance when a man slid into the seat beside him. The new arrival pretended to be absorbed by the jiggling flesh on stage as he whispered instructions for a meeting the next evening at the Floridita bar. Then he coughed theatrically at Tanner's cigar smoke and moved to a different row.

It was January 1961 and the Shanghai was a shadow of its former self. The nudes still danced, but the hardcore pornographic films were long gone and the theatre's main attraction had emigrated. Superman had packed a suitcase and boarded a plane with only the five pesetas that government regulations now allowed Cubans to take into exile. He started a new life in Miami with the equivalent of seventy-five cents in his pocket and vanished into anonymity. His old employer limped on, with the girls naked as ever but the choreography shoddier and the audiences smaller. The only people who attended with any regularity were the anti-Castro underground, who used the darkness of the theatre to hide their meetings. A neighbouring seat, some whispered instructions as the music boomed from speakers by the stage and then Hans Tanner was casually smoking a cigar as he made his way out into a sunlit Cuban afternoon.

The 33-year-old Swiss was in town on an undercover mission for the Movimiento Demócrata Cristiano (Christian Democratic Movement – MDC), an exile group based in Miami. The motoring journalist had a taste for adventure, on and off the track.

Hans Rubei Tanner had been born in Neuhausen, a small town close to the Rhine Falls, but did most of his growing up in England after his parents emigrated during the war. He turned a love of fast cars into a career criss-crossing the Atlantic as a Grand Prix reporter, becoming a ubiquitous character trackside in his dark glasses and black goatee. Away from the petrol fumes, he acted as fixer for American companies looking to do business overseas, specialising in knowing the right people at Ferrari and other high-end Italian car manufacturers. People in the industry liked Tanner without ever trusting him much. His deals often fell through, his hotel bills went unpaid and rivals claimed the lanky Swiss couldn't even legally drive due to poor eyesight. Fatally, Tanner could never fight the urge to cash in quickly when a longer-term strategy would have brought a better return.

'He might have made a great multimillionaire,' said a friend, 'but there was a dominant small-time hustler gene in his makeup.'[1]

Tanner's involvement with the MDC had begun a month earlier in a New York buried under a thick blanket of snow. He was drinking cocktails in the lobby bar of the Savoy Hilton with a Cuban friend and discussing mutual acquaintance Austin Frank Young, still locked up in a Havana prison. After a few drinks, the friend suggested Tanner talk to Cuban exiles in Florida to see if they could help. After a few more drinks, Tanner agreed. The friend had contacts in the MDC, a political movement formed in Havana by José Ignacio Rasco and Laureano Batista Falla to protest the revolution's turn to authoritarianism. Castro's Cuba was not a good place to be calling for democratic elections and the pair fled to Miami one step ahead of the firing squad. They reformed the MDC in exile and held noisy rallies by the José Martí statue in Bayfront Park; more quietly, they organised Havana-based sympathisers into an underground faction.

Tanner called at the party's Miami branch on his way to a race in New Zealand. He'd recently encouraged investors to buy shares in a company that manufactured experimental cars and was accompanying a team down under to race them in competition. It was becoming obvious the cars were fatally slow and Tanner had discreetly sold his own shares, so a detour to Miami's Little Havana district made a pleasant distraction from worrying about the reaction of the investors when they found out. He met Batista Falla, a wealthy lawyer in his mid-twenties, who told him it would be difficult to rescue Austin Frank Young from a Cuban prison but asked if the Swiss journalist cared enough about the cause to help in other ways. After the inevitable few drinks, Tanner found himself volunteering to visit Havana and pass on messages to the MDC's underground organisation. New Zealand could wait.

A flight was booked for 12 January and Tanner spent the intervening week visiting Batista Falla's paramilitaries at a rented property out in the Everglades. The Swiss, who loved guns and had done national service in the British Army, did some instructing alongside a soft-spoken American former soldier known only as

'John' who spent his downtime complaining bitterly about the CIA's all-Cuban recruitment policy for its forthcoming invasion. Together they toughened up the MDC volunteers.

'The day began at the camp with physical jerks for half an hour, each man carrying a Lee–Enfield rifle all the time,' said Tanner.[2] 'There was a daily two-mile run, in full battle order. Twice a week we had twelve-hour night marches. In the programme were map-reading, firing with rifles, Colt .45 pistols, Thompson sub-machine guns, and stripping and cleaning Browning automatic rifles as well as the rest of the arms.'

Then the week was up and Tanner was on board an airliner descending into Havana airport. He'd last been in the city for the 1958 Grand Prix and was shocked to see armed militia on every corner and the legendary casinos reduced to a few sad-looking roulette wheels marooned in an ocean of thinning carpet. Even the once omnipresent Esso petrol signs had been replaced by the green and white of a new state-owned monopoly. After a few days acting the tourist, Tanner took a seat in the fifth row of the Teatro Shanghai and waited for his contact to show.

Everyone knew an invasion was coming soon and the MDC was just one of many exile groups jockeying for position in what would soon be a post-Castro world. A few American soldiers of fortune were trying to get their own foothold in Cuba before the fighting began, including Frank Fiorini, who now led a miniature army that was behind on its rent.

• • •

The badge of the International Brigade was a black skull and crossbones on a gold shield with the words '*La Brigada Internacionale*' neatly embroidered above and below. Frank Fiorini had the work done by a Miami mascot shop. He passed the cloth insignia around the room at the Hotel de Cuba while Alex Rorke showed off a membership card for the Anti-Communist International and talked about his plans to set up a training camp in Guatemala.

It all sounded good to Kenneth Joseph Proctor, now calling himself leader of the Cuban Revolutionary Army of Liberation (CRAL). Originally from Boston, Proctor had served three years in the Air Force until an accident forced him back into civilian life, where he moved to Miami, became a trainee nurse and accumulated an extensive collection of body art.

'Numerous tattoos on arms, including wolf, cherry, rooster, "Smooze", skull and wings, a pig, ham and eggs, devil,' noted a thorough FBI agent.[3] 'On his chest he has two eyeballs plus numerous tattoos over rest of body.'

Proctor had become fascinated by the local anti-Castro scene and, in the autumn of 1960, left his nursing job to join Rolando Masferrer's group at the boarding house on 1651 West Flagler Street. The failure of the first invasion and cancellation of the second was a body blow, but the scene really fell apart in early January when six Americans from the ENC, led by 28-year-old Korean War veteran Tommy Baker, made tearful farewell phone calls to their mothers before stealing a boat and heading for Pinar del Río to join the counter-revolution. Instead, they sailed straight into the mouth of Havana harbour and were arrested.

'My boy is a peaceful boy,' Baker's mother told journalists.[4] 'He hates fighting. He doesn't even like arguments.'

The Cuban authorities didn't agree and gave Baker and his friends thirty years, although they would be out in less than two. In the aftermath, Miami police lost patience with Masferrer and cleared out 1651 West Flagler Street, throwing the fifteen or so volunteers still there out onto the street. Wilbur Gee was given some cash to pay off the remaining Americans, which amounted to about $3 each, and then Masferrer's private army was finished. Most headed back into anonymity, but Proctor and a handful of others formed the CRAL and moved into the Hotel de Cuba to live off a barely edible goulash made with whatever butcher scraps were going cheap that day.

On 25 January, Frank Fiorini and Alex Rorke turned up at the hotel looking to recruit Proctor's group into the International Brigade. Their big talk about serious financial backing and Guatemalan training camps impressed Proctor, who didn't realise the brigade was in even worse shape than his own group. Down to twelve Americans and a handful of Cubans, Fiorini's men spent their days wearing second-hand military fatigues and polishing their tiny armoury of weapons. The overseas training camps were a fiction that sprang from Rorke's recent journalistic trips to Central America and some half-hearted promises made by unimportant figures who forgot him the moment the interview was over.

Some observers believed the brigade had received start-up funds from shady Mafia figures, possibly funnelled through former Biltmore regular Bill Johnson, but, if true, the cash had disappeared fast. Fiorini was $2,000 behind on his rent and desperately hustling for more money to buy guns and ammunition. Brigade members knew their only chance of a real payday would come from a successful counter-revolution.

'Now dig! I belong to a [sic] anti-Castro counter-revolutionary force here in Miami,' wrote one brigader to an ex-serviceman pal back home.[5] 'We can use good men. If we succeed in overthrowing Castro we'll be rich, if not, dead.'

For some members, the brigade's main attraction was less the chance for action than the feminine presence of Marita Lorenz, who had turned up in Florida at the end of 1960 after a year spent with relatives in Germany. She immediately annoyed the local FBI with false stories about being protected by its agents against Cuban assassins, and then connected with Alex Rorke and Frank Fiorini, accompanying them to exile meetings in a forlorn plan to unite the various political factions. She would later claim to have visited Cuba in a failed attempt to assassinate Castro, but most people remembered her only as a glamorous figure making sandwiches for the brigade at Fiorini's house.

Proctor agreed to merge his group with the International Brigade in exchange for help landing in Cuba. Fiorini scraped together $100 to buy seven .303 Enfield rifles at a gun shop and connected Proctor with a yacht owner looking to make a false insurance claim if his vessel went mysteriously missing. The plan was barely finalised before an informer betrayed them and the FBI turned up to discourage the brigade from breaking the Neutrality Act. Proctor and Fiorini pretended to agree, but on the night of 5 February, a mixed group of CRAL and International Brigade members, both American and Cuban, pulled a gun on the chief engineer of the tugboat *Gil Rocke* as he kept watch and set off for Cuba. The tug got about six feet before the police, tipped off again by an inside man, opened fire. Speedboats chased the vessel as hijackers frantically threw rifles and International Brigade insignia over the side. The *Gil Rocke* eventually ran aground on a sand bank off the exclusive Bay Point neighbourhood, less than a mile north of where the chase had started.

In the darkness most of the hijackers managed to escape, but Proctor, two other Americans and a Cuban were arrested. They would serve thirty days for grand larceny. Frank Fiorini, who'd been at home the whole evening, claimed to know nothing about the plan and was reluctantly set free. The last invasion effort by the International Brigade came in March when 25-year-old Angus McNair Jr, remembered by his comrades as a mop of hair with glasses and strong opinions about communism, sailed off on his own mission to Pinar del Río alongside five Cubans intending to start a guerrilla group. They were captured by militia without firing a shot.

Fiorini had one last opportunity to make a mark on history. That spring, Bernard Barker asked Díaz Lanz to fly senior exile figures into Cuba once the CIA invasion had captured enough territory to make an alternate national administration feasible. Agency funds provided $1,500 for repairs to the B-25 aeroplane in preparation. Díaz Lanz wanted Fiorini to be his co-pilot, but getting CIA permission for this quickly became irrelevant when the Cuban fell out with the men he was supposed to transport and his role was terminated. The offer came and went so quickly that Fiorini was never quite sure what was happening.

The International Brigade would not be playing any part in a post-invasion Cuba but better-organised groups like the MDC still thought they stood a chance. Hans Tanner had been putting in plenty of undercover work in Havana to make that happen.

• • •

The first encounter at the Shanghai led Tanner to the gloom of the Floridita, where a bust of its most famous drinker, Ernest Hemingway, perched at the end of the bar. The author himself was less poised than his bronze replica, having left Cuba the previous summer for psychiatric treatment abroad after a campaign of harassment by the authorities sent him into a depressive spiral. Over an icy cocktail, Tanner chatted motor racing with his contact then discreetly accepted a package of messages for the MDC leaders in Miami. The next day, he was sitting in the departure lounge of Havana's José Martí airport watching police officers stare suspiciously from under a sign that read: 'Fatherland or Death! We Shall Conquer!'.

He touched down at Miami feeling a greater sense of relief than he'd ever experienced in his life only to be told by Batista Falla that the party had decided to land a group in Oriente province and needed him back in Cuba to alert the underground. In early February, Tanner returned to Havana under the pretext of tracking down some car parts that had gone missing during the Grand Prix and was driven around by men who kept watchful eyes on the police cars in their rear-view mirrors. Thunderclouds bloomed in the sky every day.

In March, Tanner made a third trip to Cuba looking to link up with MDC guerrillas in the mountains and arrange the landing. The atmosphere was now much tenser across the island, with loudspeakers booming out non-stop propaganda, pre-recorded government messages playing before every telephone call and lorries of militia troops gripping Czech sub-machine guns racing through the streets. The regime knew it had traitors within its ranks and had recently shocked the world by executing Bill Morgan against the wall of the old moat in La Cabaña prison.

After the Dominican Republic invasion, Morgan had stepped out of the political limelight to run a successful frog farm in the countryside, but he had done nothing to indicate any disloyalty to the revolution. Then, in March 1960, the French freighter *La Coubre* exploded in Havana docks and killed nearly 100 people. Shortly after, an American who had been working on Morgan's farm returned home and implicated his former boss in an interview with a Miami newspaper. Morgan shrugged off the accusation, but the authorities began tailing him, stepping up the surveillance when a group of eighty disillusioned Second Front rebels vanished into the mountains to launch a new fight against the Castro regime. Morgan refused to join them but didn't report their absence to the authorities. When agents from the US Army intelligence services subsequently made contact, he reacted favourably, despite internal opposition to his recruitment by the CIA.

'[Morgan] is perfectly capable of betraying [American Intelligence] or his own mother if it would advance his personal interests,' snapped an agency report.[6]

The Army pressed ahead and by late autumn its spymasters were discussing which secret code system to give Morgan. It was too late. On 21 October, he was arrested while making a social call on a senior officer and imprisoned in La Cabaña on a diet of shark meat and noodles. The arrest had been triggered by reports that another group of fellow Second Front veterans, including the American Juan Espiritu, had slipped away into the mountains to join the counter-revolution; Morgan had agreed to lead them once he found a safe house for his wife and child. The arrest sent Eloy Gutiérrez Menoyo, also implicated in the affair, scurrying to Florida, where an angry crowd of exiles who remembered the Dominican Republic plot shouted abuse outside an immigration office. Among them was Alex Rorke.

'Menoyo and his thugs arrested me and punched me around for nine days in 1959,' Rorke told a journalist.[7] 'Now I'm going to punch him in the nose.'

He got within three feet before a federal agent tackled him to the ground. Back in Havana, Morgan finally went on trial in early March as the rumours of a coming US-backed invasion became more feverish. He was found guilty of treason. In acknowledgement of the role he'd played in the revolution, Morgan was given the worthless honour of commanding his own firing squad. The former guerrilla stood illuminated by floodlights under the Cuban night and told the men with rifles to shoot when he flicked his cigarette away. One last drag sent tobacco smoke snaking into his lungs, and then Fidel Castro's American friend was falling dead towards the ground with gunshots still echoing around the moat.

By now, all the Americans who had fought in the revolution or joined its aftermath had left the country except for José Abrantes, who merged neatly into the Cuban military, and Richard Sanderlin, who had married a Cuban girl and was loudly protesting his loyalty to the revolution. Marine deserter Gerald George Holthaus surrendered to the US embassy in Havana in September 1959 after serving as a lieutenant in the police force; he got twelve months in the stockade for deserting his post and was busted down to private. In May the next year, Herman Marks fled the country in a stolen yacht after being accused of murdering prisoners and stealing their belongings. He would spend the next few years in and out of American prisons while the Justice Department debated whether to deport him back to Cuba. Neill Macaulay returned home with his wife and baby in a less dramatic fashion that July, having become disillusioned with the growing authoritarianism of Castro's Cuba.

'It was like a page out of the history of Nazi Germany,' Macaulay said.[8] 'The fact that the Cuban masses were as firmly behind Fidel as the Germans had been behind Hitler was no comfort.'

Back home, he contacted the CIA, failed to persuade it to

authorise a parachute mission into the Escambray mountains and became military adviser to one of the many exile groups training around the Everglades. He briefly teamed up with Frank Fiorini in an effort to convince Pedro Díaz Lanz into backing a guerrilla warfare initiative, then abandoned the military life for ever by enrolling at the University of South Carolina in January 1961 as a graduate student.

In a Havana emptied of Americans and on high alert, Hans Tanner cautiously made contact for a third time with the MDC underground. It was a world of peepholes sliding open only for a desperate voice to hiss a warning about police surveillance and the shutter to close again; of meetings in bar toilets, in private homes, at a beach club; of driving through militia roadblocks with letters from the underground crunched into a tense fist in a trouser pocket. Tanner took a road trip down to Oriente province on a freshly built highway designed especially for tanks and spent his nights in a dirty hotel where propaganda loudspeakers barked outside in the town square. Contacts sidled up in cafes to whisper about who'd been arrested that day or mourn an MDC leader killed clearing landmines off a beach.

By early April, he was back in Miami, where the MDC was rushing through plans to land men in Oriente to help the invasion and join the inevitable power grab after Castro's overthrow. Tanner helped load the boats with enough guns to equip an army.

'There were bazookas and rockets,' he remembered, '.30 machine guns, a 60mm mortar, Browning automatic rifles, at least 20 Thompson sub-machine guns and clips for the Garands, and rounds for the .45 Colts and tommy guns.'[9]

The boats were bobbing about in a stormy sea off the far eastern coast of Cuba trying to make radio contact with the shore when local patrol boats intercepted the signal and attacked. The MDC craft fled in a running gun battle, with Tanner helping to toss equipment over the side to gain speed, before finally outrunning the enemy and breaking into international waters. They arrived back in Miami on 11 April and began making plans for another landing. They were still planning six days later when the CIA launched its invasion of Cuba and turned their world upside down.

16

PORK CHOP BAY

B oris Grgurevich was a beatnik and proud of it. He liked reefer and whiskey, bebop jazz and folksingers and long talks about existentialism with the drunken poets of Greenwich Village. It was a mystery to his fellow recruits how this hipster drug dealer, smuggler and occasional junkie ended up in Guatemala being trained by the CIA. Grgurevich was equally mystified but appreciated the agency being cool with the fact he wasn't Cuban.

'Well, man, I mean they didn't make an issue of it or anything like that, not as far as I was concerned, because we had gotten sort of friendly with them, these CIA cats,' he said.[1] 'And they weren't bad guys really – I mean they thought they were doing the right thing and they thought we were doing the right thing, so we had a pretty good relationship with them.'

The spies were being polite. Thirty-one-year-old Grgurevich had been recruited under the assumption that his fluent Spanish and dark 'brutally handsome' looks could only have belonged to a Cuban.[2] The agency would never have opened the door if they'd known he was the Brooklyn-born son of Bulgarian immigrants who'd picked up his Spanish during an adventurous life that involved time in the Navy, a few years spent with American expatriates in Paris during the early 1950s, a period smuggling Mexican heroin into California that nearly put him in jail and the beatnik scene at Greenwich Village's famed White Horse Tavern. Now the CIA didn't know what to do with him.

Grgurevich's road to a Guatemalan training camp had begun when a Cuban friend called Ramón turned up at his New York apartment in early 1961 needing to leave town in a hurry over some unspecified trouble. Grgurevich knew better than to ask for details. They headed down south to soak up the Miami sun and place a few bets at the racetrack.

Ramón discovered an interest in politics after hanging around a local liquor store popular with exiles and Grgurevich tagged along when he heard the owner gave free bottles of rum to anyone who'd listen to his rants about communism. Their political engagement would have ended there if the pair hadn't lost all their money at the track and, in the same week, discovered the liquor store was a front for a CIA recruitment programme that offered $250 a month for any Cuban intent on retaking their country. Grgurevich had always assumed Fidel Castro secretly approved of the beatnik battle against American conformism, but he needed money fast. It didn't need much persuading from Ramón to sign them both up.

Grgurevich passed a physical, filled out some forms and a week later found himself in the back of a lorry crammed with Cubans heading to a disused military airport. A CIA type ('young, dapper, sort of prematurely grey, crew-cut, very square, would-be hip-looking cat') ushered them onto an aeroplane with blacked-out windows.[3] The next morning they were in Guatemala.

The training camp was halfway up a mountain on three huge terraces formed from solid lava that crunched like cornflakes beneath their boots. The place had barracks, mess halls, offices, firing ranges, a motor pool and 1,400 Cubans marching around taking orders from US Army Special Forces instructors. The recruits were mostly students or former military men in their twenties, all of them white or mixed race except for fifty Afro-Cubans led by Erneido Oliva who had fought alongside Castro during the revolution. Politics varied from disillusioned former rebels to Batista loyalists, but everyone bonded over a shared Catholicism and a dislike of the monotonously bland American Army rations served every day, which they tried to liven up with some home cooking.

'So they would have this pig,' said Grgurevich, 'a live, squealing pig, man, and they'd butcher it right outside the barracks and build a big fire and cook it. They have a ball – a kind of little fiesta, you know, singing and dancing, lushing it up, cooking this pig. It was a crazy scene.'[4]

By this time, the agency had discovered Grgurevich wasn't Cuban but let him stay rather than return to New York and tell everyone about the camp. He and the other recruits did basic training, some specialist instruction in mortars or telegraphy, and jump training for those in the parachute units. In what the instructors assumed was a morale-boosting measure, the unit was officially christened Brigade 2506 after the serial number of a volunteer called Carlos Rodríguez Santana who had died falling down the mountain during the camp's construction. By early April 1961, Boris Grgurevich (serial number 3389) was trained and fit and impatient to go into action. It was time to liberate Cuba.

●　●　●

The triggerfish was a two-foot-long silvery reef dweller with slashes of neon blue around its snout and a clean white flesh that tasted a little like sweet crab meat. Cuban fishermen called it a '*cochino*' ('pig') and the name attached itself to Bahía de Cochinos, a southern bay with pale brown beaches, clear blue water and coral reefs. The bay was surrounded by swamp and served by three main roads; the nearest sign of civilisation was the resort town of Girón with its small permanent population and a useful airstrip. CIA analysts thought the bay made a good place to land the brigade. An advance squad in rubber rafts could silently hit the beaches and guide in the larger landing craft while parachutists touched down further inland to secure the roads. Brigade aircraft would use Girón as a base to strafe government militia and deal with any Cuban planes that had survived earlier airstrikes. On the horizon, American warships in international waters would keep a watchful eye.

The plan had some drawbacks, notably that the invaders would have nowhere to retreat except the Caribbean Sea if things went wrong, but morale was high. Brigade commander José 'Pepe' Pérez San Román, a long-necked exile with a fierce stare and ten years of military experience, was convinced the Cuban people would rise up and welcome his men as liberators. He had not been told about an independent American survey done that summer which came to a very different conclusion: 'The great majority of Cubans surveyed felt that both they personally and their country were very much better off than during the days of Batista. The prevailing mood was one of hope and optimism.'[5]

Cuban optimism was tested on 15 April when eight Douglas B-26 planes came screaming from the clouds and wiped out half of Castro's air force on the ground. The following day a boatload of brigade commandos launched diversionary raids along the coast. Havana went into high alert and herded tens of thousands of regime opponents, real and imagined, into Army barracks and sports stadiums. Existing political prisoners regarded as especially dangerous were executed by firing squad, including International Brigade member Angus McNair Jr who had been captured the previous month. American officials claimed the attackers were Cuban defectors, but not even the United Nations believed them and a second airstrike to take out the remaining planes was cancelled to prevent more international outrage.

The real invasion came in the early hours of 17 April when rubber rafts full of men came gliding under the moonlight towards the Bay of Pigs. Things went wrong quickly. The rafts ripped open on reefs no one had ever bothered to mark on a map and the invaders waded ashore to find a jeepload of militia staring in astonishment. A vicious firefight woke everyone in the vicinity. Further inland, parachutists floating to earth saw their equipment drop into the swamp and sink out of sight. Alarms began to sound all over the island.

Brigaders were still unloading supplies at the beaches when daylight came and the sky was filled with government aircraft roaring in low with their machine guns stitching neat lines up the waves and into the rusty skins of the landing craft. Brigade B-26s tried to run interference but were hopelessly outgunned and outnumbered. When a freighter got hit below the waterline and began to sink, the order came in to pull all ships out of the combat zone, even those still packed with supplies. Brigade 2506 was on its own.

Out past the bay, parachutists had managed to seize two of the main roads but arrived at the third just in time to collide with a heavily armed detachment of militia rolling in the direction of the beach. White phosphorous shells stopped the leading tanks, but things looked bad until a brigade B-26 swooped in and took out an entire convoy of military cadets.

'It was awful,' said brigader Pedro Porraspita, looking down on the scene from the air.[6] 'First I saw a lot of caps flying through the air; then there were men screaming and running, and gasoline tanks blowing up. I heard later we killed about half the battalion of cadets. You could smell the burning flesh right away.'

The victory boosted morale, but the invaders wouldn't be able to depend on regular air support like this for much longer. Girón had failed to become a working airstrip after the boats ferrying in aviation fuel were chased away by Castro's aeroplanes; brigade pilots were forced to fly out of a base 720 miles away in Nicaragua with only half an hour over the target before coasting back on fumes. Not everyone made it. Four B-26s were shot down that day with only one survivor between them. Those pilots who did get home were refuelling and flinging themselves back into combat on such a punishing schedule that they were becoming sitting targets through sheer exhaustion as the day drew to a close.

That night was dark and quiet, except for a fierce midnight battle against Cuban tanks out in the swamp, where brigaders only stopped a breakthrough by spattering the advancing armour with enough tracer bullets to guide in a waiting bazooka crew. When dawn came the next day, the exiles were still locked in their beachhead and buzzards were lazily circling the piles of dead.

The invaders hunkering down for the next assault didn't include Boris the Beatnik. When names were called at the camp, Grgurevich's had not been on the list and neither was that of Ramón, a naturalised American, or those of a handful of other volunteers with problematic nationalities. The American instructors gave a thin excuse about staying on as cadre for new recruits, but everyone

Unsuccessful lawyer Fidel Castro was so horrified by Cuba's growing corruption that in late 1956 he headed into the jungles of the Sierra Maestra to launch a guerrilla war against the government.

Source: Wikimedia Commons

In 1957, American adventurer Frank Fiorini (*right*) met with former Cuban President Carlos Prío Socarrás (*centre*) to discuss a secret mission to Oriente province that would uncover Castro's real aims for the rebellion.

© California Avenue Productions, LLC

The guerrillas in the Sierra Maestra were ragged and poorly armed, but their dedication to overthrowing the authoritarian Cuban government inspired Americans like Frank Fiorini to support their cause.

© California Avenue Productions, LLC

William Alexander Morgan was a deserter, street punk and one-time carnival knife thrower who found a new life – and a Cuban wife called Olga – in the Escambray mountains when he joined competing rebel group the Second Front. Source: Wikimedia Commons

By late 1958, Castro's rebels had extended their territory to Pinar del Río in the far west, where they were joined by Army veteran Neill Macaulay from South Carolina, seen here (*right*) on horseback with a fellow rebel.
© Nancy Macaulay, courtesy of George A. Smathers Libraries, University of Florida

Teenager Jack Nordeen, pictured here in his high-school yearbook, sought adventure with Castro's rebels in the Sierra Maestra out of guilt for accidentally killing his younger brother with a rifle. Author's collection

Cuban President Fulgencio Batista (*centre, with pistol*) thought he could defeat the rebels with superior firepower but failed to realise his corrupt regime was crumbling around him.
© Bettmann/Getty Images

Frank Fiorini (*centre, with sunglasses*) smuggled guns into the Sierra Maestra until a beating by Cuban police inspired him to head into the mountains and join Castro's guerrillas.
© California Avenue Productions, LLC

German-American Ilona Marita Lorenz was the pregnant and emotionally vulnerable ex-lover of Fidel Castro when Frank Fiorini recruited her to steal documents from government offices as part of his spy ring.
© California Avenue Productions, LLC

Journalist and fierce anti-communist Alexander Rorke became a staunch enemy of the new Castro regime after being imprisoned while reporting on a failed 1959 coup in Havana. © California Avenue Productions, LLC

Many Batista loyalists went into exile in Miami, among them Rolando Masferrer, seen here in his younger days as a leftist revolutionary before he slid to the other end of the ideological spectrum and formed the paramilitary group Los Tigres. Source: *Bohemia* via Wikimedia Commons

Counter-revolutionaries continued to battle the victorious rebels even after Batista retired from the fight, but they were careful to disguise themselves in front of the camera. © California Avenue Productions, LLC

After Frank Fiorini fled Havana, he formed the International Anti-Communist Brigade and trained in the Florida Everglades to overthrow Castro's regime. © California Avenue Productions, LLC

The 1961 Bay of Pigs invasion was a disaster, but President John F. Kennedy tried to salvage some pride at a ceremony for survivors in Miami's Orange Bowl Stadium, with Brigade 2506 leader José Pérez San Román standing third from the left.

© Cecil Stoughton, White House Photographs, John F. Kennedy Presidential Library and Museum, Boston

Cuban counter-revolutionary activity continued, on a more discreet level, after the Bay of Pigs debacle thanks to CIA weapons and American government funding. © California Avenue Productions, LLC

The 6ft 6in. soldier of fortune Gerald Hemming, photographed out in the Everglades during a 1961 training exercise for his Intercontinental Penetration Force, looked impressive but sooner or later everyone stopped trusting him.

© Bettmann/CORBIS/Bettmann Archive/Getty Images

The Cold War heated up in late 1962, when covert photographs revealed the existence of Soviet nuclear weapons on Cuban territory and the resulting crisis brought the world to the brink of annihilation.

Alex Rorke and Frank Fiorini, pictured on a boat near Florida in early 1963, were good friends before falling out over a dangerous plan to provoke an international incident by attacking a Soviet ship.

Anti-Castro activities came to an abrupt end in November 1963, when President Kennedy was shot by Lee Harvey Oswald, a former Marine and Cold War defector believed by some to be a small cog in a bigger conspiracy.
© JFK Assassination Records Collection, National Archives

A 1958 attempt to overthrow Haitian dictator François 'Papa Doc' Duvalier by Haitian pilot Alix Pasquet, pictured during his pilot training at Tuskegee during the Second World War, failed miserably but would not stop other exiles and mercenaries launching their own attempts a decade later.
Source: HaitiAirmen via Wikimedia Commons

knew the real reason. It all seemed unfair to Grgurevich, who thought he was missing out on a victory parade through Havana.

'We had no idea we weren't going, and it was a big drag man,' he said.[7] 'I mean we'd been there three months, dig, and we wanted to go.'

Grgurevich and the others remaining in the suddenly empty camp huddled around a short-wave radio tuned into a Cuban broadcast. Their optimism faded away as news from the Bay of Pigs got worse and worse.

• • •

At Girón airstrip, they could hear a calm voice on the radio reassuring them US air support would be there soon. Douglas Nelson Lethbridge Aguilera, in charge of the airstrip, allowed himself to feel a surge of hope that the invasion might still succeed.

It was 19 April and the area controlled by the brigade was shrinking every hour. The previous day they had tried to break out of their beachhead, but the waves of Castro's militia pouring in from across the island had forced them back. Brigade B-26s tumbled out of the air under the guns of government planes throughout the afternoon and evening until darkness came. The promise of American jets was the best news Lethbridge had heard since landing in the country of his birth.

Douglas Lethbridge had a Cuban passport, but the CIA would have found his nationality even more complicated than that of Grgurevich if they'd bothered to look a little closer. His father was the untitled younger son of a British aristocratic family who had won the Military Cross commanding a machine-gun company on the Western Front, settled in Cuba and found love with a Puerto

Rican expat. Lethbridge was their second son and grew up bilingual on a sugar plantation, torn culturally between Europe and the Caribbean. In 1952, he found a third way by heading to Canada at eighteen years old to become a citizen, join the Air Force and cross the border into America for an Ivy League education. Marriage and divorce quickly followed.

He was drifting through life without any clear direction when Castro marched into Havana in 1959 and declared a new age for Cuba. Lethbridge returned home to support the revolution by officially becoming a Cuban citizen and sharing his aviation skills with the new Air Force. Soon disillusioned with the regime, he moved to Miami in April 1960 and eventually joined Brigade 2506. He wasn't the only man with a tangled backstory fighting in the Bay of Pigs: Herman Koch, a 22-year-old born in Havana to an American father and Cuban mother ('United States subject and citizen of Cuba,' noted the CIA), signed up as a parachutist and was lying dead in the swamp after an ambush.[8]

The promised American air support would be coming from six Skyhawk jets sitting on the deck of the USS *Essex* cruising just outside the combat zone. The pilots had orders to protect brigade B-26s but could not instigate combat or attack ground troops. No one was entirely sure who had authorised the mission, as President John F. Kennedy had rebuffed all calls for official intervention over the past few days, still clinging to the fiction that the invasion was a Cuban concern with no foreign involvement. Macho CIA operatives were disgusted by their government's show of weakness.

'It was like learning that Superman was a fairy,' spat one.[9]

Whoever had given permission, the Skyhawks were to accompany a bombing raid by brigade B-26s piloted by a mix of Cubans and American pilots from the Alabama National Guard who'd overseen the original training in Guatemala. The guardsmen were flying in the knowledge they would be abandoned by their own government and dismissed as mercenaries if captured. From Girón airstrip, Lethbridge watched the raid begin with no sign of the promised Skyhawk jets. The B-26s were torn to pieces by Castro's aircraft and four national guardsmen shot down and killed. A Cuban exile pilot heard one pleading with an American destroyer for help as his plane spiralled towards the swamp with a Castro fighter on its tail. A cool voice on the radio replied that orders must be obeyed. As the air battle raged, Lethbridge supervised the invasion's only landing at Girón airstrip when a C-46 transport plane touched down to offload bazooka shells and pick up a wounded Cuban pilot who had been shot down. It was gone in less than ten minutes.

The American jets didn't appear until after the battle, streaking high above the beach looking sinister and useless. Confusion over the time zone had seen them take off too late. On the beach, a radio crackled into life and a US naval officer told brigade leader San Román that the fight was lost and the invaders should disperse and seek cover. He complimented the Cubans on their fight.

'We don't need your compliments you son-of-a-whore,' San Román shouted into the mic.[10] 'We need your jets!'

There was no reply. By now, the brigade was a confused mess in full retreat back towards the sea, fragmenting as it went. Exiles wearing American-made duck-hunting outfits ('Happy Hunting' said the collar tags) tried to hold off government tanks with bazookas as their comrades paddled away from the beach or fell back into the swamp. They had little ammunition, food or drinking water. One group strangled a piglet to death for a meal.

'Forgive me, God,' said the man with his hands around the piglet's throat.[11] 'Look what Fidel Castro has driven me to do.'

By the next morning, it was all over. Castro's troops rounded up the survivors from Brigade 2506, although some would evade capture in the swamp for weeks. One man drifted in a boat for four days hoping for Miami but washed up instead at the Isle of Pines prison camp, where many fellow brigaders were already being held. Douglas Lethbridge was one of hundreds marched off to the Palacio de los Deportes sports arena in Havana to face taunting Castro loyalists and a public baying for blood. The brigade had lost 100 dead and over 1,000 taken prisoner, with only a handful managing to escape. The Cubans never revealed their casualties, but CIA estimates placed them between 2,000 and 5,000.

The invasion had failed.

• • •

As news emerged of the disaster at Bahía de Cochinos, hundreds of Americans contacted the recruiting offices of Cuban exile organisations in Miami to offer their services. Thirty-eight Hungarian exiles promised to come down from Delaware, while enquiries arrived from Alaska to Italy. Forty-one former Marines got as far as Chicago before the airline discovered they'd paid for their tickets with an invalid cheque and threw them off the flight. Those who got to Florida, with its exotic tang of seafood and suntan lotion, found themselves being turned away by sad-faced Cuban recruiters who knew the battle was lost and didn't want to give Havana the satisfaction of an easy propaganda target.

'[Exile groups] are determined to avoid any justification for the charges by premier Fidel Castro that the Cuban rebel forces include many foreign mercenaries,' noted the *New York Times*.[12]

A poll taken in May after the invasion had failed showed 90 per cent of Americans supported exile efforts to overthrow Castro, although only 44 per cent thought they should be funded by the US government, with 41 per cent outright opposing this.[13] Rightist groups, including armed paramilitaries like the Minutemen out of Missouri, sprang up across the country in a fervour of anti-communist activity that also boosted membership figures for veteran rightist agitators like the John Birch Society. Despite this, not everyone hated Castro. In New York, a Fair Play for Cuba Committee rally in Union Square unexpectedly attracted 5,000 people. Another 2,000 gathered in San Francisco, with smaller events elsewhere in the country.

President John F. Kennedy denied any official American involvement and promised to keep the Cuban exile population on a tight leash. Cuba and the USSR refused to believe him and would not have been surprised to learn the humiliated President had secretly authorised more efforts to overthrow Fidel Castro in what would eventually be known as Operation Mongoose. Kennedy grimly accepted it would be a tough battle to unseat a leader whose position had been helped rather than hurt by the Bay of Pigs invasion.

'He ought to be grateful to us,' said Kennedy to a confidant.[14] 'He gave us a kick in the ass and it made him stronger than ever.'

In Guatemala, Boris Grgurevich and Ramón sat around the camp feeling deflated and empty as they waited to be demobilised. To their surprise, the Americans kept the place operational and 200 new recruits arrived, all of them miserable after hearing about the invasion's failure. Training was slow and unenthusiastic until one group of recruits simply refused to take orders any more, causing the programme to collapse and everyone to be shipped back home. Grgurevich and Ramón headed to the old liquor store and picked up their pay cheques.

'Very sad scene at the recruiting place,' said Grgurevich, 'because they've got the lists of guys that got wiped or captured, and relatives and so on are falling by to look at the lists.'[15]

The pair headed back to New York and drugs, but hordes of would-be heroes were still flocking the other way to join the fight. Some had heard the CIA was paying good money for American mercenaries, while others had their own private crusades against communism. Among them was George Washington Tanner, one of nature's screw-ups, who'd been so damaged by the war years he was unable to keep a marriage alive or stop breaking the law. In the spring of 1961, his decision to join the counter-revolution would be the tumbling pebble that began a landslide of American involvement.

PART IV

BETTER DEAD THAN RED

17

MERCENARIES IN THE MAGIC CITY

MIAMI, SPRING 1961

It was as if a giant hand had lifted the country at one end and sent anything not nailed down rolling southwards towards Florida. For weeks, rumours had been circulating through the nation's bars and hunting clubs that the White House's apparent surrender was just a ruse and Fidel Castro's days were numbered. A stream of adventurers headed for Miami armed with nothing except cheap luggage and a conviction that the liberation of Cuba would be a done deal in the hands of red-blooded Americans like themselves.

They were the kind of men who got their politics from Hollywood films like *I Married a Communist*, nodded approvingly at bumper stickers that read 'Better Dead Than Red' and treated themselves to 'Fight the Red Menace' bubblegum cards (card no. 3: 'Slave Labor', card no. 19: 'Atomic Doom') from the local candy store. As far as they were concerned, communism was the devil's work and Fidel Castro his emissary in the Caribbean. This mix of ex-servicemen, teen runaways and all-round misfits emerged from the city's Greyhound bus station on Northeast First Street into the bright sunshine and headed for the nearest Cuban exile recruiting office.

The new arrivals expected to be greeted as saviours and given a secret mission, preferably by government men in dark glasses. Instead, they were turned away and directed down the street to another office where a different but equally terse Cuban did the same thing. Soon there were no more recruiting offices left to approach. The adventurers didn't know the exile groups were obeying instructions from the CIA to shut the door on any American volunteers. The agency had no idea how to continue the fight against Castro, and was already squabbling with the Pentagon and White House over tactics, but remained committed to keeping the matter an all-Cuban affair.

Some of the adventurers returned home when it became obvious they weren't wanted, but others stuck around, gathering in Bayfront Park to drink Pepsi-Cola and talk about guns and girls until it got dark. Those with no money slept under the palm trees while the rest trudged off to a shared room at the Hotel de Cuba or a bed in Glen Haven, a beige clapboard boarding house in Little Havana where grey-haired proprietor Nellie Hamilton housed a rotating cast of transients, blue-collar workers and outpatients from a local psychiatric hospital whose rent was paid by the government.

A big slice of the Bayfront Park crowd were just kids with buzzcut hair and dreams of adventure straight out of the movies. Bob Free was a nineteen-year-old who told local journalists he only wanted the chance to kill a few communists, while long-faced 23-year-old Al DuShane had abandoned a pest controller job in Houston to live out his mercenary fantasies.

'That boy just up and quit,' said his astonished boss, 'saying he was going to join an army.'[1]

Others had military experience. Dick Watley was a veteran of the United States Army Special Service Corps while Alonzo Allen, a rare black face among the mostly white Bayfront Park crowd, had done two tours in the Air Force. Ignatius Paul Alvick and the towering Gerald Hemming, now calling himself Gerry Patrick, became instant celebrities on the scene for having spent time in Castro's armed forces after the revolution. By the end of April, there were 100 men hanging around Bayfront Park every night, talking and smoking and occasionally attending exile meetings whose impassioned Spanish speeches they couldn't understand. The people of Miami figured their new guests would soon get bored and go home, but then George Washington Tanner appeared.

A tall man in his late thirties with dark brown hair and an authoritative voice, he turned up in Bayfront Park one day wearing a white shirt with military insignia and calling himself Colonel Tanner. He announced the formation of a new organisation called the Anti-Communist Legion which would train volunteers in guerrilla warfare then infiltrate them into Cuba to join the counter-revolutionary forces of the Escambray. Tanner claimed to have backing from some rich, important men who wanted to see the Red Menace eradicated from the Caribbean, and eventually the world.

Twenty eager recruits joined up immediately. Tanner made Alvick his second-in-command, Alonzo Allen his intelligence officer, and gave everyone else the rank of major or captain. He explained that the funding would arrive soon, along with uniforms and weapons, and until then they needed publicity and training and more manpower. Al DuShane offered to recruit volunteers in

Houston and was immediately sent off to the Greyhound bus terminal with the promise of having his expenses reimbursed later.

By 26 April, the Anti-Communist Legion had expanded to fifty members, who spent their days trying to recruit passers-by in Bayfront Park, usually near a monument to Cuban hero José Martí erected by exiles twenty years earlier. Gerald Hemming had the most success. At 6ft 6in. he was an imposing figure and newcomers often mistook him for the leader of the legion, a mistake Hemming rarely bothered to correct. Paul Alvick got some publicity for the group by persuading the *Miami News* to run a story under the headline '50 (All) Americans Want to Fight Fidel'. He told the journalist that the legion had assembled to help the President fight communism and needed food.

'We all gave up jobs, too, to do this,' he said.[2] 'We have no winos, no deadheads here. We're sincere in our purpose and pray God that other Americans will back us.'

Alvick announced that Colonel Tanner would be leading some anti-communist legionnaires at a training camp starting 30 April and new recruits were always welcome to join, with military experience preferred. People from outside Miami who knew Colonel Tanner as a mentally unwell war veteran and serial bridegroom were already predicting disaster. George was a disturbed mess and nothing he did ever went right.

• • •

George Washington Tanner Jr was born 9 June 1924 in West Palm Beach, a booming city that had been nothing but tents and shacks a generation earlier. The Depression knocked some of the confidence out of the place, but Tanner got a decent schooling at the Florida

Naval Academy in St Augustine and had barely turned eighteen years old when the Army conscripted him for the war against Japan. He had a smooth voice that exuded natural authority and no one was surprised when the higher-ups sent him off to Officer Training School at Fort Leavenworth.

Tanner's war years are a mystery, but the training school seems to have been a washout: he never progressed higher than staff sergeant and was back to private first class by 1947, when he left the service. Something had clearly gone wrong during his service and the Tanner who returned home to West Palm Beach was a very different individual from the one who left five years earlier. Behind the authoritative voice was a disturbed and flighty mess of a man, unable to settle down or follow a plan to its conclusion. Tanner saw several psychiatrists, all of whom agreed he had serious mental health problems but had no idea how to treat them.

'[My] son has changed considerably over the years,' said his father, 'and is now of no use to anyone.'[3]

Tanner got a job as a radio announcer and married Roberta Louise Mosher, a seventeen-year-old cashier whose brother had died in the war. Everyone hoped family life would bring some stability to Tanner, but the marriage failed and he spiralled downwards, eventually doing eighteen months in prison for stealing a car. Two more women were unwise enough to join him in holy matrimony through the coming decade, and both quickly gave up any hope of making it work. Tanner tried to check himself into a veterans' hospital, but his problems were mental rather than physical and the doctors couldn't spare a bed.

By the time the Bay of Pigs rolled around, Tanner was still on the radio and living back home with his parents. In the middle of April 1961, with nothing else going on in his life, he drove to Miami and booked a room at the Hotel de Cuba, looking to resurrect his military career. Locals directed him to a recruiting station on 17th Street and West Flagler Street where a moody Cuban told him that Americans couldn't enlist and suggested he visit Bayfront Park instead. He spontaneously introduced himself as Colonel Tanner to the mob of men soaking up the shade beneath the park's palm trees and used that authoritative announcer's voice to declare the formation of a private army to liberate Cuba. He had no backing, little money and wasn't entirely sure how to find the island on a map.

On 30 April, twenty men from the Anti-Communist Legion followed him into the Everglades west of Miami for some survival instruction. They built lean-tos, started a camp fire and waited for their leader to coach them in the mysteries of guerrilla warfare. By 1 May, it had become clear that Tanner had no idea what he was talking about.

'Tanner appears to be psychopathic,' said one disgruntled legionnaire, 'wears a white shirt with US Army colonel insignia on it and obviously has no knowledge of military matters.'[4]

That was a harsh verdict on a man who'd spent five years in the Army, but Tanner had lost the faith of his men and there was no getting it back. After some shouting, fist waving and a quick vote, Tanner was thrown out of his own organisation. He stalked off back to Miami announcing he would return when he'd got some funding from 'very important persons'. None of the legionnaires ever saw him again, although the FBI would unexpectedly run into Tanner two years later during the search for Alex Rorke.

His brief moment in the spotlight was over, but Tanner's intervention had kick-started the American side of the counter-revolution. The mercenaries of Bayfront Park wouldn't be going home anytime soon.

• • •

After the departure of their leader, the Anti-Communist Legion was left directionless, penniless and in a few cases homeless. Dick Watley took over the training camp but was moved on after a day by a park ranger who directed the group to another site about ten miles further west. They set up and tried again, but their food quickly ran out and forced them onto a diet of swamp cabbage.

Back in Miami, the legionnaires who'd stayed behind found a different kind of trouble when Alonzo Allen announced he was quitting and had a gun pulled on him by two other members in Bayfront Park for his disloyalty. Allen's friend slipped him a knife, but police arrested everyone before things got violent; Allen spent two days in jail and got out to discover his room had been burgled and the legion's records taken. He was back in Bayfront Park telling other legionnaires about the incident when two local men drove past and yelled 'Viva Fidel!' There was a chase, a fistfight and another arrest. A disillusioned Allen telephoned the local FBI office to tell them everything he knew, which wasn't much. Tanner's legion had forty-six members and had received only $100 in funding, all of it from a single Cuban exile who wanted to show solidarity. The intelligence officer thought most of his comrades were crazy.

'Allen described the majority of the members as being "misfits" and "ragged", without money and apparently completely untrustworthy,' noted the FBI report.[5]

A few days later, Al DuShane arrived back from Houston with some new recruits, most poached from a Texan anti-communist group calling itself the Liberation Forces of the Western Hemisphere that had been unwise enough to invite him to give a talk. DuShane originally hoped to bring thirty-six men south by

Greyhound bus but abandoned the plan when Tanner's promised money failed to arrive. The volunteers agreed to make their own way to Miami, but only eight, crowded into one car, completed the journey. They arrived with only a few dollars and a set of clean fatigues each, having believed DuShane's assurances that everything else would be provided, and found the Anti-Communist Legion falling apart. The training camp in the Everglades was a mess of empty Pepsi-Cola bottles and old hamburger wrappers where some unenthusiastic legionnaires put the new arrivals through their paces.

'We've been out in the Everglades on a survival test,' said one Texan when he returned to Miami looking a lot thinner, 'eating snakes, birds and dog food.'[6]

Soon the Houston boys were hanging around Bayfront Park complaining about the situation with everyone else, while Al DuShane sat on his suitcase in a remote corner looking miserable. At least the weather was good, although locals warned that tropical storms would start next month, strong enough to bend the palm trees back. The only consolation was the rain came and went so fast that your clothes barely knew they were wet before the sun came out again.

One of Tanner's original legionnaires decided now was the right time to promote himself to the position of leader. Gerald Hemming's first move was to march the remaining forty members out to a new training camp in the Everglades for more snake eating and hand-to-hand combat. His new regime proved too hardcore for some, who defected with Al DuShane and Ignatius Paul Alvick over to an office at 742 Northwest Avenue in Miami, where a private detective called Vincent J. Hanard was setting up a paramilitary organisation called the Freedom Fighters of the Americas. Alvick put a brave face on the chaos for a *Miami News* journalist.

'We are no longer trying to have one large group,' he said.[7] 'We hope to get several small, cohesive groups together who can accomplish the job of infiltration better.'

New adventurers were still arriving in Miami daily, with many ending up at Nellie Hamilton's place, where the boarders now ate in shifts and the rules included no swearing or guns at the dinner table. They hung out in Bayfront Park and discussed which of the fragmented, squabbling groups to join. Vincent J. Hanard was convinced he would soon be tsar of anti-Castro activism in Florida, while Gerald Hemming planned to dominate the Miami counter-revolution scene for years to come. Only one of them was right.

18

INTERCONTINENTAL
PENETRATION

MIAMI, SUMMER 1960

The office at 742 Northwest Avenue had anti-Castro posters in the windows and a map of Cuba on the wall. Most days a cluster of young men with the kind of straight backs only found in former soldiers hung around the pavement outside, handing recruitment leaflets to passers-by. More could be found in the back room doing jumping jacks or close-order drill as their rat-faced boss, who called himself General Hanard, looked on with a .32 pistol on his hip. The Freedom Fighters of the Americas had started in May 1961 with a dozen former members of George Tanner's legion and a few employees from Hanard's own detective agency but was finding it hard to attract any more volunteers. No one in Miami seemed to trust the general much.

Vincent J. Hanard had been a lot of things in his life. A blue-collar boy from the Bronx who served on a Navy ammunition ship in the last year of the war; a chauffeur who got arrested for impersonating a policeman and shaking down New York bars with a toy detective shield from a novelty store; a transplant to the Florida town of Hollywood; an ambulance driver who crashed so often he usually arrived at hospital in worse shape than his passengers; and now a private detective with a bad reputation.

'It is suspected by some law enforcement officials,' noted an FBI report, 'that Hanard might be engaged in blackmail and other similar practices through operation of his detective agency.'[1]

The authorities tolerated his sleaze only because Hanard regularly passed them information about local mobsters. He was currently supplying enough information about Charles Karpf, an underling of Meyer Lansky in the jukebox racket, that Miami police had been persuaded to overlook his paramilitary adventures with the Freedom Fighters of the Americas. No one thought the group would last long anyway. Members were already peeling away, full of complaints about the lack of guerrilla training and Hanard's refusal to set a definite date for an invasion of Cuba. The rest hung on because the general was paying their room and board at the Dorn Hotel, but even they turned mutinous when the cash ran out and the hotel asked them to leave. Someone discovered Hanard had spent time in a psychiatric hospital and had been diagnosed as incapable of telling truth from fiction. FFA member Steve Wilson complained about the situation to anyone who would listen until Hanard locked him in a room for the day with an armed guard on the door, which everyone took as undeniable proof of the general's mental health problems and triggered another exodus.

Leading member Ignatius Paul Alvick quit in June 1961 and telephoned the local CIA office to request funding for his own group. He was clear about the enemy.

'He indicated that he came to [the] CIA to seek financial assistance in fighting against Hanard and Castro,' noted the duty officer.[2]

The agency rejected the request and Alvick returned to New York, where he became a jobbing actor, figuring it for a more secure life. The Freedom Fighters of the Americas momentarily unified itself after a failed petrol bomb attack on Hanard's office by persons unknown, but morale quickly deteriorated after claims emerged that the detective had organised the incident himself for publicity. Even as his followers deserted him, Hanard remained plausible enough to persuade the Cuban organisation Junta Revolucionaria de Liberación Nacional (Revolutionary Junta of National Liberation) on West Flagler Street to make him their head of intelligence. The post lasted about a day before the Cubans withdrew the offer.

Hanard kept the anti-Castro signs in the window and a stack of application forms on his desk, but the Freedom Fighters of the Americas was finished by the end of June. Its remaining members drifted away and few replaced them. Most transferred their allegiance to a more promising paramilitary group: Gerald Hemming's Interpen was getting plenty of attention that summer.

• • •

In March 1951, the San Marino police had arrested a fourteen-year-old Gerald Patrick Hemming trying to break through the skylight of a sporting goods store. He had a crowbar and four school friends waiting at the front door. A night in the cells turned the gang from teen rebels into frightened kids and soon the others were accusing Hemming of being the ringleader behind a juvenile crime wave that had been well under way before the police intervened. By the time the patrol car pulled up outside the store and froze Hemming in the beam of a flashlight, the teenagers had already stolen twenty-one rifles and 3,000 rounds of ammunition from other establishments.

It had all started with reading too many books. Hemming spent his childhood enthusiastically devouring pulp fiction about wartime partisans and Depression-era gangsters and heroic agents behind enemy lines. Some parents might have regarded those kind of reading habits as unhealthy, but Mr and Mrs Hemming had nine other children in the house and a television repair shop to run. Their son was left to go his own way.

The teenagers got a stern lecture from policemen who couldn't take this junior Dillinger Gang very seriously and an equally indulgent judge gave them all a year's probation as wards of the court. The other boys immediately straightened up and flew right, but Hemming had acquired an itch for adventure that he couldn't scratch. He barely bothered to attend high school after, although the obsessive reading continued on his own time.

'I'm raised to know what it is to have a library, the classics, all this shit,' he said.[3] 'I used to play hooky and hit the used bookstores.'

One of the books Hemming picked up was an old copy of *Mein Kampf*, which he read cover to cover. He spent the next two years marching around the house in a homemade Hitler Youth outfit shouting in German until his fed-up parents suggested he join the Marines, despite being a year underage. The enlistment only lasted a few weeks before bureaucratic cross-checking revealed his true age and a reluctant Mr and Mrs Hemming took their son back until he could rejoin legally in April 1954 as a beefy seventeen-year-old.

Hemming found some stability in the Marines. His copy of *Mein Kampf* stayed in San Marino and all the adolescent fantasies about being a spy or gangster morphed into more acceptable interests in vintage firearms and guerrilla tactics. He did five years in the service, specialising in radar and control tower operation, and impressed his superiors by learning to fly light aircraft in his spare time. Hemming made it to sergeant and would have gone further if he'd been able to stop those fantasies creeping back.

Senior officers decided to put him forward for a course at Officer Training School, with the possibility of further study at the University of Mississippi. A few colleagues cautioned that Hemming's better qualities were outweighed by a strong streak of immaturity, but their warnings were ignored. The doubters were soon proved right when Hemming abruptly dropped out of the course a few days before it started and informed superiors he would prefer to be doing something adventurous in the Special Forces instead. The Navy had no interest in indulging a radar operator whose biggest military achievement so far had been a Good Conduct medal and put an unofficial block on his military ambitions.

'Not recommended for return to the US Naval Preparatory School,' noted a clearly angry commanding officer in the paperwork.[4]

Hemming got the message and quit the service in October 1958 to register unenthusiastically in the Marine reserves and return to San Marino. His family seemed happier to see him now he'd dropped the Nazi obsession, although his post-Marines worldview wasn't a huge improvement, with Hemming coming across like Friedrich Nietzsche working his way through a case of beer.

'My philosophy is the whole world is full of assholes,' he said.[5] 'Some of these assholes are chimps, some of these assholes are homo sapiens.'[6]

Hemming thought of himself as firmly in the homo sapiens category. He bummed around until his savings ran low and took a job in a scrapyard before deciding in February 1959 that it was time for some adventure. Castro's victory in Cuba was still all over the news and Hemming headed for Havana to see what opportunities were available.

● ● ●

By October 1960, Gerald Hemming was back in Los Angeles with long hair, a bushy goatee and an intimate knowledge of the Cuban prison system. Like Loran Hall and Paul Hughes before him, Hemming had been arrested for getting involved with a group of Nicaraguan revolutionaries who lacked official sanction for their operations. Deported to California, he spent his time telling friends stories about revolutionary Havana over a beer and waiting for a telephone call from the Nicaraguans to signal their operation was up and running again. When the call was slow in coming, he tried to drum up support for the cause by contacting the CIA's local office to see if it was interested in backing a revolution in Central America.

The man on the other end of the telephone seemed keener in pumping Hemming for information about Cuba. Three telephone conversations exhausted the topic but that didn't stop Hemming calling on a regular basis under the impression he was now an unofficial CIA operative. The agency regarded him as nothing more than an informer with a line in low-grade intelligence but dutifully noted his rambling calls and occasionally sage geopolitical advice.

'Hemming maintains that the United States should utilize a number of Special Forces types,' noted the file, 'who may be able to penetrate certain revolutionary movements at an early stage, attain positions of real influence within the organizations, and subsequently attempt to channel the movement's activities into areas which are most favourable, or at worst least detrimental to US interests.'[7]

He volunteered to be one of those Special Forces types, but the agency politely turned him down. After several months, Hemming finally realised his Nicaraguan friends were never going to call and a dull depression set in that only lifted when Havana acquaintance Jimmy Gentry got in touch. Gentry had been a loyal servant of the Castro regime until Cuban friends failed to help his import business survive a battle with the American authorities; now he was mixing with counter-revolutionaries in Miami and invited Hemming to join him. Hemming informed the CIA's Los Angeles office about the call but got only a non-committal answer from the agent on duty, who privately wondered if the former Marine was as patriotic a citizen as he claimed.

'It is always possible, on the other hand,' wrote the agent in Hemming's file, 'that he is still loyal to the Cuban government and at some future date will attempt to embarrass the US.'[8]

Hemming would eventually embarrass almost everyone unfortunate enough to fall under the spell of his considerable charisma, but his opposition to Castro was genuine. In Miami, he looked up Jimmy Gentry, now working in a junkyard and managing an apartment complex with his wife, and they made some tentative plans to approach Cuban exile movements. The alliance quickly collapsed when FBI agents hauled Gentry off for questioning under the impression he was still working for the Cubans. Hemming distanced himself, assured the agents of his patriotism and was soon hanging around Bayfront Park with all the other would-be mercenaries when George Tanner created the Anti-Communist Legion.

When the legion eventually imploded, Hemming pushed his way into command of the remnants and ended up with twenty men. He announced they were now called the Intercontinental Penetration Force: Interpen for short. It was time to make a mark on Miami.

• • •

On 1 July, Interpen members were milling around the tarmac of Davie airfield, near Fort Lauderdale, in camouflage suits and goggles, bumping their bulky parachutes into each other as they prepared for a demonstration jump before an audience of Cuban exiles. Hemming's men had been coming out to the disused military airfield for the past few weeks to train alongside the civilian enthusiasts of the Miami Skydiving Club where, for $7 an hour, they could hire a club aeroplane and arrange their own jumps. It wasn't safe or well supervised, but no one joined Hemming's team if they wanted to live for ever.

'I'd rather get it over fast than die slowly,' said one Interpen member.[9]

When they weren't parachuting, the group trained in guerrilla warfare on a scrub-covered island in the Everglades. Each day Hemming lectured his men about guns and tactics then handed over to a fanatically anti-communist former Navy radioman called George Williams Finegan, who gave instruction on cryptography. Later came target practice with an armoury they'd pieced together from a few old carbines and some semi-automatic rifles which would be converted to full automatic once the parts arrived. Life was tough in the swamp but even tougher back on dry land, where money was scarce and they were donating blood at $10 a pint to pay the rent at Nellie's boarding house.

Hemming hoped to make some money providing Cuban exile movements with guerrilla warfare training but got no further than a brief conversation with Eloy Gutiérrez Menoyo, an acquaintance from Cuba, who made some vague promises about taking him along on a mission some day. Everyone else refused to return his calls. Only the Junta Revolucionaria de Liberación Nacional on West Flagler Street showed any interest, but the small organisation was wary about gringos after the Hanard incident and did nothing more than allow George Finegan and his wife to use the junta's typewriters.

The situation seemed to improve when Hemming ran into Frank Fiorini one day at the junta offices. The two men knew each other slightly from Havana so Hemming was prepared to listen when Fiorini suggested that Interpen merge with his own organisation, now called the International Anti-Communist Brigade after someone pointed out the original brigades had been full of leftists. Any hesitations over the loss of autonomy were bulldozed aside by Fiorini's promises to turn Interpen into a well-funded guerrilla force that would be parachuting into Cuba within a few months.

In truth, Fiorini and Alex Rorke had no money. They'd recently visited the Anti-Communist International offices in New York on a fundraising mission that resulted in Haviv Schieber issuing a press release naming Fiorini as 'Commanding Officer and organizer of the ACI Brigade' but failed to produce any cash.[10] It was a blow, especially as Rorke's journalistic career barely covered his expenses and his wife had to beg money from her father to keep the household going, while the brigade itself was down to ten men after the Kenneth Proctor disaster. Fiorini was only keeping the group alive in case his luck changed.

'Just a paper organisation,' he said later.[11] 'Just to have an organisation to try to do something.'

Hemming soon discovered that accepting Fiorini's leadership meant little more than getting some International Brigade membership cards and a few tins of food. Fiorini's most useful intervention was to provide a box of used gas station attendant overalls and army fatigue suits so Interpen could look more like paramilitaries. Hemming soon began looking for other patrons and invited local exile figures to a parachute display at Davie Field on 1 July, downplaying the fact that the Miami Skydiving Club had organised the event and Interpen was just tagging along to borrow gear.

The display started badly when weight problems with a Piper Colt delayed their take-off and led to a long wait on the tarmac until a Cessna became available. The pilot was Howard K. Davis, another disillusioned former Castro fighter who'd been hanging around Florida since his return and getting involved in various exile activities before joining Interpen. He coaxed the Cessna into the air and Hemming was first out the door into the freezing slipstream. Five more Interpen members dived out after him, along with a Cuban from the junta who wanted some parachuting experience and a UPI journalist keen to get up close and personal with his story. The rest of Interpen watched from the ground along with Frank Fiorini, a gaggle of local journalists and Cubans from various exile organisations. There was polite applause as the men in camouflage suits floated down, got to their feet and began hauling in the parachutes. The UPI journalist landed on concrete and broke his ankle.

Gerald Hemming was feeling optimistic as he watched his men wrestling with their deflating silk canopies. He had no way of knowing his anti-communist crusade would end in failure after a long journey involving hand grenades, secret missions, international incidents, rogue members, armed robbery and grinding poverty. Hemming was a man digging his own grave under the delusion it was the foundations of a triumphal arch.

19

A REAL RAUNCHY GROUP OF MEN

CAYO GUILLERMO/MIAMI/BAHAMAS, LATE SUMMER–WINTER 1961

The *Blanca Estella* was a long way from home. A forty-foot, one-mast fishing boat which normally cast its nets off the Florida coast had no business being anywhere near Cayo Guillermo, a tiny Cuban island to the north of the mainland. The boat's three-man crew and their seven passengers were deep in enemy territory. Two of the Cuban passengers were here to survey the cay as a future invasion site, while another four planned to slip onto the mainland and join the resistance. Gerald Patrick Hemming was just along for the ride.

His invitation had come from Eloy Gutiérrez Menoyo. The former Second Front leader had made good on his promise of a mission after being impressed by Interpen's Davie Field parachute jump. Not everyone had been so happy about the event, including the Miami police, who arrested some Interpen members for vagrancy as they returned for more parachute training, and the FBI team that raided Nellie's boarding house looking for weapons. The bureau picked a day the group's guns were stashed elsewhere and agents got only some improbably wholesome-sounding answers when everyone went downtown for questioning.

'[Members] advised they were in Interpen,' noted the raid report, 'because they liked living outdoors, survival training, parachuting, keep[ing] in physical conditions, and for health reasons.'[1]

The FBI didn't believe a word but released them. Interpen returned to their boarding house to find Nellie Hamilton, a tough Arkansas native in her late sixties, had dumped their belongings on the front lawn and locked the door. She eventually softened and let most of them back inside, but Hemming was forced to find a new home for his dreams of military glory and collection of cowboy paperbacks (*They Died with Their Boots On* was a favourite) at the San Juan hotel.

Despite their notoriety, the adventurers of Interpen were penniless and living off day-old bread bought cheap from a local bakery. When twenty-five fresh volunteers arrived in town, they took one look at the group's living situation and went straight back home. Another 200 potential recruits had applied by post, but Hemming decided to ignore their applications until finances improved, a task made easier when George Williams Finegan and his wife abruptly disappeared one day and left no one to answer the correspondence. The reason for Finegan's disappearance only became clear a month later when he appeared before a Senate Internal Security Subcommittee on anti-Castro activities in Miami. The fanatically anti-communist former radioman was convinced Hemming's dismissal of potential recruits proved him to be a Cuban agent still loyal to Raúl Castro, and the senators ended the hearing more confused than when they started. The only useful information provided by Finegan was that Interpen had split from the International

Anti-Communist Brigade, disappointed at Frank Fiorini's broken promises about funding. Fiorini preferred to see the split as more organic.

'But we have never done anything with them because it was a raunchy group of men,' he said later.[2] 'Believe me. Real raunchy. And they just more or less shifted away.'

Early one August morning, Interpen got even more raunchy when Hemming met up with Menoyo's men near a dock on the Miami River and helped them load rifles and ammunition onto the peeling green-and-white paint of the *Blanca Estella*. They set off, nerves vibrating with tension, but hadn't got far when a police boat pulled up alongside them with questions about their destination. The captain came up with a believable story about a fishing cruise and they were allowed to continue. As the boat headed out of the river and into Biscayne Bay, one of the Cubans handed Hemming an automatic pistol for his own protection.

While the Interpen leader was gone, some of his followers would take the opportunity to try and start an international incident. Preferably a war with Cuba.

•   •   •

A Mark 2 anti-personnel fragmentation grenade is fifty-two grams of TNT explosive on a five-second fuse packed inside a casing that looks like a cast iron pineapple. On 14 August 1961, Joe Cavendish Garman was looking to buy one for cash, no questions asked. He and his Interpen friends wanted to blow up a Cuban gunboat.

Garman was a tall man with thinning hair and a compensating moustache from the prosperous Kentucky town of Bowling Green. His father spent the days poring over legal texts as a respected local judge, but Garman preferred to be out in the woods hunting and fishing and shooting. An experiment with marriage had led quickly to divorce when his wife realised he cared more about oiling the bolt-action on his hunting rifle than satisfying her needs. His parents hoped Joe would become a gentleman farmer, but there was a spark of wildness in his brain that recoiled from small town respectability and took him into the nightclub business instead. The criminal convictions piled up: street brawls, assault, transporting liquor without a licence. His father's influence minimised the penalties, but when Garman started dynamiting rival nightclubs and prosecutors talked about jail, it was time to leave town. In April 1961, he visited Florida and hooked up with some adventurous types in Bayfront Park who nicknamed him 'Lil Joe' and invited their new friend to an Interpen training camp in the Everglades. Soon he was wearing combat fatigues and jumping out of an aeroplane over Davie Field.

The other members liked him. As a thirty-year-old college graduate, he was older and better educated; as the recipient of $50 a week from his father to stay far away from Bowling Green, he had more money. When Garman began discussing the joys of blowing things up in his laconic Kentucky drawl, some of his new comrades were prepared to listen.

On 14 August, he and fellow Interpen man Pat Stepanick tried to get some hand grenades from a Cuban judo instructor they knew through a well-connected exile restaurant owner who gave Interpen members the occasional free meal. Garman and Stepanick introduced themselves, made some general chat and revealed their plan to blow up a gunboat being returned to Havana the next day after a long diplomatic wrangle. The grenade attack might well lead to war, but neither man had a problem with that.

'I'd rather be shot to death than bored to death,' said Garman.[3]

The judo instructor liked the plan and introduced them to some friends in the exile community, but no one had any hand grenades. They shrugged and wished Garman and Stepanick better luck next time. Everyone parted on good terms and America never knew how close it had come to an international incident on its doorstep.

Gerald Hemming didn't find out about the hand grenade incident until he got back to Miami and by then was too busy swaggering around the city boasting about adventures in Red Cuba to discipline his men. In reality, the trip had been uneventful. Cayo Guillermo had turned out to be nothing but sand and scrub, home only to a few fishermen, and the anti-Castro underground contacts had never appeared. The *Blanca Estella* team stumbled around the island for two days, sleeping on the sand, without much incident until four of the militants began talking about stealing a car and driving to Havana. The captain of the *Blanca Estella* persuaded them it was suicide and everyone returned to Miami. None of that stopped a sunburned Hemming telling his Interpen comrades tall tales of narrow escapes on Cuban territory with death never more than a few footsteps away.

He would soon be outclassed in the real-life adventure stakes by Frank Fiorini and Alex Rorke. Within a few months the pair would be flying over Cuban territory, showering propaganda leaflets over the people below.

•　•　•

In September 1961, Frank Fiorini asked a trusted friend for advice. José Joaquín Sanjenís Perdomo was a senior Treasury official who had known Fiorini since the gunrunning days and fled Cuba in early 1960 to join the exiles in Miami. His brother Sergio had been the man who saved Fiorini's life by urging him to leave Havana the year before. During the Bay of Pigs build-up, the CIA had put Joaquín Sanjenís in charge of Operation 40, an intelligence group formed to administer areas captured by Brigade 2506 after the invasion and capture key regime flunkies. The group had a strong right-wing flavour that convinced more paranoid exiles that its true purpose was to assassinate political enemies on all sides, although no one ever provided any hard proof for the accusations.

In the aftermath of the Bay of Pigs, the CIA came up with what became known as Operation Mongoose: a programme to destabilise the Cuban economy with everything from covert industrial sabotage to the distribution of morale-sapping propaganda stickers that caricatured Castro as an obese slob, Guevara as a simian Cro-Magnon and Raúl as an effete homosexual chasing butterflies. Soon thousands of exiled Cubans were on the CIA payroll in one form or another, all overseen by the agency from behind its front of Zenith Technical Enterprises, a realistic-looking business with fake sales charts on the walls that operated out of a building in the University of Miami's mostly unused south campus near the Metro Zoo. The CIA became the biggest single employer in Miami and so many agents settled in town that housing prices started to rise.

Operation 40 had been disbanded after the Bay of Pigs and Sanjenís became a senior figure in the AMOT programme, a network of Cuban informers placed inside Florida's various exile groups to keep the CIA informed of internal difficulties and ensure everyone obeyed orders. AMOT soon mutated into an intelligence service allowed so much autonomy by the agency that many Cubans felt it had become a threat to their community.

'When the Bay of Pigs went kaput, they stayed [together] as a

group and Sanjenís became a very, very dangerous and powerful guy in Miami because he had a file on everybody,' said Rafael
Quintero, a senior exile figure.[4] '[He knew] whose wife was whose
lover, how much money, etc. ... Some people tried to use that for
blackmail.'

Frank Fiorini knew little about AMOT but had convinced himself his Cuban friend was a CIA agent and made a habit of asking
him for advice. Sanjenís usually had some wise words and occasionally steered him towards exiles looking for training or a pilot;
Fiorini generally did as he was told, convinced that Sanjenís was
relaying orders directly from the CIA, although in truth the agency
was unaware of their relationship. In the wilderness of mirrors that
made up the Cold War spy scene, the AMOT chief was happy to
mislead both old friends and current paymasters in pursuit of his
own objectives. Fiorini remained a pawn in a game whose rules
and players he barely comprehended.

That September, Fiorini visited to ask about a Cuban exile from
New York looking to hire American pilots. The previous month
Alex Rorke's New York contacts had introduced him to Sergio
Rojas Santamarina, a glossy-haired former ambassador with CIA
connections who split his time between London and the Big Apple.
Rojas had a plan to invade Cuba that centred on persuading Nicaraguan leader Luis Somoza Debayle to offer up his country as a
military base, but he was having trouble persuading the dictator to
take him seriously. He thought a high-profile leafleting campaign
across Cuba would be a good start and asked Rorke to carry out the
operation with help from his friends down in Miami.

Sanjenís approved of the Rojas mission but didn't mention that
the former ambassador's CIA funding had ended a few months
back after the agency failed to come up with any convincing

reasons to keep him on the payroll. Fiorini and Rorke proceeded on the assumption that this was an official CIA mission, and no one did anything to dissuade them.

The plan involved two hired Beechcraft aeroplanes, a trip to Nassau in the Bahamas and several crates of propaganda leaflets commissioned from a Miami-based exile group with its own printing press. By October, Fiorini had hired two pilots at $1,000 each: Robert Frank Swanner III was a former crop duster from Oklahoma and Robert Thompson flew for an aircraft rental company in Melbourne, Florida. The original plan was to leaflet-bomb both Santiago and Camagüey, a large town to the east of the island's midriff, but bad weather forced the pilots to abandon the first target and head straight for the second. Swanner and Thompson did the flying while Fiorini and occasional co-conspirator Bill Johnson threw out the leaflets, and Rorke came along to photograph the experience. A 400,000-strong mix of stickers and leaflets blew out into the slipstream and fluttered down. Puzzled Cubans picked them and read: 'Set fire to transportation! Set fire to the bridges! Set fire to the warehouses! Set fire to the factories! SET FIRE TO FIDEL!'[5]

Rojas was so pleased he funded another leaflet drop in December. This one would target Matanzas in the north of the island.

• • •

The mission started badly when British authorities checked the paperwork and discovered the aeroplane Bob Swanner had just landed at Nassau should never have left America. The pilot had hired it in Miami on the pretext of a pleasure flight around the Everglades and didn't have permission to leave the country. Things got worse when the British found a crate of anti-Castro leaflets in the cabin and Swanner confessed he was involved in counter-revolutionary activities. Soon he was behind bars facing a $500 fine. Fiorini, Rorke and Johnson arrived by commercial flight the next day and were arrested on the tarmac, but the British reluctantly let them all go after they paid Swanner's fine and agreed to the confiscation of the aeroplane. All four took the next commercial flight back to Miami.

Robert Thompson was under the impression he was sitting out this mission until a telephone call came from Fiorini asking him to locate another aeroplane. He hired a red-and-white Piper Apache from his own employer and flew to Nassau to meet the others, who had managed to slip back into the country without alerting the authorities. Thompson and Swanner agreed to co-pilot each other and filed a fake flight plan. More leaflets were loaded aboard and on 15 December 1961 they wobbled into the air on the way to Cuba while Fiorini and Johnson stayed behind to fish in the bright turquoise waters and Rorke took photographs of the scenery.

The Apache failed to return. After waiting another day, the three men flew back to Miami hoping Thompson had returned the plane directly to his employer but found nothing. Rorke hired another aircraft by claiming he needed it to photograph pink flamingos for a magazine article and Fiorini took the controls for a search pattern over the Gulf of Mexico, looking for life jackets and wreckage. He found no sign of the missing plane.

The truth took a while to leak out of Cuba. Swanner and Thompson had been bringing the Apache in low over Matanzas, one of them at the controls and the other shovelling leaflets out the door towards workers in the sugar cane fields below, when Cuban anti-aircraft guns opened up. The aeroplane was hit and smashed into a sugar mill, killing both men. Cuban authorities buried the mangled bodies behind a nearby church. A solemn Fiorini visited the pilots' wives in Miami with cheques for $500 and muttered something about how their husbands had disappeared while working for the CIA then left the women to their hysterical grief. In the aftermath, Rojas fell out with Nicaraguan leader Somoza then ran out of money and plans for further operations evaporated. The crash made the newspapers but was quickly overshadowed by a five-hour speech from Fidel Castro the same month in which he claimed his belief in communism had been building since the 1953 barracks attack and had now become a guiding ideology.

'I am a Marxist–Leninist,' he said.[6] 'And I shall be to the last days of my life.'

America had a self-declared outpost of the communist bloc sitting in its own backyard. A confrontation the next year would bring the world to the brink of nuclear war.

20

BOMBE CARIBIENNE

WASHINGTON DC/CUBA/NEW ORLEANS/NO NAME KEY, WINTER 1962

The guests gathered in the East Room of the White House broke into spontaneous applause as the President of the United States of America and his wife came down the stairs looking like movie stars. John F. Kennedy wore a tuxedo with a blue boutonnière at his lapel and a beaming smile while Jacqueline looked elegant in a pale green off-the-shoulder gown by Oleg Cassini. The United States Marine Band struck up a strident version of 'Hail to the Chief' as the couple greeted their guests.

'Jack and Jackie actually shimmered,' said author William Styron.[1] 'You would have had to be abnormal, perhaps psychotic, to be immune to their dumbfounding appeal.'

On that warm evening of 29 April 1962, a selection of America's Nobel Prize winners and a crowd of fellow high achievers had assembled at the White House for a banquet to celebrate the nation's intellectual talent. Guests ate filet de boeuf Wellington and drank a Mouton Rothschild 1955 as the hum of conversation modulated the clank of cutlery and clink of glasses. William Styron's wife Rose chatted to Albert Szent-Györgyi about seafood under the impression the Hungarian scientist was an expert on saltwater mussels and not, as she later found out, human musculature. Mary Hemingway, widow of the troubled writer who'd committed shotgun-suicide the previous year, chided President Kennedy over his combative attitude to Cuba. He diplomatically disagreed. Afterwards there was coffee, followed by speeches, a reading from an unpublished Hemingway novel and a nice line from the President in his familiar Boston Brahmin accent: 'I think this is the most extraordinary collection of talent, of human knowledge, that has ever been gathered together at the White House, with the possible exception of when Thomas Jefferson dined alone.'[2]

That got big laughs. Kennedy had charisma enough to cover up an ocean of sins, political and personal. Everyone present knew he owed his election victory to vote-rigging by the Chicago Democrat machine and cheated on his wife with an obsessive passion that made no allowance for a crippling back pain and its accompanying pill addiction. The more politically savvy were aware the administration's much-publicised concern with civil rights never stretched further than the opinion polls dictated and its foreign policy broke every international law on the books in a quest for American hegemony. None of that stopped laughter and applause ringing out across the tables in the State Dining Room.

In the afterglow of cigars and cigarettes and chamber music, nobody saw any significance in the dessert prepared that evening by White House chef René Verdon. *Bombe Caribienne* was a moulded ice cream dish of vanilla, pineapple, cinnamon and rum topped with a sculpture of spun sugar.

'Much too sweet,' muttered a drunk William Styron to himself.[3] 'A real bomb.'

Within a few days of the Nobel dinner, Soviet premier Nikita Khrushchev would make the decision to move his own bombs to the Caribbean in the form of nuclear warheads. Havana welcomed this deterrent against another invasion as an act of Marxist–Leninist brotherhood, but the geopolitical reality had more to do with Soviet concerns over America's far larger nuclear arsenal, especially the Jupiter missiles overlooking the Black Sea from Turkey. An outgunned Khrushchev thought placing a real *Bombe Caribienne* on America's doorstep would balance out the situation. On 9 September, the first Soviet missile unit arrived by freighter at Casilda, a quiet Cuban port used mostly by fishing boats. The mission was so secret that Russian technicians disembarked wearing heavy winter boots they'd been assured were essential footwear for their destination.

The eighty cruise missiles, twelve short-range missiles and six nuclear bombs that would eventually be installed on Cuban territory were strategically insignificant compared to the fleet of Soviet nuclear submarines prowling America's coasts, and their delivery time wasn't substantially quicker than those launched directly from the USSR, but the symbolism meant everything. The Soviets were convinced that Kennedy would back down when he discovered the warheads, just as he had over the Bay of Pigs. They were wrong.

• • •

The camera nestled in the belly of the Lockheed U-2 spy plane gliding calmly over Cuba at 70,000 feet recorded the landscape below in a thousand high-resolution black-and-white photographs. When it landed, American technicians extracted and developed the film before rushing it to CIA analysts who hunched over light tables to decode the grey smudges and white scars in the images. By the evening of 15 October 1962, the analysis was complete: Cuba had nuclear missiles aimed at the United States of America.

President Kennedy was informed the next day and assembled a team of fourteen advisers, including his 36-year-old brother Robert, to formulate a response to the provocation. Everyone agreed the issue was political rather than military. In the event of nuclear war, the missiles would not get off their launch pads before an American strike blotted out the island and, even if they did, would not significantly increase the megatons of death already raining down.

'A missile is a missile,' said the famously cold-blooded Secretary of Defense Robert McNamara.[4] 'It makes no great difference whether you are killed by a missile from the Soviet Union or Cuba.'

That pragmatism was never shared with the public. Kennedy had campaigned for the presidency with a hawkish approach to the Cold War and some strategic lies about a 'missile gap' putting America at the mercy of the Kremlin. The average Kennedy supporter was a patriotic anti-communist who'd been shocked by the failure of the Bay of Pigs and would regard weakness over the missiles as a deal-breaking humiliation. Some at the White House shared that view, like Robert Kennedy, who demanded another invasion of Cuba as 'the last chance we will have to destroy Castro', while cooler heads suggested a blockade or strategic airstrike.[5] As the President's men grappled with their options, a decision was made to inform the American people of the situation. At 19:00 on 22 October, all major television networks in the country carried a live televised address from Kennedy that informed viewers about the missiles, Soviet aggression and the threat of nuclear war. At the same time, US forces around the world went to Defcon 3 ('Air Force ready to mobilize in 15 minutes') and civilians were evacuated from the naval base at Guantánamo Bay at such short notice that pots were left boiling on stoves.

Polls showed that 84 per cent of Americans backed Kennedy's confrontational stance, even as panicking suburbanites dug makeshift bomb shelters in their gardens and the *Washington Star* did good business with a fifty-cent booklet titled 'You Can Survive Atomic Attack'.[6] Less optimistic newspapers informed readers that a nuclear war could result in 20 million American casualties and advised parents to buy dog tags so their children's burned corpses could be identified. Sales of dried food, chemical toilets and radiation protection suits skyrocketed. Warning sirens went off periodically in major cities through testing or error and caused a wave of nervous breakdowns among those already living on their nerves. Churches opened twenty-four hours a day and psychiatrists had more new patients than they could handle. The world seemed to be ending.

'All of our thoughts and comments were selfish,' said Patti Lynn, then a nineteen-year-old college student.[7] 'We weren't considering the Cuban people or those in South Florida. It was all: "How will I be able to finish college ... the world is going to be destroyed ... Russia is going to blow us up ... I'm going to die a virgin..."'

An emergency meeting on 25 October of the United Nations Security Council achieved little and American forces went to Defcon 2: 'Armed forces ready to deploy and engage in less than six hours'. President Kennedy had now sided with his brother and was pushing for an invasion against the counsel of his advisers while, on the other side of the Caribbean Sea, Fidel Castro was demanding

Moscow launch a pre-emptive strike if American troops landed on Cuban soil. Through secret back channels an alarmed Khrushchev offered to withdraw his missiles if America removed its own Jupiter missiles from Turkey, but Kennedy refused. On the morning of 27 October, a U-2 spy plane was shot down over Oriente province and the pilot killed; later that day, US Navy destroyers used depth charges to bring a Soviet submarine to the surface in the waters off Cuba, unaware it was armed with nuclear weapons and the captain was barely being restrained from using them by his own crew.

The events shocked some sense into both sides. That evening, Kennedy agreed to the mutual removal of missiles and guaranteed the end of military action against Cuba with a letter written in strangled diplomatic language the next day: 'The United States of America will respect the inviolability of Cuban borders, its sovereignty, that it take the pledge not to interfere in internal affairs, not to intrude themselves and not to permit our territory to be used as a bridgehead for the invasion of Cuba, and will restrain those who would plan to carry an aggression against Cuba.'[8]

Fidel Castro refused to believe the Yankee promises and had to be strong-armed by Moscow into dismantling the missiles and sending them home. He expressed his disgust by hiring a team of Waffen-SS veterans who had fought for Nazi Germany during the war to train his militia against any future American invasion. He could have saved his money. Operation Mongoose had been officially cancelled and CIA agents were scrambling around Miami to stand down their Cuban proxies.

The exiles obeyed orders, but the agency had no authority over independent groups like Interpen, which had spent most of the missile crisis obliviously training in the Everglades and arrived back in town to find the world on the brink of nuclear war. Gerald

Hemming came up with a plan of action that would probably tip it over the edge.

• • •

It had been a strange year for Interpen. First, Jack Nordeen turned up limping in Miami and asked for help in overthrowing the Nicaraguan government. He promised Hemming the liberated country could be used as a launch pad against Cuba, but the plan stalled through lack of money and Nordeen left town never to make contact again. Then representatives of the Movimiento Revolucionario 30 de Noviembre, a group of disillusioned leftists led by the brother of revolutionary martyr Frank País, approached Interpen to provide training for an upcoming infiltration mission. Hemming and his more experienced lieutenants took the Cubans out into the Everglades and only discovered how violently unpopular the group was with other exiles when death threats began arriving back at Nellie's boarding house. A guilty-looking trainee who called himself 'Captain Sosa' gave them pistols for self-defence out of an arsenal originally provided to the movimiento by the CIA.

'[Hemming] stated that these weapons had been issued to them,' noted an FBI report, 'because other underground Cuban groups in Miami had been "giving them trouble" by putting sugar in gas tanks and tossing small grenades in their quarters.'[9]

The trouble eventually faded away but so did the training fees and soon Interpen's members were back begging for food from Cuban grocers. Hemming tried to turn his amateur adventuring into something more professional by joining the CIA, to which he was still making occasional calls with information about the exile scene, and filled out a long application form with truths, half-truths and outright lies. While waiting for an answer, he took a Greyhound bus to Los Angeles for a fundraising trip among anti-communist American businessmen whose names he'd found in the newspapers. Hemming gave his usual spiel about fighting Castro and victory being only a donation away but got nothing. On what was meant to be his last day in town, the local police found an unlicensed Remington Rand .45 pistol, donated by Captain Sosa, lying on the front seat of Hemming's hire car and pulled him in for questioning. The Interpen leader made things worse by claiming to be a CIA agent and demanding the return of his gun.

Eventually, the police released him and Hemming headed for Mobile, Alabama, to visit a former Interpen member. His friend was involved in cheque fraud and car theft, and Hemming spent a week in jail before convincing the sheriff he had just been passing through. Back in Miami, a CIA official got in touch to advise Hemming that impersonating an agent and associating with known felons might adversely affect his job application. It surprised no one when a rejection letter arrived a few weeks later.

Interpen was now down to around a dozen men, including 'Lil Joe' Garman, Howard K. Davis, the petty crook and former Freedom Fighters of the Americas member Roy Hargraves, Hemming sidekick Ed Collins, the 33-year-old Finnish-born hospital worker Ed Kolby (who claimed to be a Special Forces veteran with a Purple Heart), former FFA and Anti-Communist Legion member Steve Wilson and a handsome Canadian called William Dempsey, whose withered left arm hung four inches shorter than the right. They sat around outside Nellie's boarding house drinking cheap beer and making big plans for military glory that would never materialise. On more motivated days, they field-stripped their guns on the back lawn before doing some close-order drill around the garden, sometimes joined by a dwarf called Pete who lived at Nellie's and enjoyed trotting behind the toweringly tall Garman. The boarding house could be a sketchy place and the police once raided a clapboard cottage out back in search of a man on the run, only to be disturbed by Interpen and Pete marching past ('Hup, two, three, four') and causing so much confusion the suspect slipped through a back window and escaped.

Other Glen Haven residents now included men like Robert K. Brown, a crop-haired 29-year Army veteran from Colorado who'd once supported Castro's rebels but was now in Miami working on his master's thesis about the Cuban labour movement and playing a small role in some exile operations, and homosexual alcoholic Dennis Harber, who taught English to Cuban locals and begged members of Interpen to ration his whiskey so it would last the day. Nobody at the boarding house did much in the way of overthrowing Castro.

'I was wasting time like everyone else', said 'Skinny' Ralph Schlafter.[10] 'A great excuse. You no longer had to work for a living – you could sit there and do nothing, and feel worthwhile. Instead of saying you were unemployed, you said you were a soldier of fortune.'

As the summer of 1962 rolled in, Hemming was considering doing something drastic, like getting a proper job, when a middle-aged sailor called Larry LaBorde turned up with talk of boats and guerrillas. LaBorde was a New Orleans native whose various adventures as harbour master and small boat operator invariably ended in disgrace due to a combination of alcohol and firearms. Around the start of Operation Mongoose, he'd been captaining a temperamental subchaser called the *Tejana III* when the Cuban owner loaned it to the CIA operation in Florida. No one at the agency had intended to hire any Americans for the operation, but the *Tejana III* was too useful to turn down and LaBorde was the only person who could coax the motor back to life during its frequent break-downs. Langley reluctantly signed him up as a contractor to ferry Cuban commandos across the sea. Agents soon discovered their new recruit was an erratic alcoholic, prone to cornering them in restaurants for loud talk about top-secret missions, and no one was sorry to see him go when the agency switched from private boats to its own fleet.

An unemployed and bitter LaBorde continued blundering around Miami, his red nose and bloated belly a familiar sight at exile meet-ings. He approached Interpen with a two-pronged plan to blow up a boat called the SS *Williams*, which was allegedly smuggling machin-ery into Cuba, and then rob a CIA warehouse full of weapons being stockpiled for exiles. It was the kind of idea Hemming would have dismissed as crazy the previous year, but times had changed. He and Ed Collins began practising underwater sabotage techniques with aqualungs in the sea off Key Biscayne. They were close to launch-ing the attack when LaBorde's drunken boasting in bars alerted the authorities to the plan and the aqualungs were confiscated by some unsmiling men in dark suits who refused to show identification and advised Interpen to leave town for a while.

Hemming chose to visit New Orleans with LaBorde, who intro-duced his new friend to local Cuban exiles as a CIA operative hoping to revitalise the city's moribund paramilitary scene. Im-portant Cubans liked the idea and provided some firearms, which encouraged Hemming to announce plans for a training camp staffed by his friends and paid for by the exiles. None of the Cubans stopped to wonder why the agency wanted their money, rather than the other way around.

Land for the camp was donated in the town of Covington, forty miles outside New Orleans, by a 47-year-old businessman and former tennis champ with alleged links to organised crime called Michael Julius McLaney. He'd made a fortune through casinos in Havana and hoped to recover them if Castro was overthrown. Hemming invited his Interpen comrades to help prepare the camp, but at the last moment senior exile figure Luis Rabel ran a background check on the new arrivals through friends in Florida and wasn't happy with the results.

'Local Cubans and a shadowy American adventurer have been working feverishly – but unsuccessfully – for over a month to set up an anti-Castro guerrilla training camp base near Covington,' reported the *New Orleans States-Item*.[11] 'Luis Rabel, local delegate of the Cuban Revolutionary Council, confirmed last week the Miami Council Headquarters nixed the Covington base for undisclosed reasons.'

Those undisclosed reasons were the revelation that LaBorde and Hemming were penniless adventurers who had been lying about their agency affiliation. Rabel cut all contact with the men from Miami and the training camp collapsed before it had even begun. Hemming tried to raise money from other sources in New Orleans for a few unsuccessful days, then returned to Miami leaving his hotel bills unpaid. Larry LaBorde stumbled off into his own erratic orbit and the Interpen men were back in the front room at Nellie's boarding house, selling their blood to pay the rent.

• • •

The October missile crisis found Interpen's members training in the Everglades, oblivious to it all. They'd spent the autumn tangled up in various abortive schemes hatched by exiles, like the group that hired them to transport a guerrilla unit to Cuba but dropped out at the last minute when the funding fell through. Hemming and friends decided to make the trip themselves but were stopped by the Coast Guard before getting far from Miami.

Their failures and misfires were only emphasised when Frank Fiorini introduced his friend Alex Rorke at a Miami diner. The International Anti-Communist Brigade had been busy all summer with leafleting raids, attempted phosphorous bomb runs and ferrying exile guerrillas across the Florida Straits by boat. A few insiders sensed some tensions between the brigade's two leaders, but to Hemming they looked like an enviable success story. He turned on enough backslapping camaraderie to make the three men inseparable for a short while, but the three musketeers act was never going to last. Hemming felt too resentful at the ease with which a well-spoken college boy like Rorke had become a celebrity of the anti-Castro struggle. Locals greeted him on the street, a film producer was convinced Rorke's life would make a good movie and important people in New York were starting to pay attention. The trio soon drifted apart.

In September, things improved for Interpen when Rolando Masferrer, who'd been banned from Florida after his disastrous 1960 invasion attempt and had exiled himself to New York, asked them to train a group of Cubans at No Name Key for a secret project. Hemming couldn't resist the publicity boom of inviting local journalists along to watch the action, but the resulting stories provoked a raid on the camp by US Border Patrol agents. They found the Interpen trainers and nine Cuban men miserably eating swamp cabbage in a tumbledown hut, and whatever project Masferrer had in mind collapsed in the aftermath.

Hemming and the others returned to No Name Key late the next month for some more survival training and were still out there, isolated from the world among the rabbits and raccoons, when the missile crisis erupted. They drove back to town on 26 October to find the world on the brink of nuclear war. Miami was crawling with soldiers, locals were panic-buying tinned food and many Cuban exiles had abandoned their guerrilla operations to sign up with the US Army. Interpen sat around Nellie's front room and began planning for World War III, but the crisis ended a day later, leaving the world relieved that peace had triumphed and Hemming disappointed the chance to fight Cuba had been lost.

He came up with a plan for Interpen to avenge America's honour by infiltrating Cuban territory, separating into two groups of five and spending the next two weeks launching sabotage attacks on any military installations in sight. Mission complete, they would reunite, steal a Cuban boat and head for the Bahamas. It was a suicide mission that could only push the world back towards nuclear war, but to the unemployed soldiers of fortune at Nellie Hamilton's place it sounded like a solid idea.

They pawned their possessions and put down a $200 deposit on the *Sally*, a 35-foot Chris-Craft motorboat. Just after midnight on 4 December 1962, the Interpen team were loading guns, ammunition, hand grenades and blood plasma at the Marathon docks in the Florida Keys when customs agents raided the place and arrested all thirteen men. Things looked bad until a local lawyer called Charles Ashmann took the case and accused customs of entrapment, then threatened to drag CIA agents into court to ask awkward questions about the agency's operations in Miami. In January 1963, the charges were dropped.

The group was more broke than ever. Hemming got a job mowing lawns, while other members drifted back home. Rival faces were already emerging onto the Miami scene with more energy and drive, and longer criminal records. They were looking past Cuba to another Caribbean dictatorship, this one controlled by machetes and voodoo, which might prove to be the first domino that toppled all others in the region.

21

STRICTLY A NO-GOOD PUNK

DEERFIELD BEACH/MIAMI/BAHAMAS, AUTUMN 1963

The office of the *Sun-Sentinel* in Deerfield Beach was full of cigarette smoke and chattering typewriters. At a desk near the door, a balding man with glasses and sharp features was smoking a cigarette as he pecked gloomily at his keyboard. A taller man with a family resemblance sat on the edge of the desk. Both looked up when the stranger who'd just walked into the office approached them.

'Jim Buchanan?' the man asked.[1]

Buchanan was a fiercely right-wing newsman whose support for the counter-revolution stretched back to sheltering Austin Frank Young in a Havana hotel room during his brief 1959 jail break, while brother Jerry was a familiar face with the International Anti-Communist Brigade when he wasn't in prison for various petty crimes. Together they acted as gatekeepers to the world of Cuban exile groups in Miami. They looked warily at their visitor, who remained cockily cheerful as they peppered him with questions and peered at his driving licence as if the small print could tell them something. Eventually, the stranger led them outside to where his car was cooking in the August sun and opened the trunk to reveal three old Mauser rifles, a Lee–Enfield .303 with telescopic scope and a cardboard box full of automatic pistols. When the man looked over his shoulder, both Buchanan brothers were grinning.

The man with the guns was 28-year-old Edward Ivan Arthur from Columbus, Ohio. Back in the *Sun-Sentinel* office, dingy after the bright sunlight, Arthur told the Buchanan brothers about his hatred of communism, desire to free Cuba and current sleeping arrangement on the couch of a friend in nearby Pompano Beach, a humid city of lush lawns and dripping sweat. Like many, he had originally supported Castro's rebels and even visited Havana in 1957 for a failed attempt to join the struggle, but the regime's transformation into a Marxist–Leninist dictatorship horrified him. During a recent trip back to the Cuban capital, posing as a tourist, Arthur had secretly drawn any official building that looked impor-tant, but the Ohio FBI showed no interest in his amateur espionage. A friend in Ohio recommended he contact the Buchanans for an introduction to the anti-Castro scene, so he filled the trunk of his car with guns and set off to join the fight.

Jim Buchanan liked the new arrival's straightforward approach. He agreed to pass the guns to an exile group known as 'Comman-dos L', a recently formed guerrilla outfit that distinguished itself by actually carrying out missions rather than just squabbling with other Cubans, and recommended Arthur form his own organisa-tion to fight Castro. The journalist himself was more activist than observer: he ran the International Anti-Communist Brigade's official publication, a regular newsletter whose masthead was crammed with right-wing slogans like 'Serving America 24 Hours a Day', '*Con Dios Todos – Sin Dios Nada*' ('With God Everything

– Without God Nothing') and 'Re-Instate the Monroe Doctrine'. He arranged a meeting between Arthur and brigade founder Frank Fiorini about how best to help the cause.

Arthur visited Fiorini at his Miami home and was impressed by the man but disappointed by the advice. The veteran anti-communist had recently fallen out with his friend Alex Rorke and recommended avoiding any involvement in the Cuban scene unless the aim was to end up disillusioned and broke. Although he still carried out occasional missions for Joaquín Sanjenís and others, Fiorini spent most days working as a used-car salesman and was hoping to open a detective agency that specialised in divorce cases. He seemed bitter at the result of recent fundraising efforts among local exiles.

'We were struggling when we were not getting financial assistance from the Cuban colony,' Fiorini said.[2] 'It was a struggle, you know.'

He advised Arthur to go home and get a proper job. Instead, the Ohio native gave his usual cheerful grin and headed off to talk with a lawyer recommended by Jim Buchanan. The *Sun-Sentinel* man had advised him to get some paperwork drawn up for his new or-ganisation before he landed in Cuba.

• • •

Charles Ashmann was the 28-year-old boy wonder of the Miami legal scene. A former aide to a Democrat senator, Ashmann made his name by beating the Cuban government in court when it failed to pay the advertising firm of Harris & Co. for an ill-fated cam-paign to encourage American tourists to visit the newly nation-alised fleshpots. Ashmann convinced a judge to allow the seizure of Cuban property on America soil in lieu of payment and went round the country flamboyantly confiscating goods, boats and even Castro's private aeroplane when it arrived in New York for a United Nations meeting.

The victory gave Ashmann, a native New Yorker transplanted to Florida, a taste for international intrigue and he reinvented himself as a legal eagle for the Cuban exile scene and the American adventurers it attracted. In late August, he agreed to take a meeting with a young man from Ohio who called himself 'Captain Arthur' and hoped to incorporate a non-profit under the name Americans for Freedom. Ashmann gave his client the standard speech, warning that raiding Cuba direct from the US was illegal under the Neutrality Act but authorities couldn't do anything if the Bahamas was used as a neutral base. Ed Arthur seemed more interested in discussing the chances of his newfound political engagement changing people's minds about him back in Ohio.

'Arthur claimed his purpose in involving himself in revolutionary activities,' noted an FBI report, 'was to combat communism and tyrannical dictatorships, and to thereby atone for his past.'[3]

That past involved an extensive criminal record which had begun with delinquency at eight years old, then flowered into multiple counts of armed robbery, extortion, fraud and assault and battery, most recently on a female acquaintance. He had spent most of his adult life unemployed and had the tattoos to prove it, with daggers, dice and hearts inked across his arms and hands. He made occasional attempts to straighten up and fly right, like the time he conned his way into the National Guard at thirteen for a brief spell and did the same thing two years later with the US Army. Later came an attempt to join guerrillas in the Sierra Maestra, which came to nothing when he couldn't locate any M26J activists. Arthur was trying to put his criminal past firmly behind him, but no one who had seen his Columbus police record would have been optimistic about his chances of rehabilitation.

'Good looking lad, attracts women easily,' wrote an officer.[4] 'Spent time at Lima State Hospital for Insane; has split personality. Fathered one illegitimate child. Was paroled from Boys Industrial School. Steered "suckers" to crap games at Los Angeles, California. Doesn't like to work. His speciality is "rolling queers", and he is strictly a "no-good punk". He engaged in a homosexual act with Ed Myers and blackmailed him to the extent of $6,000.00. He lives with known queers.'

Charles Ashmann believed in giving people a second chance, especially if they were paying clients, and started the wheels turning on the incorporation of Americans for Freedom. The group started small and stayed that way. Arthur persuaded an old prison friend from the Ohio State Reformatory called Eddie Lombardo to join up, along with fellow jailbird Robert Ayala, a 49-year-old Army veteran of Spanish descent. The three tried to raise money by offering *Life* magazine the chance to bankroll a mission into Cuba to the tune of $100,000 in exchange for exclusive photographic rights. *Life* turned them down and whatever money the trio had quickly drained away in the Miami bars. Soon they were sleeping in their cars and selling personal possessions to buy food.

Jim Buchanan kept in touch and bought them the occasional morale-boosting diner breakfast. Behind the scenes, he was involved in some Caribbean intrigue and thought Americans for Freedom might have a role to play.

•　•　•

The official name of the men with the straw hats and machetes was the Volontaires de la Sécurité Nationale (National Security Volunteers), but Haitians knew them as the Tonton Macoute after the voodoo bogeyman who ate children for breakfast. A paramilitary unit loyal only to President François Duvalier, they tortured, raped and murdered anyone who threatened their master's grasp on power. Thousands had fled the Tonton Macoute for exile in neighbouring countries since the President took power in 1957, with many ending up in the British-run Bahamas, where a tired-looking 58-year-old former consul called Clément Benoît attempted to organise them into the Parti Révolutionnaire Haïtien (Haitian Revolutionary Party).

On 23 August, Benoît announced he had 3,000 men ready to overthrow Duvalier as soon as someone provided the guns, ammunition, training and boats. No one took him very seriously, with the CIA calling Benoît 'an opportunistic dreamer' who appealed only to cane cutters and illegal immigrants, but his announcement triggered an official complaint from the current Haitian consul and led to a deportation order.[5] Benoît was searching for a country prepared to take him when Charles Ashmann got in touch, described himself as an attorney who opposed dictatorships and offered to arrange a temporary US visa and a bodyguard. On 9 September, a smiling Ed Arthur turned up in Nassau to escort the Haitian exile back to Florida.

Ashmann and Buchanan were mixed up in a plan to invade Haiti, with the intention of using it as a base to raid Cuba, and thought Benoît would make a good figurehead. The former consul had his doubts about the idea, most of which had started on the flight over when Arthur drank too much and boasted about being head of a large military organisation with a huge arsenal of weaponry, although in reality this amounted to two broken automatic rifles being looked after by a wheelchair-bound gun dealer in Florida. Arthur dropped heavy hints that Benoît would be wise to fund his group then fell asleep for the rest of the flight. In Miami, the pair took up residence at the McAllister Hotel, where the Haitian was distressed to discover that twenty-five followers who arrived in Florida hoping to join him had been rounded up by the Immigration Service and repatriated. He got more distressed when Ashmann made it clear his free legal services didn't extend to paying the hotel bill or funding the invasion.

A meeting with a local doctor who had expressed an interest in backing the plan went well until Benoît asked for $75,000, and then ended abruptly. Arthur and his fellow Americans for Freedom went door to door to solicit funds but only raised $25, at which point Robert Ayala quit the scene and reduced the group to Arthur and Lombardo. The pair sat around in bars wondering what they had got themselves into.

'Who the hell cares about Duvalier or Castro?' Arthur asked Lombardo one night as they pounded beers.[6]

A depressed Benoît moved into a cheaper hotel with a more liberal attitude about allowing him and his white wife to share a room. He was talking about leaving Florida altogether when Buchanan stepped in with some good news: a group of Canadian Jesuits unhappy with Haiti's turn towards voodoo had agreed to fund an exile invasion from the Dominican Republic to be led by former Haitian Army Chief-of-Staff Léon Cantave and involving a simultaneous attack from Florida under Rolando Masferrer. The Cuban was as aggressive as always ('I'll crack [Duvalier]'s balls like hazelnuts,' he promised) and already planning a subsequent invasion of his homeland.[7] Alex Rorke had also been hired to provide air support.

Even more promising, Buchanan told Benoît, was the participation of another flying soldier of fortune. The son of a famous military hero had recently contacted the journalist to offer the use of his own private air force in the fight against Papa Doc's regime. Benoît couldn't stop himself looking sceptical.

•   •   •

When Major-General Claire Lee Chennault died of lung cancer in 1958 he was a war hero, a public figure and the father of ten children by two different wives. He had made his name fighting the Japanese before America even entered the war as commander of the all-volunteer Flying Tigers air unit which scored victories across China and Burma. After Pearl Harbor, he was one of the leading figures in the campaign to reclaim the Far East and not even having a face like a belligerent saddlebag could keep him off the cover of *Time* magazine. Now one of his sons wanted to do for Cuba what the old man had done for China.

In June 1963, Lieutenant-Colonel Claire Arthur Chennault rang Frank Fiorini from San Francisco to offer twelve fighter planes with pilots for an attack on Cuba, all available for a down payment of just $700. Fiorini passed him on to Jim Buchanan, who persuaded the lieutenant-colonel to paint the planes in Dominican colours and change the target to the Haitian capital instead, hoping to cause a messy Caribbean war that would allow Masferrer and Cantave to overthrow the Duvalier regime in the resulting chaos. If they were really lucky, things might become so bad that the US would be forced to intervene.

By now, Ed Arthur and his miniature army played an increasingly minor role in Buchanan's plans. The independent-minded

Ohioan with the extensive criminal record wasn't good at taking orders and Buchanan was considering taking over Americans for Freedom and putting Chennault in charge. The son of a famous war hero would be good publicity for fundraising. Buchanan was wondering how to break the news when the invasion fell apart.

The first group of Rolando Masferrer's Cuban mercenaries had arrived in Miami and were sleeping in cheap motels when the FBI swooped in and wrecked everyone's plans. Haiti may have been a bloody dictatorship but it was also a friendly nation and President John F. Kennedy had no intention of allowing a gang of adventurers to unleash chaos on America's doorstep. Agents interviewed everyone involved, warned them off and put a stake through the invasion's heart by revealing that Lieutenant-Colonel Claire Arthur Chennault was really Arthur Chen Jr, a 28-year-old born in Shanghai with no relation to the famous aviator.

Chen had emigrated to Berkeley, California, with his family a decade earlier, then served in the US Army as a private for a few months before being discharged as a paranoid schizophrenic. His father continually had to rescue him from various messes, usually caused by Chen impersonating Air Force officers, CIA officials, a Korean War veteran and a US intelligence officer looking to defect to the Soviets. He wandered across America and Europe, and in 1961 ended up in a West German jail from which his father extracted him with difficulty. Back in California there was talk about having Chen institutionalised, but he managed to stay out of trouble for a few more years until he married a Cuban girl in San Francisco and became interested in exile activities. He started calling himself Claire Arthur Chennault and made contact with Frank Fiorini. He had no aircraft and couldn't fly a plane.

'[At] times he becomes very tense and worried, and does things he cannot explain on these occasions,' noted FBI agents who tracked Chen to an address in San Francisco, where he had a job delivering newspapers.[8]

The invasion plan collapsed. General Cantave launched his own attack without any foreign support and watched his force quickly pushed back across the border into the Dominican Republic by the Tonton Macoute. The authorities in Santo Domingo deported him to France to avoid any diplomatic embarrassment. Ed Arthur returned to Ohio that October to give anti-communist speeches anywhere that would take him and use the money to support Commandos L. He obtained weapons from a Los Angeles paramilitary group who spent their days training to stop an unlikely Chinese communist invasion via Mexico, and also from a faction of the paramilitary Minutemen prepared to disobey their fox-faced leader Robert DePugh ('I don't like the idea of all those greasers pouring into this country and causing problems,' he told Arthur) in order to do business with exiles.[9] Arthur spent his days driving trailers loaded with guns down south and hoping he didn't get stopped by police.

The other major figures in the plot followed his lead and gave up on Haiti. Clément Benoît moved to St Croix in the American Virgin Islands and became a French teacher. Charles Ashmann was arrested for defrauding various clients and pleaded insanity in a doomed attempt to avoid prison time. Rolando Masferrer returned to New York, abandoning many of the men who had come to Miami at his request and were now stuck in motels with bills to pay. Jim Buchanan was doing his best to help them out when news came in that rocked the world of Florida exiles.

Alex Rorke had disappeared somewhere over the Caribbean Sea.

22

INTO THIN AIR

The more talkative man, with the black hair and blue eyes, claimed they were in the seafood business and needed an aeroplane immediately. His shorter, blond friend nodded in agreement. The pair had arrived at the offices of Beach Air Services Inc. in the early afternoon of 24 September 1963 looking to hire a light aircraft for a trip to Honduras in connection with a 'lobster-hauling contract'. Beach Air's owner, a former Navy pilot called Edwin Mahood, didn't quite understand all the seafood talk, but the men had cash and that was enough to rent them a blue-and-white twin-engine 1958 Beechcraft Travel Air plane for four days. The blond man showed a pilot's licence in the name of G. Sullivan and filed a flight plan for Tegucigalpa in Honduras. The black-haired man, who called himself Alex, headed off to make a telephone call to his wife.

Alexander Irwin Rorke Jr and Geoffrey Sullivan were at Broward international airport in Fort Lauderdale thanks to some missed connections and a lot of bad weather. The whole mess had started four days earlier when Rorke met with Frank Fiorini and Bill

Johnson at Opa-locka, a busy commercial airport outside Miami. It was only the second time Rorke and Fiorini had seen each other since a bad argument that spring, which the gossip-mongers in Miami were claiming had been all about money.

'Frank don't love him no more,' wrote Gerald Hemming to a friend, "cause "Fat Daddy" ain't getting his cut no more.'[1]

The money in question came from a fierce anti-communist lecture on Cuba that Rorke had been touring around the nation's colleges and right-wing clubhouses for the past year. It was lucrative enough to buy him a 35-foot cabin cruiser called the *Violynn III* and enrol the eager students who flocked around his speaker's podium into a group called the US Freedom Fighters (USFF) which ferried exile activists out to the Bahamas. Some of Rorke's friends thought the fame had gone to his head. He ran the US Freedom Fighters as his private army and referred to them as 'Rorke's Raiders' even though the USFF had originally been created by Fiorini as a non-profit fundraising group. More worrying was a pamphlet he circulated about his availability for media appearances entitled 'Alexander the Great' and illustrated with a large picture of the Macedonian warrior-king on the cover.

Rorke's activities with the USFF took him further away from Fiorini but, despite Hemming's suspicions, money was never the problem. The fracture in the pair's friendship had originated in Rorke's habit of calling the local CIA office with information about the exile scene, under the impression this regular contact was proof the agency supported his activities. When a *Violynn III* sea mission threatened to fail due to an equipment shortage, he asked the CIA for help and was genuinely surprised by the curt refusal that came down the phone line.

'Repeated previous stand that Kubark [i.e. the CIA] would not support uncoordinated uncontrolled activities,' noted the agent who took the call, 'but again offered [to] report any information Rorke might wish volunteer. Rorke declined.'[2]

That seemed especially unfair as, in Rorke's opinion, some of the feedback he'd received during the phone calls seemed closer to operational guidance. He retaliated by sitting for a television interview with ABC in which he claimed the agency had secretly approved all International Anti-Communist Brigade's missions, something Frank Fiorini apparently believed was true thanks to his contact with Joaquín Sanjenís. The programme was never broadcast after someone important made an exasperated phone call to ABC executives and had it axed. The CIA stopped accepting information from Rorke and advised its agents to avoid contact, but it couldn't halt his ongoing crusade against communism.

In early April 1963, Rorke obtained some high explosive from Fiorini and Bill Johnson with the intention of blowing up a Soviet ship off the Cuban coast. Rorke's friends thought the idea crazy when they found out and immediately dumped the explosives into an Everglades swamp. He dismissed them as cowards and attempted to run the mission on his own until an anonymous phone call got the *Violynn III* with its crew of Cubans and Harvard students impounded in the Bahamas. Rorke suspected Fiorini had made the call and the friendship between the two men crumbled.

The journalist had no intention of giving up his crusade and bought a C-45F twin-engine Beechcraft aeroplane on an instalment plan. Mutual friends in New York then introduced him to Swiss motor journalist Hans Tanner of the Movimiento Demócrata Cristiano and an arrangement was made for a bombing mission over Cuba. Anyone hanging around the private hangers at Palm Beach international airport on the evening of 25 April would have seen a group of men loading the Beechcraft with duffel bags coloured a faded military green. The bags contained improvised napalm bombs.

• • •

The Beechcraft took off from Palm Beach a little after 19:00 that April evening. At the controls was Geoffrey Sullivan, a 28-year-old former US Air Force flyer who had spent eight years in the service before quitting to become a commercial pilot. He was a fun-loving, risk-taking type who flew his plane under bridges to impress his young daughter and lived up in Waterbury, Connecticut, where he was a regular at any rally with a patriotic theme. Three years earlier, he'd met Alex Rorke at an event and been drawn into his world of exile politics. Now the two men were sitting in the cockpit of the Beechcraft as it droned through the night towards Havana and the Ñico López oil refinery. In the cabin behind them were MDC head Laureano Batista Falla and a 22-year-old aeronautical MIT student with glasses and crew cut called William Leroy Wilson, both smoking cigars.

They were circling low over the capital when the towers and silos of Ñico López emerged out of the darkness below. Batista Falla and Wilson lit fuses on the homemade bombs with their cigars and threw them out of the Beechcraft's door into the cold air. Most of the napalm failed to explode, but one of the larger bombs hit an oil tank and sent an orange blast roiling up through the night. When the last jar had been dropped, Sullivan yanked at the controls and sent the Beechcraft racing out of Cuban airspace. They were back in Jacksonville, Florida, by 00:30 with fuel tanks nearly empty. Batista Falla reminded everyone to keep quiet about the raid until the

MDC claimed responsibility through its Venezuela office, a tactic that should prevent the authorities discovering the Neutrality Act had been breached. A few hours later, Rorke woke Hans Tanner with a brief telephone call.

'The party that we planned went well,' he said.[3] 'I'll fill you in on the details later.'

Later that day the bombing team were in Washington DC at a press conference given by the Anti-Communist Liaison Committee, another of Rorke's front groups, for what was intended to be a general update on anti-Castro activities. Journalists attending what they thought would be a routine rant against Cuba got themselves a scoop when Rorke, still buzzing with adrenaline, couldn't stop himself talking about the raid. As Batista Falla sat there shaking his head in fury, Rorke read out a heavily fictionalised account of the attack and flashed an ironic smile at more outlandish elements involving a seaplane and a speedboat intended to throw authorities off the scent. The story was all over the newspapers by the next day and Rorke, 'a tall man with a deadpan delivery' according to one journalist, got a starring role in the action while the MDC was barely mentioned.[4] Havana initially denied the attack, then confirmed it and raged against America.

Rorke followed up the press conference with some television interviews in which he boasted about film footage taken inside the aeroplane during the raid and tried to stir up trouble with strange claims of 'Russian underwater missiles on the ocean floor off Cuba.'[5] His thirst for publicity quickly backfired. Batista Falla and the MDC distanced themselves, while the FBI confiscated the Beechcraft and launched an investigation. Rorke was looking at jail time for violating the Neutrality Act until his film footage turned out to be murkily unusable and everyone involved stuck to the cover story about a mysterious seaplane crewed by exiles. The charges were dropped, but no one in authority seemed keen to return Rorke's confiscated vessels and he was forced to buy another aeroplane on credit in August to join Cantave and Masferrer's planned attack on Haiti. He and Geoffrey Sullivan received a $1,000 down payment, before the invasion was called off.

A few weeks later, the two men were summoned to customs headquarters in Florida and sternly warned to quit their adventuring and stay out of trouble. Fiorini and Johnson had been called in the same day for a similar warning and the shared experience brought about a reconciliation. Rorke suggested they meet up at Opa-locka airport in a few days time to discuss an important proposition involving Central America. When they reconvened, he spent a while complaining about his money problems – 'being behind in his car payments, payments on his plane, payments on the *Violynn III*', as Johnson remembered it – then got to the point.[6]

'Rorke explained that he had some connections with Nicaraguan President Luis Somoza, who had offered Rorke an airstrip, free gasoline and free weapons,' Fiorini told the FBI later, 'but that Rorke had to be in Nicaragua by the following Thursday if he were to take advantage of this opportunity.'[7]

It sounded like a good deal: a mission launched from Central America would prevent interference from the American authorities and ease up the financial pressure. Rorke's B-26 plane was being closely watched by customs officers, so Johnson agreed to rent a Cessna from a work colleague, as long as someone else paid for it. They arranged to meet back at Opa-locka on the morning of 24 September 1963 and go see Somoza together.

● ● ●

It rained so hard at the small airfield that Bill Johnson couldn't get the Cessna off the ground. After hours of waiting for clearance, he surrendered to the weather and taxied the plane back to its owner. Frank Fiorini, waiting for a phone call to confirm the trip was still on, assumed everything had been cancelled and went about his day. That left Rorke and Sullivan at the airport waiting for a Cessna that would never arrive.

At first they passed the time chatting, with Rorke being overheard mentioning he needed to get back to New York as soon as possible to cover some bad cheques he'd written to raise funds. Then a Cuban called Enrique Molina Garcia, an MDC member who seemed to be their connection with the Nicaraguan authorities, arrived and was greeted warmly by the two men. The hours ticked on. Eventually, they approached a friend of Johnson's who worked at Atlantic Aviation Company and asked about hiring an aircraft. He directed them to Beach Air Services Inc. at Broward international airport, a twenty-minute drive away.

The Beechcraft Travel Air took off from Broward a little after 15:00, much later than the trio had intended to start their journey, and headed for the underdeveloped island of Cozumel off the north-eastern coast of the Yucatán Peninsula. At 19:00, they touched down at the airport, barely changed since its days serving the military during the war, and refuelled. An hour later, the plane took off into the darkening sky on a flight plan to Tegucigalpa in Honduras across the Caribbean Sea.

Rorke was a devoted husband, father and son who always found time to telephone his loved ones during his travels. After two days of silence, his wife Jackie called Beach Air Services Inc. and was told they'd heard nothing but weren't worried as the plane was rented until Saturday. They admitted the Beechcraft carried no life jackets, life raft or flare pistol. When 28 September came and went, Edwin Mahood contacted his insurance company while a tearful Jackie Rorke telephoned Frank Fiorini and begged for help. He rang around friends and managed to get Naval Intelligence on the case. They discovered Rorke's plane had never arrived at Tegucigalpa.

'They immediately sent out, I believe, Coast Guard aircraft and I believe possibly Naval Air Force,' Fiorini said.[8] 'I'm not sure, you know, what they did, but they did provide the necessary search mission for locating the aircraft.'

The search party found nothing. By 1 October, the disappearance was all over the media and newspapers were printing neat maps showing the plane's flight plan as a series of dots that ended with a question mark somewhere in the Caribbean Sea. Ominous reports claimed a nervous-looking Geoffrey Sullivan had given a cherished St Christopher medal to his wife before he flew down to Florida. Rorke's father began a letter-writing campaign that targeted everyone from the FBI to Central American radio stations, appealing for information and talking movingly about his 'mental anguish'.[9] A second Coast Guard search was launched on 4 October after Jackie complained to the press that not enough was being done to find her husband. She was convinced the Beechcraft had crashed.

'Suppose the plane went down at sea and they're holding on to a little piece of something with a hurricane coming,' she sobbed to a reporter.[10]

Gerald Hemming managed to insinuate himself with the Beach Air insurance agent and offered to find Rorke in exchange for a cut of the $31,000 that would otherwise have to be paid out to the plane's owners. Interpen had finally fallen apart earlier in the year, but the few members still talking to their former leader climbed into orange jumpsuits and boarded a hired aeroplane for a four-day search of Central America. They visited Mérida and Cozumel in Mexico, Belmopan in Belize and then Puerto Barrios in Guatemala, where the Americans tumbled out of the aeroplane without visas or passports. The authorities placed them under arrest at an Air Force base in Guatemala City. Hemming and a few others got stupidly drunk, lied a lot to the pilots and 'talked at great length against US government officials, US government policy, and the corruption and ineptness of the US Central Intelligence Agency'.[11]

The Guatemalans began to suspect Hemming was a Cuban spy and a fistfight with an Air Force officer was only narrowly avoided when the group was hustled off into house arrest for a few days. On 6 November, they were allowed to fly back to Florida, although not before a belligerent Hemming had insulted the American officials who helped them. There was still no sign of the missing Beechcraft.

• • •

In early November, a former FBI employee now working in a Dalton, Georgia, employment agency told the bureau he had found Alexander Rorke. On 31 October, the journalist had registered at a local hotel under a false name and boasted to the desk clerk about being active in the anti-Castro struggle. He claimed to be in town to cash some government bonds left by his wife after she committed suicide.

The local bank refused to touch the bonds, so Rorke had tried to borrow $25 from a cashier, failed, and headed to a nearby employment agency, where he registered for work and talked about the evils of communism. The ex-FBI man working there had seen a photograph of Rorke in a newspaper and thought the candidate with a different name sitting across the desk looked similar enough to merit a phone call to his former employers. Agents arrived in Dalton to find Rorke had vanished, leaving behind only a suitcase full of clothes ('brown striped short-sleeved sport shirt, bearing label Taddle and Saddle, Size 15-15 1/2, Styled by Reliance,' noted the conscientious FBI men) and a lot of confusing documentation about bonds.[12] It looked like Rorke might be involved in some kind of financial scam and the case only started to make sense when the agents discovered the man's real identity: George W. Tanner, the former head of the Anti-Communist Legion.

Purely by coincidence, the founding father of Miami's paramilitary scene had found himself mixed up in the search for Rorke. Both were tall, dark-haired and prone to boasting about their activities, but the similarities ended there. Tanner had left the anti-communist struggle after the training camp debacle and settled back into his life of radio announcing, petty crime and short-lived marriages. The FBI quickly dropped the lead. Rorke's father took matters into his own hands and advertised a $25,000 reward for the 'delivery of the men to any United States port' in widely distributed leaflets with text in English and Spanish.[13] He reached out to Frank Fiorini, the emotional strain showing when an answer was slow in coming: 'I cannot understand why you have not replied,' he wrote.[14] 'My son's wife and children as well as Mr Sullivan's wife and child have been deeply distressed and I expected a good friend of theirs, like yourself, would be interested.'

Rorke's father-in-law Sherman Billingsley approached the FBI for information, being honest enough to admit he hadn't liked the man but didn't want to leave his three grandchildren without a father. The bureau filled him in on Rorke's activities but could provide no information about the lost plane. Billingsley was one of many who assumed Rorke and Sullivan had launched a covert mission over Cuba and been shot down or captured. He publicised the $25,000 reward for their return during a press conference at the Stork Club and information came in fast, but it was hard to sift the truth from lies. Gerald Hemming claimed Molina Garcia was widely suspected of being a Castroite agent in the exile communities, although few knew whether to believe him. Journalist John Chamberlin confirmed the plane had been heading for Nicaragua but thought Rorke had been looking to start a business importing tropical fish for private aquariums in order to make enough cash to reclaim the *Violynn III*. George Adams, a wealthy businessman connected with the Anti-Communist International, boasted about donating $20,000 to Rorke for a bombing mission over Havana which had ended when the Beechcraft was shot out of the sky. He denied everything when the FBI visited his office for an interview. Haviv Schieber also liked to give the impression Rorke had disappeared on a mission for the ACI but refused to go into details. Geoffrey Sullivan's wife received a phone call stating that Rorke was dead and her husband due to be released from a Cuban prison; her hopes were crushed when the caller rang back two days later to apologise for having been given incorrect information.

Alexander Rorke, Geoffrey Sullivan and Molina Garcia were never seen again after leaving Cozumel in the evening of 24 August. No trace of their Beechcraft Travel Air was ever found. Rorke's friends in Miami concluded his plane had crashed into the sea on the Honduras leg of the night flight to Nicaragua, while his family preferred to believe he had diverted east to Cuba for a raid and been shot down. Whichever story was believed, no one had long to mourn before bigger news arrived. A month after Rorke's disappearance, someone murdered the President of the United States as he sat in a motorcade snaking its way through Dallas under the blazing sun.

23

THE VIEW FROM THE TEXAS SCHOOL BOOK DEPOSITORY

DALLAS/LOS ANGELES/MIAMI, NOVEMBER 1963

The Texas School Book Depository was seven floors of orange-brown brick in downtown Dallas that sat on the corner where Elm Street met North Houston Street. Up on the sixth floor, workmen were laying down plywood sheets to protect the cartons of books from oil that had begun seeping up through the floor, a greasy reminder of the building's past incarnation as a grocery wholesaler. Someone had taken advantage of the chaos to build a nest of cardboard boxes around a window with a good view of Dealey Plaza down below.

At midday on 22 November 1963, most book depository staff were outside in the sun hoping to get a glimpse of President John F. Kennedy's motorcade passing through the plaza. One temporary worker, employed for just over a month, remained up on the sixth floor. Lee Harvey Oswald had made it clear he wasn't a fan of the President.

Oswald was a 24-year-old political extremist whose illusions kept getting shattered by reality. He had grown up poor in New Orleans to a widowed mother and spent his youth moving around: some time with aunts, some time in an orphanage when his mother couldn't cope, Dallas with a new stepfather, school in Louisiana, school in Fort Worth, some time in New York after his mother got divorced, some time in a youth home. He was back in New Orleans by the time he was fourteen years old, feeling like an unmoored outsider who didn't belong anywhere. He embraced his misfit status by writing to the Socialist Party of America for literature and taking an interest in Marxist theory. His other interests were more typical of teenage boys, including a fascination with guns, an interest in flying intense enough to attend a few meetings of the Civil Air Patrol Cadets and an urge to join the Marines. Oswald tried to enlist at sixteen but was rejected as too young and had to wait a year.

He spent three years in the service, most of it in Japan and the Far East as a radar operator. He taught himself Russian and shared his left-wing and increasingly pro-Soviet views with sceptical fellow Marines, who nicknamed him 'Oswaldskovich'. An eccentric but tolerated figure, he caused no problems until he accidentally shot himself in the elbow with a pistol hidden in his locker, then fought the sergeant who reported him. Later he got into more trouble for randomly firing his rifle into the jungle during guard duty in the Philippines. The resulting disciplinary issues soured Oswald on the Marines and radicalised his politics further.

In September 1959, he obtained an honourable discharge, told everyone he was going home, then flew to Moscow with the intention of starting a new life in the Soviet Union. The Russians assumed they were dealing with a spy and were halfway through deporting him when Oswald attempted suicide in a hotel room.

He was allowed to stay and spent the next three and a half years working as a lathe operator in Minsk, Belarus. Life in the workers' paradise was not what he had expected.

'I am starting to reconsider my desire about staying,' he wrote in his diary.[1] 'The work is drab, the money I get has nowhere to be spent. No nightclubs or bowling alleys, no places of recreation except the trade union dances. I have had enough.'

With time on his hands, Oswald slept his way through a parade of easily impressed Belarusian girls before falling for a pharmacology student called Marina Prusakova. They got married and, after jumping through all the bureaucratic hoops the USSR had to offer, received permission to emigrate to America. Oswald stepped off the aeroplane expecting to be greeted by hordes of newspaper reporters but was deflated to find no one seemed to care about his return. The couple settled in Fort Worth, where Oswald took, then lost, various menial jobs, before moving to the steamy heat of New Orleans for more of the same. He felt marginalised by his experiences and unhappy doing minimum wage work ('surly, immature, spoke little and was a poor worker,' was how one colleague remembered him), while back home the birth of a daughter had failed to solve the problems in his marriage.[2]

Oswald's disillusionment with the Soviet Union had not made him any less left-wing. He was increasingly drawn to Castro's version of Marxism–Leninism and became furious when General Edwin Walker, a retired right-winger in Dallas close to the John Birch Society, publicly called for US military intervention in Cuba. Oswald bought a revolver and a 6.5mm rifle by mail order using the name 'A. J. Hidell' and forced his reluctant wife to photograph him in the back garden posing with the guns and a sheaf of left-wing newspapers. He began to talk about shooting Walker.

'Well, what would you say if somebody got rid of Hitler at the right time?' he told Marina when she protested.[3]

On 10 April 1963, Oswald left a note for his wife hidden inside a cookbook and took a bus to Dallas. That evening, he hid in Walker's garden and aimed his recently acquired Carcano rifle at the bright square of a dining room window. The bullet hit the wooden frame and showered splinters over Walker as he sat at his desk. Oswald fled the scene and got the bus back to New Orleans.

The resulting manhunt scared Oswald away from direct action and back into conventional political activism. On 29 May 1963, he received a letter authorising him to set up a New Orleans branch of the Fair Play for Cuba Committee ('Dear Friend ... Enclosed are your card and receipt, along with our thanks and welcome,' began the unsuspecting form letter), although the main organisation was already crippled by political schisms and barely functioning.[4] Oswald optimistically printed up 300 membership forms and became head of the organisation as A. J. Hidell. He remained its first and only member.

He handed out leaflets on the streets of New Orleans, mischievously giving his address on some copies as that of a local Cuban exile group's headquarters, and tried some clumsy infiltration of the opposition by approaching a local Directorio Revolucionario Estudiantil official with offers to help. Oswald had his cover blown four days later when the official encountered him distributing FPCC leaflets and a fistfight broke out.

In late September, Oswald and his wife decided to move to Dallas, where the job situation seemed more promising. A heavily pregnant Marina and her daughter went ahead and settled with a friend in the nearby city of Irving. Oswald was supposed to follow but instead took a bus down to Mexico City with the idea of getting a visa for Cuba. He succeeded only in annoying the embassy official with a scrapbook of cuttings about his Fair Play for Cuba Committee activities and was told that people like him did more harm than good to the revolution. Oswald returned to America angry and frustrated, convinced he'd been denied entry because of his homeland's opposition to the Castro regime. A friend got him a temping job at the Texas School Book Depository that October and he moved alone into a single-storey Dallas rooming house, seeing his wife and daughter only at weekends. The couple told acquaintances the arrangement was to save Oswald's commute, but few believed them.

Oswald's new co-workers at the book depository were excited to read in the newspapers that President Kennedy's motorcade would pass through Dealey Plaza, a pool of green grass cupped in the city's concrete hands outside their building. On Thursday 21 November 1963, Oswald made an unusual weekday trip to Irving and returned to Dallas for work the next morning. He left behind his wedding ring and some money but brought along a large paper bag he told everyone contained curtain rods. The next day at lunchtime he took the bag into the nest of cardboard boxes on the sixth floor.

• • •

At 12:30, the presidential motorcade was winding its way along the broad road that cut through the plaza's sloping lawns and oak trees. President John F. Kennedy and his wife Jackie waved regally from the back seat of a midnight-blue open-top Lincoln Continental while Texas Governor John Connally and his wife Nellie occupied the row in front. Groups of people either side of the road waved back and cheered as the motorcade rolled along at a steady eleven miles an hour. Secret Service men in black suits and dark glasses trotted alongside, alert as hunting dogs.

'Mr President, you can't say Dallas doesn't love you,' said Nellie Connally.[5]

'No, you certainly can't,' agreed the President.

There was a cracking noise that some onlookers thought might be a firecracker. Nellie Connally looked back and saw Kennedy clutching his throat with both hands. Beside her, Governor Connally turned his back and slumped away.

Two workers who had been watching the motorcade from the fifth floor of the Texas School Book Depository heard shell cartridges dropping on the floor above them. Across the road a 44-year-old local steamfitter called Howard Brennan looked up and saw a man in a sixth-floor window of the book depository aiming down a rifle. The third shot blew off the back of Kennedy's head and showered skull fragments and brain matter over the interior of the car. Brennan watched the man framed in the window like a figure on a playing card.

'He drew the gun back from the window as though he were drawing it back to his side,' he said, 'and maybe paused for another second as though to assure himself that he had hit his mark.'[6]

The midnight-blue Lincoln Continental peeled away from the motorcade as Jackie Kennedy cradled her dying husband in her lap. Within ten minutes of the last shot, Lee Harvey Oswald was on a bus making slow progress through the Dallas traffic. As a gridlock formed, he jumped off and took a taxi to his rooming house, where he grabbed his jacket and a revolver. In Parkland Hospital, Kennedy was declared dead ('gunshot wound, skull') by the doctors.

Brennan's description of the man with the rifle was already circulating to police. At 13:15, policeman J. D. Tippit stopped his patrol car to talk to a slim young male walking briskly along East 10th Street who matched the description. It was Lee Harvey Oswald. After a brief conversation, Tippit got out of his car to continue the questioning and Oswald shot him four times in the chest and face, then strode off reloading his revolver.

'Poor dumb cop,' Oswald muttered to himself as Tippit lay bleeding to death in the road.[7]

As sirens started to scream, he slipped into the Texas Theatre cinema and hid in the back row. The ticket clerk brought up the house lights on *War is Hell* as the police arrived and overpowered Oswald. He was dragged out of the cinema screaming to passers-by about police brutality.

The United States of America went into collective shock as news of its President's death went out by radio and television. Many heard the news from Walter Cronkite on CBS as the news anchor pinched away the tears after being handed the bulletin live on air. Americans cried and prayed in their homes, sat in shock at office desks and gathered silently outside department stores to watch the televisions in window displays. Vice-President Lyndon Johnson was sworn in as President on board Air Force One with a stunned Jackie Kennedy at his side, her clothes still splattered with blood. A mob of locals attacked General Edwin Walker's house that afternoon in the belief the radical right had been behind the assassination.

• • •

Loran Hall's first reaction on hearing about the President's death was to get himself an alibi. A reporter on television was speculating the assassination had been the work of rightist subversives and Hall had recently been in Dallas talking with the kind of conservatives who kept machine guns under their beds.

Four years ago, Hall had been in a Cuban prison after getting mixed up with some Nicaraguan revolutionaries, and right now he was unemployed in Los Angeles. In between had been several years of low-paid work to support his family until a chance encounter with Gerald Hemming in January 1963 reawakened the old itch for adventure and inspired him to join the anti-Castro struggle down south. Hall drove to Florida expecting to join a well-organised military unit but instead found Hemming nearly bankrupt and Interpen falling apart.

Hall's new commander, along with his new wife, had been evicted from their apartment for non-payment of rent and the only cash coming in was from occasionally mowing lawns in the neighbourhood. Hemming's men spent their days hanging around outside Nellie's boarding house drinking beer and trying to scrounge up money for the rent. The closest they'd come to any action had been back in February when Interpen member Roy Hargraves teamed up with some of Rolando Masferrer's followers to hijack a Cuban fishing boat and hold the crew at gunpoint in a remote part of the Bahamas. Hargraves was lucky to be back in Florida collecting fuel for the boats when the Cuban Navy stormed in to free the fishermen and capture the kidnappers. The world barely noticed this attempt to provoke an international incident.

Some men would have gone straight home after seeing the situation at Nellie's, but Hall liked guns and right-wing politics and frittering away the days. He fitted in fine, even if his comments about how Jews secretly ran the country grated on other members. The days rolled on humid and aimless until Hemming, desperate for money and action, teamed up with a visiting arms dealer and former Minuteman from Illinois called Richard Lauchli to rob a gunrunner they believed to be pro-Castro. Late in the evening on 18 June, the two men, along with Joe Garman and three Interpen members, took the dealer and his family hostage at a house in Miami. At some point in the raid, with half the man's guns already transferred to their cars, they discovered the rumour had been badly garbled and the arms dealer was a fierce opponent of Castro. An apologetic Garman was trying to make friends and reverse the damage when a police car pulled up outside the house. Hemming and Lauchli escaped, but the others were arrested.

The arms dealer kept his mouth shut and all charges were eventually dropped, but Interpen disintegrated in the robbery's aftermath. Garman and the others were convinced their leader had run out on them, with some suspecting he'd called the police himself, while Hemming protested his innocence to a diminishing circle of supporters. Hall stayed loyal enough to be invited along when Hemming left for Dallas hoping to persuade some wealthy anticommunists involved in the oil business, whose names he'd got from the newspapers as usual, to finance a new version of Interpen. No one was interested. The two men drove back to Miami deep in their own thoughts, with Hemming brooding on his failure and Hall wondering if he could do a better job of fundraising on his own. That autumn, Hall booked some solo speaking engagements at John Birch Society events in Texas and California but didn't tell Hemming.

The talks went well. Hall had a talent for impressing the radical right and no qualms about posing as a Cuban veteran of the Bay of Pigs, an act made believable by a good command of Spanish and a swarthy skin tone. Not everyone bought the Cuban act, with one Birch branch putting him through a polygraph test that turned up results of 'weak truthfulness'. Hall steamrollered the rest into accepting him at face value with plenty of '*¡Sí!*' and '*¿Qué volá?*' and some spicy talk about the treachery of President Kennedy. Within a week, he'd collected enough money to buy a few rifles and some medical supplies for a forthcoming mission that existed mostly in his imagination.

Back in Miami, he connected with Lawrence Howard, a stocky former Interpen man of Mexican descent who'd quit the group early in the year to work with Cuban paramilitaries in the Florida Keys. The Cubans had made occasional raids towards their homeland by boat, never getting very far, but had high hopes for a forthcoming mission if they could obtain enough guns and supplies. Hall suggested combining forces. In October, he took Howard on another fundraising drive that netted enough money to buy more rifles and some explosives. A wealthy Dallas oil man called Lester Logue hid the equipment in a trailer at his home while arrangements for the mission were finalised down in Florida.

In mid-October, Hall and William Seymour, an Interpen veteran and friend of Howard, returned to Dallas for the trailer but managed to get themselves arrested when local police found a bottle of methamphetamine diet pills in their glove compartment. The drug helped them stay awake on long drives across the country but was illegal without a prescription. They made bail after the usual mugshots and fingerprints, but it seemed like something more than bad luck when customs swooped on the trailer back in Miami and confiscated everything.

Hall and Howard blamed each other for the loss, while others thought it significant that Gerald Hemming had been ranting furiously to anyone who'd listen about the treachery of former comrades exploiting his Dallas contacts. Hemming even filed a police report after discovering Hall had redeemed one of his own pawned rifles and added them to the mission stockpile. Out in the Florida Keys, the Cuban paramilitaries shut down operations after the guns were confiscated and both Hall and Howard soon gave up the mercenary life. A few weeks later, news of Kennedy's assassination broke across the media and the two men separately came to the conclusion that the kind of hard-righters they'd met in Dallas had been responsible. It was a relief when the news programmes announced that Lee Harvey Oswald was a man of the left.

The Dallas police mugshot caught Oswald with a defiant smirk on his face that vanished when he appeared in front of the television cameras to protest his innocence. Officers and FBI agents questioned him for twelve hours, but Oswald denied everything, claiming to have been elsewhere in the book depository when the shots were fired and dodging questions about the Carcano rifle found among cartons on the sixth floor. He requested legal representation from John Abt, chief counsel to the Communist Party USA, but was told the lawyer wasn't available until Monday. On 24 November, Oswald was being escorted through a scrum of reporters in the basement of police headquarters when local nightclub owner Jack Ruby pushed through the crowd and shot him in the stomach. Oswald died in Parkland Hospital two hours later. The killer claimed he wanted to spare Jackie Kennedy the agony of testifying at a trial.

Oswald may have been a leftist, but the resulting government crackdown seemed aimed more at the right. Lyndon Johnson was astonished to discover the extent of CIA activities in Miami ('We had been operating a damned Murder Inc. in the Caribbean,' he said) and ordered the agency to rein in its remaining Cuban paramilitaries, while Robert Kennedy promised to tackle domestic right-wing militias.[8] A venomous response from Minutemen leader Robert DePugh didn't help: 'If Robert Kennedy had in the past been as concerned over left-wing anti-Americans as he had been concerned over the right-wing pro-Americans, then his brother might be alive.'[9]

The crackdowns and investigations swept up Loran Hall, who was trying to put his mercenary days behind him with a straight job in Los Angeles. FBI agents knocked on his door after a Dallas-based exile called Silvia Odio del Torro informed them about a September fundraising visit from a group which included an American who resembled Oswald. The bureau suspected a link to Hall's activities. Under questioning, the Interpen man couldn't remember Odio but tentatively suggested a case of mistaken identity involving himself, Howard or Seymour. The FBI already had some reservations about Odio's mental state and the investigation quickly closed, but it was enough to convince Hall he'd made the right decision in quitting Miami and its paramilitary adventures.

Not everyone gave up that quickly. A hardcore troop of former Interpen men was still clinging on at Nellie's boarding house and looking for new targets. Someone suggested they take a look at Haiti.

PART V

VOODOO SOLDIERS

24

THEY CALL HIM PAPA DOC

MIAMI/PORT-AU-PRINCE, SUMMER 1966

obert K. Brown was packing books at his home in Boulder, Colorado, when the first telephone call came. Since leaving Miami, Brown had been through a disastrous marriage and worse divorce that convinced him rejoining the military for a tour in Vietnam would be restful by comparison. Army bureaucracy took one look at his security clearance, littered with red flags from Havana to Miami, and declared Brown would be better off staying a civilian. That afternoon, in the early autumn of 1966, he was taking a break from trying to change the minds of the brass with some manual labour at Panther Books, a small mail-order operation he ran that published manuals on guerrilla warfare. It was all legal under the First Amendment, even if the authorities remained unimpressed. The ringing telephone was an unwelcome distraction, especially when it was Joe Garman on the other end of the line asking if he had any mortar rounds.

'No, Little Joe, I do not,' replied Brown.[1] 'I have better things to do, like making a living.'

He hung up and went back to work. Thirty minutes later, Martin F. X. Casey called to ask the same question. A black-haired, heavy-drinking Irish-American in his late twenties, Casey was a former Marine who'd bummed around Central America and got expelled from Mexico before washing up in Miami after the Bay of Pigs. A local journalist introduced him to the adventurers of Nellie's boarding house and he moved in, taking a room next to a former psychiatric patient who did nothing but watch television and eat peanut butter all day. Casey never officially joined Interpen, mostly due to an instinctive distrust of Gerald Hemming, but he hung around the fringes and was well liked enough to become a leading voice among those who remained after the group broke up.

Casey explained that he and the boys were plotting to invade Haiti and asked Brown to join them. For a moment, the publisher was tempted. He'd enjoyed those days spent sitting around the dining room at Glen Haven discussing how to liberate Cuba while Nellie Hamilton packed them lunch boxes for a day training out in the Everglades. The nostalgia quickly passed when Brown remembered how all their plots had come to nothing. He wished Casey luck and went back to his books, but ten minutes later Bill Dempsey was on the phone asking for some machine guns. The persistence of the calls and something about the Canadian's serious tone convinced Brown that perhaps the Haitian adventure was worth investigating first hand. He offered to visit Miami and help out. Delighted mercenaries from Nellie's reassured him that the operation was strictly professional and no part would be played by Hemming, who had quit Florida and was back in California trying to get a regular job.

'Gerry double-crossed too many people, stole too much and lied too much,' said a former Interpen member.[2] 'He had to blow Miami but fast.'

Brown booked a flight to Florida and soon discovered how much things had changed since his last visit. New waves of immigration had brought in thousands of Cuban émigrés more interested in building a new life abroad than in joining the counter-revolution, and the kinds of young men who would once have been raiding the Cuban coast now preferred to start businesses, get married and settle down. Those exile groups still active had their missions regularly squashed by the CIA if there was any chance of embarrassing the American government. Agents confiscated most of the MDC's armoury when it refused to play along and arrested Movimiento Insurreccional de Recuperación Revolucionaria (MIRR) leader Dr Orlando Bosch for towing a radio-operated torpedo through Miami's rush-hour traffic, something that would have seemed almost normal only a few years earlier. Eloy Menoyo moved his Second Front headquarters to the Dominican Republic in early 1965 to escape American restrictions but was captured in Oriente province soon after with a guerrilla group. Bosch retaliated with a series of bombing raids on Cuba, but the authorities swooped again when American mercenaries working with MIRR were involved in some high-profile crashes, including a fatal incident involving pilot Jack Wright in the Bahamas. Everyone still talked about overthrowing Fidel Castro, but the reverses of the past few years had torn the heart out of the paramilitary community.

Only Nellie's boarding house seemed untouched by the passage of time. The resident soldiers of fortune slapped Brown on the back as he carried his kitbag through the front door and told him about their recent adventures. There wasn't much to tell. They trained out in the Everglades, bought and sold a few weapons and tried to keep the mercenary dream alive with minimum-wage jobs and blood donations. 'Lil Joe' Garman got closest to some action when the Los

Pinos Nuevos exile group enlisted him to help a raid on Cuba. After looking over their equipment and finding most of the guns rusted or inoperable, Garman advised the Cubans to quit the counter-revolution business and retreated back to the security of Nellie's.

Martin Casey briefed Brown about the Haiti plan. It had begun in New York earlier that year when Duvalier's enemies collected enough money to hire Rolando Masferrer for another invasion. The Cuban's reputation in his community was worse than ever ('a blood-thirsty, power-hungry barbarian who had all the earmarks of a brutal, feudal warlord, interested only in personal gain', in the words of one exile) and the Haitians were now the only group who would risk dealing with him.[3] Masferrer teamed up with senior exile figure Father Jean Baptiste Georges, recruited some idealistic Haitians to supplement his remaining Cuban cronies and asked the mercenaries at Nellie's boarding house to join the operation. Victory would depend on surprise, superior firepower, a popular uprising and luck. Brown was unimpressed.

'It wasn't going to be a repeat of the Normandy invasion that was for sure,' he said.[4]

The boys at Nellie's reminded him that a group of Americans had been involved in a similar attempt to overthrow Haitian dictator François 'Papa Doc' Duvalier only a few years earlier. Brown pointed out that all those men had died.

• • •

Haiti had green mountains, blue seas and a bloody history. It had been a French colony until a slave revolt at the start of the nineteenth century kicked out the foreigners, killed any whites who tried to stay and set the country on a wobbly century and a half of monarchy, schism and coup-ridden republic. Power stayed in the hands of a mixed-race minority descended from slaves and their French owners while the downtrodden Afro-Haitian majority did all the work. In 1957, the short, plump, unsmiling Dr François Duvalier, known to his patients as 'Papa Doc', managed to harness the racial resentment of the underclass and got himself elected President on a platform of pan-African solidarity that promised a fairer distribution of the country's wealth. His first move was to expel the mixed-race elite from the Army and government. Many left for America to plot his overthrow.

Among the exiles was Alix Pasquet, an elegant Army officer in his late thirties with an air of poised cool who had played professional football before embracing the military life. He had been one of only three Haitians selected to receive pilot training at Tuskegee in Alabama during the war, although his main memory of the time was hiding in the barracks to avoid racist locals. When he moved to America after Duvalier's election, Pasquet settled in Miami.

At a cocktail party one evening, Pasquet recruited an ambitious local deputy sheriff called Arthur T. Payne into his plan to overthrow Duvalier and turn the clock back to the days when the mixed-race elite ran things. Convinced it was easy money, the thickset lawman went fundraising among a dubious crowd of investors, including sketchy hoteliers, contractors after juicy construction contracts and some Italian-American businessmen looking to build casinos in Port-au-Prince. Miami-based M26J supporters got involved in the hope they could use post-revolutionary Haiti as an operational base against Batista. The money collected was intended to fund an underground network made up of Pasquet's friends, but a visit to Haiti by Payne, posing as a tourist, ended badly when he was deported and the money confiscated.

Pasquet decided on more direct action. He enlisted his brother-in-law Lieutenant Henri Perpignan and another exiled Army officer into a seaborne invasion of their homeland and persuaded Payne to bring along three of his fellow deputies. The plan involved landing the fishing smack *Molly C*, captained by Joe D. Walker, then taking over the Casernes Dessalines military barracks behind the National Palace and rallying troops loyal to Pasquet. A plane full of weapons would fly in from Miami to arm the newly assembled revolutionary forces. The plan was about as suicidal as a salmon aiming to choke a bear by leaping down its throat but simple enough that Pasquet convinced himself it would work. Payne seemed to have gone along mostly so he wouldn't have to explain where all the money had gone to his financial backers.

In the late afternoon of 28 July 1958, the *Molly C* reached the coast around Montrouis in an area known as Délugé and immediately wrecked itself on a reef. The invaders carried their weapons and equipment through the pounding surf, with Payne and his fellow Americans dressed as tourists while the Haitians wore their old uniforms. Four Haitian Army soldiers went out to investigate the wreck and a firefight broke out on the beach that killed two of them and wounded Payne in the leg. The invaders hijacked a truck and set out on the hour's drive to Casernes Dessalines in Port-au-Prince, where they bluffed their way into the understaffed barracks for another firefight that killed three more soldiers and took another fifty prisoner.

The invasion began to unravel when Pasquet telephoned his old comrades to join the revolution, only for them all to make excuses and hang up. Back in Miami, the aircraft full of guns had been impounded by customs. Things got worse when Duvalier, who had been making plans to flee, discovered that the invasion force amounted to only eight men. No one was sure how the information reached him, although a popular story had a Haitian plotter, possibly Perpignan, naively sending a prisoner out to buy a pack of cigarettes and expecting him to come back. The Haitian Army counter-attacked under the command of a newly energised Duvalier, who looked pudgier than ever in baggy combat fatigues and a helmet a size too big. A grenade thrown through the window of the commandant's office killed Pasquet while he was on the telephone; Arthur Payne, desperately claiming to be a journalist, was shot dead by soldiers when they burst into the barracks. A Florida deputy called Levant Kersten slipped out during the fighting and tried to blend into a crowd of watching civilians until he was discovered and executed. The others were killed in the assault and their bodies dragged through the streets of Port-au-Prince. The American government denied any involvement in the invasion, which Duvalier's entourage refused to believe.

'If Haitians join Americans to plot against Duvalier,' warned Jacques Fourcand, Duvalier's personal physician, 'blood will flow in Haiti as never before. The land will burn from north to south, from east to west ... The dead will be buried under a mountain of ashes because of serving the foreigner.'[5]

In the aftermath, Duvalier's regime hardened into murderous authoritarianism. The President raised neon signs over the capital reading 'I Am The Haitian Flag One And Indivisible, Dr F. Duvalier', although the effect was dimmed by the regular power cuts that had begun to affect Port-au-Prince.[6] He championed voodoo, a spiritual stew popular with the country's rural poor that mixed African animist religions with Roman Catholicism and animal sacrifice, and encouraged Haitians to see him as a supreme sorcerer with supernatural powers. On the earthly plane, his Tonton Macoute paramilitaries hacked opponents apart with machetes and left the dismembered bodies by the roadside. Tonton leader Luckner Cambronne became known as the 'Vampire of the Caribbean' both for his bloodlust and for his profitable sideline selling plasma, donated by terrified locals, to overseas markets. The tourism which had once sustained the mostly agrarian society dried up as the luxury liners ceased to call and the only international flights still touching down at the Port-au-Prince airport always seemed to arrive empty and leave full.

America valued Duvalier's anti-communism enough to donate millions of dollars in aid, but the relationship soured in the aftermath of the abortive 1963 invasion by Benoît and Masferrer when the Tonton Macoute displayed the severed heads of their enemies, real and imagined, on spikes around Port-au-Prince. President Kennedy withdrew his support and put heavy pressure on Papa Doc to step down, but events in Dallas three months later derailed any plans for regime change.

The next year, a rigged referendum established Duvalier as President for life. Exiles and opponents continued to try to overthrow his regime but always failed, until Father Jean Baptiste Georges and Rolando Masferrer teamed up in 1966 with a plan they thought would change Haiti for ever.

•　•　•

The crowd at Nellie's boarding house thought Robert Brown should meet the invasion leadership. Everyone assembled in the living room of Father Jean Baptiste Georges, a former education minister in Duvalier's government who cut a cool figure in dark glasses and a sharp suit with a cigarette dangling from his lips. Rolando

Masferrer was his usual intimidating self at the priest's side, while a short American in his late forties with dark hair and an extravagant moustache was introduced as Mitch Livingston WerBell III, an arms dealer who had useful contacts in the Dominican Republic.

Brown squatted on the carpet with pencil and paper to demonstrate how the invasion should be organised. As a captain in the Army reserves with Special Forces training, he was the best-qualified man in the room on military matters and any sensible exile leader would immediately have made him commander. Father Georges didn't put much store in sensible and made it clear all military matters would be decided by himself in consultation with his backer 'Francisco'. Brown accepted a spear-carrying role in the mission and was secretly glad not to be commanding anything. By the time the meeting had ended, he'd formed a distrust of Mitch WerBell, who liked to pour forth endless streams of unlikely stories about being involved in top intelligence operations during the war, his father being a Russian Cavalry colonel in the Tsarist Army and the CBS television network bankrolling the invasion.

'WerBell was one of the most if not the most flamboyant snake-oil salesman I've run across in my nefarious career,' said Brown.[7] 'If he said the sun was going to rise in the east in the morning, I would say, "Mitch, I'll wait and see."'

In September, orders came to move out. The gang at Nellie's were sitting around polishing their AR-15s when a telephone call sent them across town to a two-storey white house with a 'for sale' sign on the lawn. The house contained forty Haitians, a few Cuban exiles, a lot of rifles and rucksacks and no furniture. Fifteen minutes after they arrived, a policeman knocked at the door to ask why so many men of military age were crammed together in a suburban house. Brown claimed they were attending a Boy Scout convention and couldn't afford a hotel room. The policeman narrowed his eyes and left. As the patrol car peeled away from the curb, Brown ordered everyone to load their guns into the trunk of his car then sped off for Nellie's boarding house to hide the arms in a garden shed. While he was gone, the police raided the house. As the door burst open, Joe Garman noticed a hand grenade lying overlooked in a corner and shoved it into his underwear. It stayed there, pineapple serrations clearly visible through his fatigue trousers, while police officers searched the place and interrogated everyone. They failed to notice the grenade.

After the raid, the invasion force remained in the house waiting for word from Masferrer that a boat, a two-masted yacht called the *Poor Richard*, was available to start the mission. Hours turned into days, all passing in a haze of French, Spanish and English chat, with the police regularly driving past the house at a slow enough speed to make their presence felt. Some of the Cubans made trips to Little Havana for a coffee and a chat with family, all while wearing their camouflage uniforms. One day a Cuban volunteer's mother appeared in front of the house in a state of distress, screeching: 'José, José, you can't leave your mama alone!'[8]

It was the last straw for Brown, coming hard on the heels of his discovery that WerBell had, somehow, not been lying about the involvement of CBS in the invasion and a camera crew had recently spent time in the Everglades filming Haitian volunteers on training exercises. Brown doubted the wisdom of having a national television network involved in the illegal invasion of a country not at war with America, but his friends from Nellie's were prepared to stay and see how the situation unfolded. He wished Casey, Garman and the others good luck and departed for Colorado to pack more books and argue with the Army over his security clearance.

The telephone call about the boat never came. Instead, Rolando Masferrer announced the invasion had been rescheduled for January the next year, when Port-au-Prince would fall into their hands like a ripe plum and Havana would inevitably follow.

25

BAY OF PIGLETS

NEW YORK/MIAMI/COCO PLUM BEACH, WINTER 1966–EARLY 1967

The Columbia Broadcasting System had only itself to blame. If Jay McMullen had asked a few more questions and spent a bit less money, then the television network wouldn't have ended up being grilled in the House of Representatives about its reasons for funding a mercenary invasion of Haiti. McMullen was the top CBS investigative journalist, a double-chinned 44-year-old from Minneapolis with a combover and a reputation for diving fearlessly into the sordid underbelly of American society in search of a story. He'd joined the CBS radio service after the war and made a name for himself producing hard-hitting pieces about gang violence on the streets and corruption in the adoption business. A transition into television introduced modern surveillance techniques, like the 8mm camera hidden in a lunchbox used to film an illegal Boston bookmakers, and brought a strong social crusading note into McMullen's work. A 1964 piece on mail-order amphetamines was powerful enough to inspire a change in the law.

His bosses loved the ratings but didn't appreciate the meticulous approach ('painfully slow,' complained the president of CBS News), which could see McMullen spending a year on one story.[1] The journalist ignored the griping. McMullen wanted in-depth reporting and striking visuals and didn't care how long it took to get them.

In March 1966, fellow journalist Andrew St George took him out for lunch. The Hungarian had been keeping an eye on Cuban affairs for *Life* magazine ever since his days interviewing Castro up in the mountains and had recently discovered an exile plot involving Haiti.[2] This was the kind of juicy story McMullen loved and, conveniently, would neatly fit the gaping hole left by the recent collapse of an investigation into arms dealing. St George had visions of producing the show himself, but McMullen burst that bubble by taking over production and reducing the Hungarian to a paid adviser role. The $500-a-week salary was generous enough that St George didn't complain much.

Their first move was to visit key conspirator Mitch WerBell III at his expansive home in Powder Springs, Georgia. Unlike Robert Brown, McMullen immediately warmed to the drawling, whiskey-drinking arms dealer and did enough background research to discover that many of the man's apparently bizarre stories were true. WerBell's father really had been a wealthy Tsarist officer who fled to America after the Bolshevik revolution, and his son had earned a serious reputation for spycraft with American Intelligence in the China–Burma–India theatres during the war. WerBell currently ran an arms company called Sionics Inc. and liked to present himself as a new breed of technologically advanced gun dealer responsible for advancements in the field of firearm suppressors significant enough to earn him the nickname 'The Wizard of Whispering Death'.

WerBell would sell to anyone but preferred to see his weapons used in the service of a ferociously elitist anti-communism.

'Communism is the substitution of a peasant dictatorship over the aristocracy,' he said.[3] 'And I prefer the aristocracy.'

His hatred of subversion led to stints as adviser to the Batista regime and time in the Dominican Republic fighting a leftist insurgency, which he carried out with sufficient relish that friends in Santo Domingo had agreed to allow the Haitian expedition to use their country as a base. McMullen never asked why the Red-baiting arms dealer had joined a conspiracy to overthrow the bloodthirsty but equally anti-communist despot François Duvalier, but he would later claim WerBell indicated the CIA was involved. In turn, WerBell would deny ever giving that impression. The only thing both men agreed on was that WerBell had offered CBS exclusive rights to film the gunrunning, mission training and invasion itself for a fee of $80,000 payable in instalments. McMullen informed his bosses, who agreed and asked their corporate lawyers for a way to finesse the illegality of what was happening.

'If you're involved in filming guns and training exercises, obviously you have knowledge of a violation of law,' CBS president Richard Salant said later.[4] 'But our general position is where the violation is generally known, or there is reason to believe law enforcement agencies know about it, then we proceed without notifying them.'

There was no evidence at this stage that the authorities knew very much, although some agencies had begun sniffing around the edges of the plot. In June, McMullen and a camera crew visited the house of Masferrer's brother Kiki to film an arms cache but were surprised by a visit from immigration officials looking for Rolando, who was still officially confined to New York after his paramilitary adventures in the sunshine state. McMullen thought the men were FBI agents and hid his crew in a cupboard until they left. Afterwards he stressed the importance of secrecy, unaware his cameraman was about to go straight to the CIA.

• • •

James Wilson had no objection to filming natural disasters, human tragedy and the reality of crime on American streets, but he drew the line at facilitating a coup attempt in the Caribbean. The freelance cameraman's liberal values had never been seriously challenged in the five years he'd worked with CBS until Jay McMullen invited him to join 'Project Nassau' at a lunchtime meeting near network headquarters in New York. Initially enthusiastic, Wilson became uneasy about the job when he found himself hiding in a cupboard at Kiki Masferrer's suburban Miami house. McMullen's vague assurances that it was all 'a CIA operation' didn't help.[5]

In July, CBS gave Wilson a temporary assignment in Houston, Texas, for a story about NASA and he took the opportunity to call the local CIA office. The agency passed him on to the FBI, who denied jurisdiction and put Wilson in touch with US customs. Finally finding someone who would listen, the cameraman spilled his concerns about the part his employer was playing in a forthcoming invasion of Haiti. Customs agents told him to stay with the invasion group, keep quiet and report back everything he saw. Wilson returned to Miami and found McMullen digging himself deeper into the story by passing over increasingly large sums of cash to the plotters: $3,000 to Rolando Masferrer for various expenses; $500 so Father Georges could perform voodoo rites to inspire his Haitian volunteers; $380 for a failed attempt to film an arms shipment being transported from New Jersey to Miami; and $750 for Wer-Bell to finalise arrangements for a base in the Dominican Republic, only for negotiations to fall through and leave the plotters forced to launch the invasion from American soil.

Martin Casey and the boys from Nellie's boarding house tried to stay away from the CBS cameras as financial tangles saw the invasion boat *Poor Richard* repossessed, Robert K. Brown return to Colorado and the invasion put back by a few months. Masferrer's Cubans were less camera-shy and happily allowed McMullen to film a training session at Kendall Park, a lot of green space and trees south of Miami, as long as he paid $350 for the privilege. Former Marine and war veteran Donald Miller, who had provided training to various Cuban exile groups since the Bay of Pigs but had nothing to do with the Haiti mission, was persuaded to turn up and act as a drill instructor for the cameras. After two hours of un-convincing jumping jacks, marching and belly crawling, someone on the CBS crew suggested a live fire exercise.

The Cubans had some old M1 Garand rifles in the trunks of their cars. The camera zoomed in on a ragged line of prone men aiming down their sights and then a faulty rifle exploded when the trig-ger was pulled and blew out volunteer Julio Cesar Hermilla's right eye. As he lay on the grass screaming, his comrades delayed taking him to a doctor so McMullen could get footage of the injury. Don Miller was disgusted by the whole situation.

'This was all recorded on film by the CBS camera,' he said after-wards.[6] 'But the CBS people later refused to accept the responsibility for seeing that the boy's injury was properly treated. It was only after I insisted that someone from CBS accompany me that Andrew St George agreed to come along with me and the boy to the hospital.'

Hermilla sued the television network from his hospital bed and was quietly paid $15,000 to make the complaint go away. After treatment, he returned to his work at a Miami factory and lost three fingers in a punch press because of his reduced depth perception. When he asked for more money, Rolando Masferrer threatened to gouge out his other eye.

The Haiti plot began to crumble. US customs agents visited McMullen after the hospitalisation to announce they knew all about the invasion and would not allow Masferrer's men to leave port. The journalist discussed the matter with St George, who cautiously reached out to friends in the FBI and State Department but got only boilerplate responses about the Neutrality Act from men who thought he was talking theoretically. McMullen kept on filming. In October, the bilge pump on a small boat being piloted by St George exploded and put him in the burns unit of the hospital. The Hungarian dropped out of the plot, claiming Masferrer had sabotaged the boat as revenge for some personal slight, and WerBell got $500 a week from McMullen to step in as 'story editor'.

Things got stranger when Martin Casey, eager to meet the mysterious 'Francisco' behind Father Georges ('Francisco says this. Francisco says that,' remembered the mercenary, 'I assumed that Francisco was one of the conspirators'), followed the priest through Miami to a rendezvous with a Cuban witch who charged good money for communicating with the undead.[7] Francisco was a spirit summoned up in the back room of an occult shop to help guide the invasion from the afterlife. After this discovery, it didn't seem especially unusual when Masferrer and WerBell tried to blackmail the Haitian consul in Miami into joining the plot and then demanded $200,000 to call off the invasion when he refused. They claimed to be waging psychological warfare against Papa Doc, but McMullen came to believe the invasion had degenerated into a scam to squeeze money from the gullible, a category which he was starting to suspect might include himself. When an airborne invasion fell apart in November due to a lack of suitable planes, the journalist withdrew his crew and went back to New York to piece together a programme from the existing footage.

A senior CBS man looked over a rough cut of the proposed hour-long show and was so unimpressed ('the non-adventures of a ragtag crew next to whom Duvalier looks good') that the piece was never broadcast.[8] Nine months and tens of thousands of dollars had been wasted. The invasion of Haiti by Father Georges, Rolando Masferrer, Mitch WerBell III and the crew at Nellie's boarding house was over, or so it seemed.

• • •

Coco Plum Beach was an artificial island in the Florida Keys made from rubble piled into the shallows with a two-storey concrete block house on top. Early in the morning of 3 January 1967, two young cousins who lived nearby heard a rumour that police had been there the previous evening. The cousins drove over at dawn to check out the story and found a man standing in the middle of the road. When they pulled over, he leaned in the window with a hand grenade in each fist.

'Go Miami,' he said in a heavy Cuban accent.[9]

They went Miami. The next ninety miles were spent driving erratically along US Highway 1 while the man held a grenade between their skulls and tried to explain in broken English that he hated Fidel Castro and communism. In Miami, he jumped out of the car, threw a $10 bill into the driver's lap and ran into a nearby house. The carjack was over.

The cousins had got themselves mixed up in the aftermath of Rolando Masferrer's last throw of the dice to overthrow Duvalier. In December, he and WerBell had bought a 55-foot shrimp boat called the *Sandona* and assembled an invasion force at Coco Plum Beach. Kitbags were stowed in the block house, rifles greased and arrangements made to ferry in the remaining supplies. After a few days of activity, a serious-looking man in a nondescript car parked up to watch them work. When Martin Casey strolled over to investigate, the car sped off only to be replaced a few hours later by another man in another unmemorable car. The authorities were keeping Coco Plum Beach under surveillance. This didn't bother Casey and his friends, who still half-believed the CIA supported the invasion, but Masferrer muttered to Father Georges about moving up the launch date.

Late on 2 January, the invasion force got the order to head for Haiti. They were loading the last wooden crates on board the *Sandona* by torchlight when a phalanx of cars roared up to the dock with sirens blaring. Customs agents jumped out to find themselves outnumbered by 100 men in camouflage uniforms and hunting outfits, most Cuban with twenty Haitians and a handful of Americans. In the confusion some of the men ran off into the darkness, while others surrendered and the rest lined up in military formation to march off the island, claiming they were headed to Miami to protest their arrest.

'We want to fight communism, but not in Vietnam, only in Cuba,' shouted one marcher waving around a small bust of José Martí.[10] 'So why stop us?'

Sherriff's deputies formed a roadblock and corralled most of the marchers back onto Coco Plum Beach but lost a few who took the opportunity to slip away into the night. Martin Casey crawled half-way through a copse of pine trees before bumping into the boots of a waiting deputy. Back in the blockhouse, customs agents found 100 M1 rifles, fifty carbines, ten automatic rifles, twenty-five machine guns and some mortars. Chartered buses took the prisoners into town, where fifty-one men were booked into a Miami jail and an-other twenty-five processed in Key West. Police still searching the scrubland for stragglers the next day hauled in five more Cubans. Bail was set at $100 for each man and $5,000 for Masferrer.

Local journalists were all over the case and visited Nellie Hamilton at her boarding house to find out more about her tenants. She put on an air of wholesome confusion and failed to mention that Bill Dempsey and 'Fat' Ralph Edens, a former Navy radio operator, were hiding upstairs having hitchhiked their way back to Miami. Nellie did her best to cover for the other members currently in custody.

'They were nice boys, no different from other boarders,' she said.[11] 'I didn't know what they were up to. Sure, some had guns but I thought it was for target practice.'

In the end, only seven people were indicted: Father Jean Baptiste Georges, Rolando Masferrer and his helpers Julio Constanzo and Antonio Leon Rojas, Mitch WerBell III, the former Haitian Army officer René Juares Leon, who had once served as assistant to General Cantave, and Martin Casey. All were charged with violating the Neutrality Act. They refused to plead guilty and announced their defence would focus on proving the CIA had been behind the operation all along.

• • •

The Central Intelligence Agency wasn't happy the case was going to trial. Its agents hadn't been involved in the Haitian affair, but file cross-referencing revealed thirteen of the Cubans who took part had worked for the agency in the past as informants or members of Brigade 2506. Another two were still employed as assets but hadn't bothered to notify their handlers about Masferrer's invasion plans. That looked bad, but even worse was the prospect of past CIA operations against Castro being revealed during the trial.

'Possibly more damaging in the long run,' noted an internal report, 'would be the surfacing of questions concerning the "right" of the Agency to engage in "illegal" activities from US soil.'[12]

When charges against Mitch WerBell III were dropped in September, his fellow defendants assumed the CIA had put pressure on the judge to free one of its own. In truth, WerBell's connections to American Intelligence were limited to his wartime exploits and a brief stint as an agency informant earlier in the decade that was ended by the unreliability of his information ('subject is characterized as an unscrupulous conman,' noted an internal report) and an obvious desire to use the relationship to benefit his own activities.[13] WerBell probably owed his freedom to a recent business venture with the inventor of the Ingram machine pistol, a miniature engine of death which had caught the eye of Special Forces units serving in Vietnam. His value as an arms dealer overrode any desire to see justice done.

The trial took place towards the end of 1967 and was covered by a local press pack clearly jaded about conspiracies involving Cubans. Attempts to call CIA agents to the stand were rejected by the judge and accusations about illegal government operations were thrown out. In the end, Masferrer got four years, Casey nine months and the rest received sixty days. All were freed on bail pending an appeal.

In the aftermath, Joe Garman turned his back on the mercenary life and returned to his family in Bowling Green, Kentucky, who set him up as a gentleman farmer, or at least as close to one as a violent anti-communist obsessed with guns would ever get. CBS thought it had escaped any negative publicity until a 1970 House Commerce Subcommittee investigating the affair uncovered the full extent of the network's role. The report was scathing about McMullen's involvement and the blind eye he turned to self-evidently criminal activity. Fellow journalists wallowed in the discomfort of a rival, with the *Washington Post* smirking over the plot's 'comic opera' tone and 'zany details', while newsrooms across the country chortled at the idea of McMullen buying beer and sandwiches for the would-be invaders.[14] CBS denied any wrongdoing, claimed it had paid only $5,000 to Masferrer's men and managed to escape any legal penalties. Amid all the fallout, quiet but persistent rumours that Mafia money had helped finance the invasion in exchange for gambling concessions in Port-au-Prince went uninvestigated.

Martin Casey's first action after getting out on bail was to head back to Nellie's boarding house and persuade his comrades to continue the mercenary life. They were unaware that 800 miles way in New Orleans a district attorney called Jim Garrison was making waves re-investigating the Kennedy assassination and had become convinced Interpen had been involved.

26

MR GARRISON INVESTIGATES

It was a few days before New Year's Eve when Loran Hall discovered he was being subpoenaed. Reporters knocked on the door of his Kernville, California, house with the news and found the former mercenary still yellow from the hepatitis-induced jaundice that had recently put him in a veterans' hospital. He condemned the subpoena as harassment, announced he would fight it and denied being part of a conspiracy to kill President John F. Kennedy.

'Sure I wanted to beat Kennedy,' he told reporters, 'but with ballots not bullets.'[1]

Hall had become tangled up in a controversial investigation launched the previous year by a rogue district attorney in New Orleans. As usual, Gerald Patrick Hemming was partly to blame. The former mercenary leader had dragged Hall's name into the proceedings when he stopped off in the Big Easy that summer to visit the office of James Carothers Garrison and offer his help. Hemming's motives were less than pure: he didn't much care who'd killed the President but had heard rumours Garrison was looking into Interpen's failed 1962 New Orleans training camp and, wanting to avoid unwelcome publicity, was hoping to divert the investigation into other avenues. If that required stabbing a former friend in the back, then he was prepared to make the sacrifice.

In New Orleans, Hemming was introduced to the man behind the investigation. Jim Garrison was a dark, intense-looking district attorney in his forties, convinced that the American people had been sold a lie about the death of their President. He unreeled an alternate history to his visitor in which Kennedy's murder had not been the work of a self-radicalised Marxist–Leninist in a failing marriage but instead the product of a well-funded conspiracy out to behead the government. Hemming thought the district attorney might be onto something until Garrison explained the assassination had been 'a homosexual thrill-killing' by a cabal of wealthy anti-communist sadomasochists linked to a transvestite cabaret at a club called 'Bottoms Up'.[2] Then the mercenary began to worry about Garrison's mental health. He wasn't the first.

Garrison had grown up in the humid port of New Orleans on the Mississippi River. The Big Easy was a bubbling cauldron of French colonial buildings, drunken sailors on leave and racial strife which united once a year at Mardi Gras for a riotous parade down Bourbon Street before fragmenting back into squabbling factions fighting for control of the city's deeply corrupt political establishment.

The future district attorney joined the Air Force at twenty years old and flew thirty-five combat missions during the war. He came out the other side with a case of shell shock so severe that military psychiatrists refused his application to re-enlist for Korea and declared Garrison 'moderately severely incapacitated' by his mental health problems.[3] At least one psychiatrist thought him schizophrenic. Garrison did four and a half years of psychotherapy and declared himself cured. He went on to earn a law degree at Tulane and served two years in the FBI before devoting himself to the legal profession. He was tall, dark and gifted enough a speaker that in 1962 the people of New Orleans elected him their district attorney. Garrison immediately ordered highly publicised raids on the vice scene in the French Quarter but seemed keenest to shut down gay bars by any means necessary. Regulars found themselves charged with 'being a homosexual in an establishment with a liquor license', a crime no one could remember being inscribed in the statute books.[4]

When Garrison was re-elected a few years later, New Orleans assumed he would continue with his anti-vice crusade. The city was shocked when the *New Orleans States-Item* newspaper reported in February 1967 that the district attorney's office had quietly spent $8,000 investigating the assassination of President John F. Kennedy. The revelation forced Garrison into making a bold public statement.

'My staff and I solved the case weeks ago,' he said.[5] 'I wouldn't say this if we didn't have evidence beyond a shadow of a doubt.'

The news came as a surprise to the people of America, who were under the impression the case had already been solved. The President's Commission on the Assassination of President Kennedy, known as the 'Warren Commission' after its chairman, had released a mammoth report three years earlier that unequivocally named Lee Harvey Oswald as the lone assassin. Only very few disagreed with the verdict and those who did, like former State Department intelligence analyst Harold Weisberg in his self-published book *Whitewash*, seemed mostly upset that Oswald's actions had discredited leftist politics for the foreseeable future.

Somewhere around 1966, Garrison read *Whitewash* and became fascinated by the idea of a plot against the President, particularly as Weisberg insisted dubious members of the far-right had actually pulled the trigger. With most public officials, this would have remained a private obsession to be indulged off duty and shared only with friends, but Lee Harvey Oswald had been a New Orleans native and that gave Garrison the legal standing to launch an official investigation. His staff began to re-examine the evidence and ask around town for anyone who remembered Oswald.

• • •

One of the first people interviewed for the inquiry was Jack Martin, an alcoholic private detective with more lines on his face than a relief map of the Rocky Mountains. He sat trembling across the desk from Jim Garrison and slurped coffee as he told his story.

Back in late November 1963, Martin had become entangled with the original Kennedy investigation thanks to a good memory and a failed friendship. For years he had been close to David Ferrie, a far-right pilot who wore fake eyebrows and a homemade wig to cover his alopecia, and had lost his job at an airline after accusations of misconduct involving teenage boys. None of that bothered Martin much, whose main connection with Ferrie was a shared interest in obscure religious sects, but their friendship soured when the pair squabbled over a post in the tiny Holy Apostolic Catholic Church. Martin nursed a grudge until the Kennedy assassination offered him a platform for public revenge. He remembered that a group photograph on display at Ferrie's apartment featured a young man who looked a lot like Lee Harvey Oswald and called the FBI.

The bureau investigated and found the photograph had been taken at a meeting of a Civil Air Patrol group run by Ferrie when Oswald had been a young cadet. Martin was convinced this was evidence of his former friend's involvement in the assassination, but the theory seemed to fall apart when agents discovered Oswald had attended only a few patrol meetings as a teen and Ferrie had not seen him since. The FBI wound up its investigation by noting that Martin had spent time in a psychiatric hospital and Ferrie was a probable paedophile, then closed the file with a sigh of relief.

Three years later, Martin had more to say. He told Garrison that on the night Kennedy was assassinated he'd been beaten up by Guy Banister, his boss at the detective agency. The FBI had already heard the story and dismissed it as a drunken row triggered by Martin making unauthorised long-distance phone calls from the office, but now the detective claimed he'd been attacked for reminding his boss that a group comprising Oswald, Ferrie and some Cubans had once visited the agency.

After that revelation, Garrison couldn't get any more out of him and Martin stumbled out of the office in search of a drink, leaving the district attorney frustrated but convinced he had uncovered a conspiracy. Proving it would be more difficult. Guy Banister had died of a heart attack in 1964 and no one apart from Martin remembered Oswald visiting the detective agency. Oswald's only verified contact with the building was slyly using its address on some of his Fair Play for Cuba Committee leaflets to cause trouble for an exile group once based there, but Garrison remained convinced that if he kept tugging on the thread, then the truth would be revealed.

The *New Orleans States-Item* broke the story of Garrison's investigation a few months later and a bemused, sick-looking Ferrie found himself accused of masterminding the killing of the President. He died of a brain aneurysm a week later in his filthy apartment in the Broadmoor district of the city. Garrison told friends the pilot had been murdered to stop him talking.

With no one left to prosecute, Garrison's staff recommended dropping the investigation, but the district attorney ploughed on, now convinced that Ferrie's homosexuality was central to the case. On the basis of some insubstantial rumours, he focused on a discreetly gay businessman called Clay Shaw and ordered his investigators to find a connection with Ferrie. After a lot of dead ends, they turned up a 25-year-old insurance salesman called Perry Russo who claimed he might have seen Shaw and the pilot together in a car once. Garrison insisted the young man undergo a hypnosis and sodium pentothal session, administered by a psychiatrist with no aversion to asking leading questions, and soon Russo remembered having seen Ferrie, Oswald and Clay Shaw together at a party for gay sadomasochists, discussing the assassination of the President.

On 1 March 1967, a bewildered Shaw was arrested and charged with being the kingpin behind the murder of President Kennedy. Garrison now believed the shooting had been carried out by a gay cabal in which Oswald was a male prostitute; his killer Jack Ruby a homosexual nicknamed 'pinkie'; Officer Tippit a homosexual policeman; and an important role played by Breck Wall, a transvestite performer who appeared in a cross-dressing revue called 'Bottoms Up' in Dallas. As for motive, the district attorney was convinced Ferrie and Shaw had acted out of jealous, impotent rage at a handsome and heterosexual President. Cubans still bitter over the Bay of Pigs debacle might also have been involved, although Garrison remained undecided on that point.

The investigation made headlines for months and wormed its way into the soul of the nation. Men's magazine *Playboy* devoted one issue to a lengthy interview with Garrison. Not everyone was convinced, but the American consensus on a lone assassin began slowly to shift. Things were about to get even more conspiratorial.

Within a few months, the plot by a gay cabal would mutate into a CIA coup d'état with Interpen and Loran Hall at its heart.

• • •

Interpen's abortive 1962 attempt to set up a training camp in New Orleans had been big news at the time and had passed into urban legend over the past five years, with many convinced the camp had been operational. Some of Garrison's investigators suspected Banister and Ferrie, both weekend right-wing activists with links to the Cuban exile scene, had been involved and might even have helped run the place. Gerald Hemming's appearance at the district attorney's office was the perfect opportunity to do some digging.

Hemming was cheerful, cooperative and infuriatingly prone to long digressions about irrelevant topics, but he managed to convince his interviewers that Interpen had no connection to any conspiracy. The camp had failed to get off the ground and he'd never met any of the people whose photographs were slid across the desk to him. Once free of suspicion, he immediately stuck the knife into Loran Hall, never having forgiven his former friend for stealing a rifle years earlier. Hemming casually mentioned that when he heard about the Kennedy assassination, his first response had been to call Lester Logue in Dallas and see if his former Interpen colleague was in town.

'[Gerald] Patrick [Hemming] said he did this because he believed at the time that Hall very well could have assassinated the President,' noted a Garrison investigator.[6]

Hall's name was pinned to a board in Garrison's office with all the other suspects while Hemming headed to California, promising to track down more leads. His amateur investigation consisted of little more than regularly calling New Orleans with requests for money to cover his expenses. Garrison refused to pay and the telephone calls stopped. The Interpen connection would probably have expired there if Garrison hadn't plucked a random letter from the endless stream pouring into the office that autumn and discovered another link to Hall. The letter writer suggested the investigation look into Edgar Eugene Bradley, a Hollywood right-winger who acted as West Coast front man for a New Jersey fundamentalist preacher and had allegedly been overheard discussing an assassination plot. Although there was no obvious connection to Clay Shaw, the letter fitted with Garrison's growing belief the conspiracy extended beyond a group of New Orleans homosexuals to include elements of the American hard-right.

'If you go far enough to either extreme of the political spectrum, Communist or Fascist,' Garrison told journalists, 'you'll find hard eyed men with guns who believe that anybody who doesn't think as they do should be incarcerated or exterminated.'[7]

The letter directed investigators to a neat house in Van Nuys, Los Angeles, where they found Carol Aydelotte, a Californian housewife who mixed in extremist circles and had managed the difficult feat of getting expelled from the fanatically anti-communist John Birch Society for being too right-wing. She claimed Bradley had once tried to convince a young Ku Klux Klan activist of her acquaintance to take a shot at President Kennedy; when asked if Bradley had any associates who might also have been involved, Aydelotte named former Interpen men Loran Hall and Lawrence Howard. As the conversation developed, she revealed some background that should have rung alarm bells among the investigators: her ejection from the John Birch Society had been triggered after she approached Bradley at a meeting for a donation to her favourite cause, which happened to be the American Nazi Party. He thought she was 'a kook' and told her so, a response which snowballed into a political civil war and ended with Aydelotte's eviction.[8] Hall and Howard's names were thrown into the mix because she had donated to their 1963 mission into Cuba and felt betrayed by its failure.

Garrison's men chose not to believe this lead was just bitter score-settling among the Californian far-right and advised their boss to subpoena the three men as material witnesses. That December, Loran Hall found his name all over the newspapers and Interpen more famous dead than it had ever been alive.

• • •

Hall arrived in the steam bath of New Orleans still pale yellow from a brush with hepatitis and eager to clear his name. His lawyers had managed to beat the subpoena in a Californian court but that had only provoked the Garrison investigation into a fresh barrage of legal threats and a compromise was reached. Hall agreed to take a few days off from his job bartending at Duffy's Tavern to go tell Jim Garrison all he knew in exchange for immunity from prosecution.

The interview was surprisingly civil, with the district attorney cracking jokes about going on a mission to Cuba to bring back cigars, as Hall walked him through the 1963 fundraising trips to Dallas and California: the endless talks given in suburban tract houses to middle-aged audiences in shirts and ties or pastel-coloured dresses; the polite conversation over cups of coffee with wide-eyed fanatics who inevitably wanted to talk about the Jewish influence on American culture; listening politely to rants from National States Rights Party types about white supremacy and race war. Hall glossed over how many of those radical right viewpoints he shared.

The fundraising never came to much, with the most Hall ever collected in one evening being $130 and the average take closer to $26. It was a lot of effort for little return, especially when the donors demanded receipts to check Hall was spending their money on guns and nothing more frivolous. Most of his audiences had less interest in overthrowing Castro than in raging about their own President and it was never unusual for some loudmouth to start spluttering that the country would be better off if someone shot Kennedy.

'It's like at that meeting,' Hall remembered, 'when the old boy jumped up and said rather than give two thousand dollars for this thing here I'd rather donate to a fifty thousand dollar pot and have Kennedy killed.'[9]

Despite his willingness to talk, Hall couldn't give Garrison anything useful. No one had ever seriously asked him to kill the President; he had only met Bradley once and barely remembered him; he knew nothing about Clay Shaw or David Ferrie; his memory remained hazy about the Silvia Odio del Torro affair, although it was possible they had met during his fundraising trip to Dallas. Hall was politely thanked and sent back to Kernville, California. His former comrade Lawrence Howard also visited New Orleans for an interview of even less use and returned home calling Garrison 'a very nice man'.[10]

Only Edgar Eugene Bradley refused to cooperate, but his lawyers were able to prove he had been on a bus travelling through El Paso at the time of the assassination. Garrison immediately dropped him from the investigation, although not quickly enough to stop a vigilante taking a shot at Bradley through his front window. The investigation was soon pushed in a different direction when fake stories planted by the Soviets in leftist Italian newspapers persuaded the district attorney that the CIA was the hidden hand behind the plot. This view was amplified by the hiring of a new investigator called William Wood, a former spy who had never forgiven the agency for kicking him out after a 1953 alcoholism-induced nervous breakdown.

Wood guided his new boss into increasingly paranoid waters until Garrison started to believe that President Lyndon Johnson had ordered Kennedy's murder to get the top job for himself and would do anything to cover up. The district attorney convinced himself Mafia hitmen were on his tail, talk show host Johnny Carson worked for the CIA and homosexual men were waiting in airport bathrooms to entrap him. He regularly muttered 'Fuck you, J. Edgar Hoover' into the mouthpiece before dialling out under the impression FBI agents were tapping his telephone.

As the trial date for Clay Shaw got closer, the investigation spiralled further out of control. Garrison's chief witnesses now included a paranoid schizophrenic conman known as 'Slidin' Clyde', an increasingly erratic Perry Russo who told different versions of his story to anyone who asked, and a desperate heroin addict who would say anything to avoid a prison sentence. Harold Weisberg, author of *Whitewash*, joined the investigation team and confidently announced he had identified 'Skinny' Ralph Schlafter of Interpen as a gay New Orleans hustler named 'Red' who could be placed in Dealey Plaza during the assassination. Garrison began threatening anyone who contradicted his theories with legal action. Things got so crazed that even Gerald Hemming distanced himself when the district attorney's men got back in touch. An interviewer who travelled to Los Angeles during the spring of 1968 noted the former Interpen leader was taciturn for once and full of 'extreme scepticism of the validity of our investigation'.[11]

On 1 March 1969, the jury took fifty-four minutes to find Clay Shaw innocent. The following month, Garrison was arrested for fondling a thirteen-year-old boy at an athletics club, confirming long-standing rumours and throwing a different light on his obsessive campaign against homosexuals. Charges were dropped, but Garrison's days as New Orleans district attorney were numbered.

In Miami, the remnants of Interpen were locked in their own downward spiral, determined to make one last attempt to overthrow Papa Doc in Haiti. It would end with a suicidal bombing mission over Port-au-Prince in a shot-up aeroplane that didn't look like it would make it home in one piece.

27

DÉJÀ VU OVER PORT-AU-PRINCE

PORT-AU-PRINCE/MIAMI/BAHAMAS, SPRING 1968–SUMMER 1969

The only thing stopping Martin Casey falling to his death from the Lockheed Constellation's cargo bay was a steel chain hooked to a belt around his waist. He stood in the aeroplane doorway balancing a barrel filled with kerosene as the houses and streets of Port-au-Prince rushed past 300 feet below and the wind ripped through his hair. 'Fat' Ralph Edens and the Haitian Charles Smith were rolling more barrels down the cabin towards him while Howard K. Davis was up by the cockpit door swivelling his head between the rattling plane interior and the Haitian capital appearing over the shoulders of the pilot. They were coming in low towards the blindingly white presidential palace but not yet over the target when Casey lit the marine flare taped to the barrel that served as a fuse.

'No, no, no!' yelled Davis.[1]

In the roar of the wind Casey heard 'Go, go, go!' and pushed his makeshift bomb out of the cargo door. To the side, Bill Dempsey began tossing glass bottles of white phosphorous into the slipstream with his one good arm. The first barrels landed among the shacks of the poor camped outside the palace walls and then the Lockheed was turning in the sky to begin a second run. This time, the barrels hit the villas of Duvalier's cronies and gouged craters into the concrete courtyard of his palace. The pilot was bringing the Constellation around on a third run when the anti-aircraft guns down below opened fire and tried to knock the plane out of the sky.

That morning of 4 June 1969 was the latest attempt by the boys from Nellie's boarding house to overthrow Papa Doc Duvalier. As bullets smashed through the Perspex windows of the cockpit and smoke poured into the flight deck, it looked like it would be their last. Two years earlier, their plan to invade Haiti had ended in arrests at a Florida dock and criminal charges, all of which had temporarily convinced the former Interpen men to abandon their Duvalier plans and refocus on Cuba. An exile friend called Francisco Avila Azcuy had been captured while on a secret mission to his homeland and Nellie's crowd agreed to kidnap a Cuban fisherman in revenge, then arrange a trade. Not everyone thought the plan would work.

'Castro couldn't have been blackmailed,' said 'Skinny' Ralph looking back.[2] 'He would just [have] shot the guy and called our bluff.'

They never got a chance to find out. The generator on their boat gave out near the Bahamas with all spare batteries dead so the mercenaries drifted for three days until a sport fisherman saw them waving for help, but he ignored them and sailed away. A furious Casey shot at the boat as it disappeared towards the horizon. They eventually flagged down some Cuban exiles on their own mission and persuaded them to donate a spare battery. On the way back to Miami, a huge freighter almost ran them down and 'Skinny' Ralph fell in the ocean and had to be hooked out. Once ashore, they tried to restore their spirits by cooking a fish reeled in during the trip but discovered it tasted of soap because they'd forgotten to rinse out the cooking pan. Then it was back to hanging around Nellie's, drinking beer and scrabbling for money to pay the rent. Avila stayed in prison.[3]

In May 1968, they read in the newspapers of a fresh attempt by Haitian exiles to overthrow Duvalier, this time using a different collection of American adventurers. Jay W. Humphrey was a tall Korean War veteran and pilot who spent his spare time eating health food and lifting heavy enough weights to win the bodybuilding title 'Mr Washington State'. Early in the year, he had been offered good money by exiles connected with the Jeune Haiti movement to bomb Port-au-Prince and land commandos at Cap-Haïtien, where the local garrison had agreed to join them. On 21 May, two B-25 aeroplanes, one piloted by Humphrey and the other by an American called Carl Davis, who had experience flying missions for Cuban exiles, took off from the Bahamas loaded with bombs and Jeune Haiti volunteers. They swooped in low over the capital, aiming for the presidential palace.

'With that bastard Duvalier bombed to death,' said Davis, 'the Haitian Army would be demoralised.'[4]

No one had considered the Oerlikon anti-aircraft guns on the manicured palace lawn and the B-25s were almost shot down, their bombs tumbling short. They pressed on to the airport at Cap-Haïtien, where nervy Jeune Haiti commandos killed an Army officer who jogged out to meet them, only realising afterwards that he was their contact with the rebel garrison. As the commandos took over the local radio station, a gunship appeared off the coast and began shelling the town. Humphrey, Davis and some senior Haitian exiles immediately climbed back into one of the B-25s and took off for

Miami, leaving the commandos behind to be slaughtered by the Tonton Macoutes.

Newspaper articles in America talked about prosecutions for breaching the Neutrality Act but then went silent. Behind the scenes, both Humphrey and Davis were claiming to work as contractors for the CIA, while the Haitian exiles insisted Jeune Haiti had been funded by the agency before the invasion. Prosecutors quietly dropped the case after 'extensive correspondence with Department of State ... explained problems that might arise during a trial', which convinced some observers the Jeune Haiti crowd were telling the truth.[5] The more cynical believed that exiles with loose agency connections had gone rogue and embarrassed the CIA into quashing a trial that would otherwise have revealed too many secrets.

The Haitian exile community shrugged off the disappointment and kept fighting Duvalier. In early 1969, Colonel René Juares Leon, who had been involved in the failed plot two years earlier with Rolando Masferrer, went back to Nellie's boarding house and rehired the men who had failed the first time around.

• • •

The camp was two miles off the nearest road and fifty miles west of Miami in a clearing hacked out of the thick brush of the Everglades. Martin Casey had set up a makeshift obstacle course, planted punji-stake traps around the perimeter and hung paper plates in the trees as targets. In the early days, the Haitian volunteers lacked firearms and ran around in combat gear shooting the plates with air rifles.

Colonel Leon managed to access some of the remaining Canadian Jesuit money through a lawyer in New York and handed over enough cash for real rifles. Casey bought them from a Georgia arms dealer, although only after a furious argument when both men forgot the codewords they'd agreed for the sale and accused each other of being undercover agents. The Haitians at the camp progressed to live fire exercises under a rotating cast of instructors from Nellie's. It went well enough that some of the former Interpen men allowed themselves to daydream about the rewards they would enjoy after Duvalier was overthrown.

On 11 March, the 22-year-old exile Gerald Baker was accidentally shot in the chest during a training exercise. The trigger had been pulled by Charles Smith, a fanatical Haitian patriot who'd joined the US Marines but never got higher than a private because he kept deserting to join failed invasions of his homeland. Baker collapsed with blood bubbling on his lips and everyone panicked. He was being driven to the hospital when Monroe County deputies stopped the car to find a nervy driver with an unconvincing cover story and the Haitian dying on a back seat. They raided the camp two days later and 'Skinny' Ralph had to run around the perimeter pulling up the punji sticks to avoid crippling the deputies who came crashing through the undergrowth. The authorities found twelve men still present among the hammocks and lean-tos, including William Dempsey and Ed Kolby, all in the process of packing up their rifles and survival gear.

'From the way they were dressed and armed,' said the astute Monroe County sheriff, 'I'd say they were planning an invasion of Haiti.'[6]

Charles Smith was charged with murder, despite his protests that the gun had gone off accidentally, while everyone else was arrested for breaching the Neutrality Act. They spent eleven days in jail before Baker's death was ruled accidental and the charges dropped.

In the wake of the shooting, cash from New York dried up as

Haitian exile groups distanced themselves from the chaos down south. Colonel Leon tried to persuade the backers to reconsider, while Howard K. Davis and Ed Kolby headed to San Francisco to beg the flamboyant lawyer Melvin Belli for funds on the assumption he might get involved just for the publicity. Belli refused, but an associate, introduced over a meal at a nearby barbeque restaurant, almost invested in the invasion before his enthusiasm drained away in a meeting with the main protagonists in Miami. Later, a Florida stockbroker put them in touch with diplomats at the Israeli embassy in Washington who liked the idea of creating a friendly nation in the Caribbean. The Israelis floated the idea of training Haitian commandos in the Sinai desert, but the plan fell apart when Tel Aviv stepped in to avoid causing trouble in America's backyard.

'After that,' said Casey, 'no one wanted to know our names. Everything went downhill. We couldn't get any money.'[7]

It would have been a good time to quit the mercenary business. No one had any cash, Casey was still out on bail as he fought his nine-month sentence from the 1967 arrest and the others were dangerously close to becoming unemployable layabouts. Only 'Skinny' Ralph was smart enough to walk out, waving goodbye to his friends and hello to married life. His departure reduced the group at Nellie's boarding house to Martin Casey, Bill Dempsey, 'Fat' Ralph Edens and Ed Kolby, with Howard K. Davis renting a house elsewhere in town with his wife. Despite the setbacks, the arrests and Gerald Baker's death, they were determined to keep going.

● ● ●

On 3 June 1969, the conspirators were waiting at a disused airfield on South Caicos, a sparsely populated island known mostly for sea salt and flamingos. Colonel Leon and Charles Smith had come up with a new plan to invade Haiti which, the Americans quickly realised, was an exact replica of Jay W. Humphrey's previous failed attempt. Leon assured them that things would be different this time and the gang flew out to the picturesque island on the edge of the Atlantic Ocean to wait for their ride.

Howard K. Davis had visited Miami International the previous day to help a bald, middle-aged pilot called Lawrence Carlin load a Lockheed Constellation with fifty drums of kerosene and a case of bottles containing white phosphorous. Leon had scraped together enough cash to hire the four-engine plane and bribe the pilot but not enough to buy off the two-man crew. Carlin fed his employees a tall story about a cargo run around the Caribbean and ignored their questions when six men climbed into the Constellation at South Caicos in combat gear and began stacking armloads of rifles like firewood.

As the engines juddered to life, the new arrivals realised the plane was an ancient wreck, with a broken intercom system and internal systems that barely seemed to work. Carlin dismissed their complaints but had to abort his take-off twice when the engines and hydraulics malfunctioned, before coaxing the plane into the air on the third attempt. From South Caicos, they headed to Great Exuma in the Bahamas, where Leon's contacts had put together a fifty-strong invasion force which would take the rifles and invade Haiti by sea while the Lockheed bombed the palace at Port-au-Prince. They touched down to find the beaches white, the sea icy blue and the landing strip deserted. The invasion force had obviously been the product of wishful thinking on someone's part and the group stood around in the Caribbean sun arguing over whether to abort yet another failed mission. Casey and the others were leaning towards going home when 26-year-old Canadian Bill Dempsey,

with his withered arm and handsome face, convinced them to keep
going.

'Are we going back to Miami with our tails between our legs
like we always do?' he said.[8] 'What the hell, we might as well try
something.'

They climbed back on board and the Lockheed Constellation
lumbered off the runway, set course for Port-au-Prince and came
over the hilltop outside the Haitian capital at 10:30 that morning. The
first two bombing runs missed the presidential palace and then the
anti-aircraft guns opened up. The Lockheed took thirty-four hits in a
matter of minutes and a piece of shrapnel sliced through the cockpit
floor to knock one of Carlin's crew unconscious in his seat.

Two more bullets punctured the window and missed the pilot's
head by inches as smoke poured into the flight deck and the engines began to scream. They banked away from the ground fire
and headed for Cap-Haïtien, where Colonel Leon thought a group
of anti-Duvalier guerrillas were waiting, but found the runway
blocked with trucks. They aborted the mission and headed north,
with the Constellation shivering in the sky as dials shorted out one
by one in the instrument panel. Carlin hoped to ditch on a remote
Caribbean island, but bad weather and the effort of keeping a shot-
up plane airborne pushed them off course until the fuel tank was
bone-dry. Flying on fumes, the Constellation finally touched down
at an airstrip belonging to the American missile-tracking station
on Grand Bahama Island. Everyone staggered out onto the tarmac
in their orange flight suits looking wild-eyed and glad to be alive.

'Just out for a spin,' Martin Casey told the technicians who gathered around the Lockheed to stare at the bullet holes in its skin.[9]

The mercenaries hired taxis to take them to the nearest bar while
the technicians called the police. Eventually, everyone got deported

to America except for Bill Dempsey who was sent back to his parents in London, Ontario, where he refused to talk to reporters ('Beat it!') and somehow managed to escape any charges.[10]

A trial followed for violating the Neutrality Act, in which the two crewmen hired under false pretences testified for the prosecution. The mercenaries were saved from more serious charges by most of the bombs having failed to explode, something 'Fat' Ralph blamed on Smith not lighting the marine flares properly, and by American scepticism over Duvalier's claim the six people who died in the bombing had included a six-month-old baby burned to death when a shack caught fire. Papa Doc's credibility had been undermined by his claims the bombing raid was a communist operation launched from Cuba. No one even seemed able to agree on how many bombs had been dropped, with Duvalier claiming four, a crew member eight and 'Fat' Ralph Edens convinced twenty-eight barrels had gone out of the door.

In the end, all eight men were found guilty of violating the Neutrality Act and jailed: Leon got three years, Smith two and the others received terms between nine and eighteen months. Casey sacked his lawyer during the trial and had to undergo a court-mandated psychiatric report ordered by a judge who refused to believe any sane man would represent himself. All would serve only a few months before being freed, but it was the end of the road for the crowd at Nellie's boarding house. Ralph Edens became an ironworker, got married and had a son; Casey also got married and had three children; Davis returned to his flying career. The others drifted away.

The Miami mercenary dream was dead, but there were still a few twitches left in the corpse. Frank Fiorini was finally about to bring down the widely disliked leader of a country. Unfortunately, that country was America.

28

WEIRD TIMES AT THE WATERGATE

WASHINGTON DC, JUNE 1972

Foggy Bottom was a deceptively homely name for a Washington DC neighbourhood only a twenty-minute walk from the White House. Popular with well-connected powerbrokers, its most fashionable address in 1972 was a $78 million complex of curvy but soulless poured concrete with views of the Potomac River. The Watergate boasted apartments, offices, restaurants, shops, a hotel and the kind of eye-watering prices that only those at the heart of the establishment could afford.

That summer, most Watergate residents were working for Richard M. Nixon's Republican administration, now campaigning for a second term, but the place was so conveniently located that their Democrat foes had rented an entire office floor to serve as an election headquarters. Activists spent long hours there trying to close a dispiritingly large gap in the polls, but by midnight on 16 June everyone had gone home for the day and the building was dark. Night guard Frank Wills came on duty and prepared to make his first sweep. Working security at the Watergate Office Building was undemanding work that suited Wills, an asthmatic African-American who'd quit the Ford assembly line in Detroit and come to Washington in search of a job easier on his lungs.

The security guard was swinging a torch beam around the underground parking garage when he noticed masking tape stuck across the steel latches of doors which gave access to the stairwell. The tape had been applied so the doors would close but not lock. Wills assumed it had been left by a daytime maintenance crew sick of hunting for their keys and peeled off the tape, noted the incident in his logbook, then forgot about it. Back in the lobby, he encountered Bruce Givner, a young volunteer from Democrat headquarters who'd stayed late and was on his way to the Howard Johnson's Motor Lodge across the road for coffee and a cheeseburger before going home. Wills went with him to break the monotony of the night shift and returned alone after a while with a bag of takeout. On his next sweep of the building, he found more tape on the garage doors. This wasn't maintenance workers.

At 01:47 on 17 June, Wills called the police and waited anxiously in the lobby. The first unit to respond was an unmarked car carrying three members of the 'bum squad', long-haired officers in hippy clothes who had spent their evening hunting drug dealers. Calls like these usually turned out to be false alarms, so the officers were in no hurry as they turned off the elevators, locked the outer doors and searched the building floor by floor. The mood changed when Wills led them onto the sixth floor.

'When we turned the lights on, one person, then two persons, then three persons came out, and on down the line,' said Wills.[1]

Five men were hiding in the Democratic National Committee offices. The bum squad pulled their guns and discovered they had three Cubans and two white Americans, all in their forties or older with short-hair and conservative suits. They didn't look like burglars. The men refused to talk except to give fake names, with two Cubans laughing when they got confused and gave the same one. A quick pat down uncovered surgical gloves, walkie-talkies, lock picks, cameras, crowbars, electronic equipment, miniature flashlights, hotel keys and tear-gas guns. Down at the station, a nervy desk sergeant wondered if the electronic equipment might be a bomb and called in the FBI, who confirmed it was a listening device. The hotel keys led to rooms at the Howard Johnson's, where officers found $2,300 in sequential notes and a cheque signed by 'E. Howard Hunt'.

By the next day, the FBI had identified the burglars. Virgilio González was a Miami locksmith active in exile politics; Eugenio Rolando Martínez had led CIA marine missions against Cuba until a few years ago and remained an informer for the agency; James McCord was a security consultant who had retired from the CIA two years earlier to work for the Republican Party; Bernard Barker was a former CIA agent now working in Miami real estate.

The fifth man was Frank Fiorini.

• • •

Bernard Barker had a reputation as a man who held on to his money so tightly that it squealed in pain. When he had invited Fiorini for a meal back in the spring, it was clear nothing had changed.

'And you know where we ended up having lunch?' remembered an exasperated Fiorini.[2] 'In the cheapest hamburger joint in Miami. Barker kept telling me: "Eat four of these burgers if you like. Eat five. They're not very big." You bet they aren't – they cost fifteen cents a piece.'

Barker had been eased out of the agency six years earlier after his bosses realised there was little point employing a secret agent whose identity was known to everybody in Miami. His political work in the lead up to the Bay of Pigs had been too public to allow a retreat into the shadows afterwards, but Barker managed to cling on to his job for a few years by reporting on the Cuban exile scene, relying on information sourced from Frank Fiorini, until the agency realised it had others who did the same job better. Back in civilian life, Barker worked as a boxing promoter and manager of a real estate firm which had a reputation for selling worthless swampland.

In 1971, he was contacted by his former CIA boss E. Howard Hunt, who had used the cover name 'Eduardo' when they worked together, and asked to meet at the Bay of Pigs monument in Miami. Hunt, a mournful and balding fifty-something, had retired from the CIA a year earlier and was working part-time in the White House with the 'plumbers team' trying to stop leaks to the press. Now he was branching into political dirty tricks. Anyone looking to understand Hunt's mindset could have done worse than reading the pseudonymous paperback thrillers he'd churned out over the past few years in which a suave CIA agent takes on an unholy alliance of Satanists, hippies and communist freaks determined to destroy America. The books reflected, in a garish pulp mirror, Hunt's own fears of the leftist counterculture sweeping his country.

At the Miami monument, a sawn-off black obelisk topped with an eternal flame, he told Barker that the Cuban government was funding the Democrats and asked for his help in defending America. His former subordinate didn't hesitate and was soon working alongside a team of White House employees prepared to do anything for the Nixon administration and ranging from the businesslike to the unbalanced. At the far end of the scale was G. Gordon Liddy, a moustached former FBI agent now working for the Committee to Re-Elect the President, who had made willpower the driving force of his life. To conquer a childhood fear of rats, Liddy forced himself to kill and eat one; to prove his inner strength, he held lit matches to his flesh. His forearms and hands were such a mess of scars that doctors had warned he could soon lose the use of his fingers. The Nixon loyalist prided himself on doing whatever was necessary to keep America great and dismissed moral concerns as the intellectual static of inferior minds. Barker thought him deranged.

Orders came down to burgle the office of a psychiatrist treating a RAND Corporation analyst called Daniel Ellsberg who had passed compromising documents about the Vietnam War to journalists. Barker took part but turned up nothing incriminating. Liddy remained convinced that dirty tricks remained a necessary weapon on the political battlefield and in early 1972 received permission from some shadowy figures in the White House to bug the Democratic National Committee at the Watergate.

Hunt oversaw the operation. He got old friends at the CIA to provide a wig, tape recorder, camera and false identification papers but wouldn't reveal their intended use. Barker was sent to Miami with orders to recruit some reliable men and in April 1972 Frank Fiorini found himself eating hamburgers in a cheap restaurant while listening to a lecture about Fidel Castro's support for the Democratic Party. To test his commitment, Fiorini was asked to join 'a group of ten Cubans' and go crack some heads at a forthcoming anti-war demonstration in Washington.[3] He agreed.

• • •

Fiorini had been out of the counter-revolution game for several years by this point after a series of disastrous setbacks. In 1967, he'd driven a car packed with explosives into Mexico in an attempt to sink a Cuban freighter but aborted the mission when the ship turned out to be sailing under a British flag. He buried the bombs in the desert but was arrested coming back across the border by suspicious customs officials. After hours of questioning, Fiorini wriggled out of any charges, although his demolitions expert did jail time after being unable to remember how to spell the name on his fake driving licence.

The next year, Fiorini came up with a plan to hijack a Soviet freighter and recruited a team of American mercenaries through a newspaper advert that promised adventure and good pay. He got eleven war veterans from Miami who drank too much. The operation seemed doomed from the moment they arrived at their hotel in Mexico to discover it had been demolished several weeks earlier. Things got worse when the money ran out and they had to sell their guns to buy food. Fiorini's team hung on long enough to rent a boat and head for Cuba, but the captain got lost on the way and ran aground in British Honduras, where local police arrested everyone. Back in Miami, Fiorini gave up on the paramilitary life to concentrate his energies on marriage and a respectable job as a salesman at the Pan American Aluminum Corporation.

Charges over the British Honduras affair were still grinding their way through the legal system when Barker appeared on the scene and asked him to smack around some hippies protesting the war in Vietnam. It would have been a smart move to avoid involvement, but Fiorini was loyal to his friends and the boys fighting in southeast Asia, a group which now included Ed Arthur strafing the Viet Cong as a helicopter gunner. Fiorini flew to Washington and discovered the promised ten Cubans had been reduced to Barker and a friend. Undiscouraged, Fiorini waded into the protest and got arrested for punching out a demonstrator but had the charges dropped by a sympathetic police officer.

Afterwards, Barker quietly asked if he would join a team breaking into the Watergate in search of documents linking Fidel Castro with Democrat fundraising efforts. It was a big leap from street violence to burglary, but Fiorini had recovered his taste for action and agreed to reconnoitre the complex with Eugenio Rolando Martínez, a prematurely white-haired friend of Barker who seemed to be under the impression the whole operation had been authorised by the CIA. A series of unsuccessful break-ins followed, including a farcical attempt when E. Howard Hunt hid in the building after workers went home but was unable to open the front door and spent the rest of the night in a cupboard periodically urinating into a bottle of Johnnie Walker Red Label. A more successful burglary took place on 28 May when Fiorini and the others planted a listening device on the sixth floor and photographed documents. Barker had the film processed by a commercial photography shop down in Miami and the long-haired young man working the afternoon shift found himself developing shots of Democrat documents gripped in surgically gloved hands. Barker gave him $40 to keep quiet.

On the evening of 16 June, another burglary was organised after former CIA electronics expert James McCord discovered a listening device planted in the Democrat office needed repairing. It was decided that Fiorini, Martínez, Barker and a lock-picking contact from Miami called Virgilio González would escort McCord inside to fix the device, while Hunt and Liddy monitored the situation from room 723 in the Howard Johnson's across the street. McCord had already visited the Watergate during the day under the pretence of a business meeting and taped open the locks to the underground garage.

A light burning on the sixth floor delayed the mission and the burglars remained in the hotel room taking shifts watching the Democrat offices through binoculars. A young man seemed to be hard at work as the clock crept past midnight and everyone else went home.

'This was some dedicated Democrat,' said Liddy, impressed despite himself.[4]

The worker was Bruce Givner, abusing the office's telephone privileges to make free calls to friends and family back home in Ohio. Eventually, he hung up for the last time and left the building together with Frank Wills, heading for the Howard Johnson's restaurant section. Fiorini and the three Cubans slipped out of the hotel above and crossed Virginia Avenue to find the tape had been removed from the interior garage doors. After a whispered discussion, Virgilio González picked the locks and re-taped them to keep the doors open for McCord, who would enter the building separately.

When the bugging specialist, a fleshy forty-something, arrived sweating on the sixth floor, he had forgotten to remove the tape behind him and then nagged Barker into turning down the volume on a walkie-talkie spitting static. The team didn't hear Liddy's warnings about the police arriving until it was too late to run. In the van taking them to the station, McCord ordered everyone to keep quiet and wait for the White House to spring into action.

• • •

Richard Milhous Nixon had taken the presidency in 1968 on a wave of blue-collar Republicanism that despised hippies, draft dodgers, Black Panthers and troublemakers but wasn't keen on sending its sons to die in Vietnam. Nixon's promises of peace, at home and abroad, had squeaked him into the White House by the narrow margin of 500,000 votes and any scandal could be fatal to his re-election chances. When news reached the Oval Office that members of the Committee to Re-Elect the President had been involved in a break-in, Nixon ranted about their recklessness then ordered his staff to cover up any connection to the government.

A press spokesman described events at the Watergate as a 'third-rate burglary attempt' and brushed off revelations in the *Washington Post* that some of those arrested had worked with the Republican Party.[5] The contents of E. Howard Hunt's office safe were quietly destroyed and Attorney General John Mitchell ordered his wife Martha, an indiscreet drunk known around Washington as 'The Mouth of the South', be held incommunicado at a California hotel after she tried to inform the media that James McCord was a party activist. The story could have died there, but senior FBI man William Mark Felt was feeling resentful at White House interference in his investigation and began feeding hints to *Washington Post* reporter Bob Woodward. The revelation that funds from the Committee to Re-Elect the President had been used to pay the burglars led to the arrest of Liddy and Hunt, and it quickly became obvious senior figures in the Nixon administration had known about Watergate.

The public didn't seem to care. On 7 November 1972, Richard Nixon won the presidential election by one of the biggest landslides in American history. The next January, Fiorini and the three Cubans appeared in court to give their occupations as 'anti-communists' and admit the burglary charges – 'We decided to plead guilty to the charges against us because we were, in fact, guilty,' they said, surprising observers who didn't expect that much honesty from criminals.[6] Hunt also pled guilty, but Liddy and McCord fancied their chances with a jury and went to trial. Both men lost. Provisional sentences for everyone averaged around fifty years.

Fiorini found himself in a medium-security Connecticut federal prison, sleeping in a busy dormitory where steel doors slammed and toilets flushed all day. He remained silent about the affair but felt increasingly angry that Barker had got him into this mess; Barker, in turn, felt betrayed by Hunt for the same reason; Martínez was bitter at the CIA, which he still believed had been behind the operation; while Hunt and McCord raged against the White House for having allowed them to be imprisoned. Liddy regarded them all with contempt for lacking his iron willpower when faced with the prospect of dying in prison.

On the other side of the bars, the *Washington Post* continued digging into Watergate and found more incriminating evidence. In April 1973, a number of Nixon's top aides resigned and the following month a televised Senate committee began an investigation into the burglary and its suspected cover-up. Millions of Americans watched the great and the good lie, deflect and only reluctantly tell the truth. The stake through the heart of the affair was the revelation that Nixon had secretly recorded hours of White House conversations in which his inner circle discussed how best to conceal the Watergate burglary. On 27 July 1974, Richard Nixon was impeached. He resigned two weeks later. Many of his White House staffers went to prison. No American politician would ever be completely trusted again.

Frank Fiorini watched Nixon's resignation speech from his Miami home, having been released on parole at the start of the year after the judge withdrew the provisional sentences, only ever intended to intimidate the prisoners, and passed shorter terms. McCord was already out after cooperating with investigators, while Barker, González and Martínez would be released soon after. Hunt served thirty-three months, most of it spent mourning his wife, who had died in an air crash, while Liddy did four and a half years then wrote a self-serving memoir called *Will* that impressed and appalled readers in equal measure.

Fiorini was glad to be back with his wife and stepson but soon signed up with a local Cuban exile group, still determined to spend the rest of his life fighting Castro. He wanted to bring down the man who had begun as an idealistic rebel in the Sierra Maestra and become an oppressive dictator. It was, Fiorini believed, only a matter of time before Castro was overthrown

29

COMMUNISM, COCAINE, CONSPIRACIES

On 19 February 2008, the website of *Granma*, the official newspaper of the Cuban Communist Party, carried a letter from Fidel Castro announcing his resignation. He had ruled the country for forty-nine years and the vigorous, cigar-smoking guerrilla of the revolution was now a wispy, grey old man with liver-spotted skin and serious intestinal problems. His brother Raúl took over and the former 'maximum leader' retired his combat fatigues to spend the last eight years of his life as a respected elder statesman before dying of natural causes late in the evening of 25 November 2016 at the age of ninety.

To outsiders, Havana didn't look much different to when he had taken power. Locals had mobile phones and laptops but, thanks to the ongoing American sanctions, the cars were the same 1950s models that had roamed the streets under Batista. For a long time after the revolution, Cuba's only foreign visitors were the Venceremos Brigade, an 'anti-imperialist Education Project' drawn from the leftist ranks of America's Students for a Democratic Society, who visited the island to cut sugar cane and patronise the locals.[1]

The venceremos volunteers watched Cuba stagger through the next few decades until the collapse of Eastern bloc communism in the late 1980s removed access to huge, subsidised markets and the economy crumbled. The government turned to foreign tourism and began marketing the island as a destination for anyone who liked sun, sea and cheap drinks.

By 2018, around 4.7 million tourists visited the country each year, including a substantial number of Americans who had to enter via Canada or Mexico to avoid legal action for breaching sanctions. Film companies took advantage of the old cars and unchanged streets to shoot period movies in Havana, even if cynical locals muttered that the city had looked less dilapidated in the past.

Castro had been unhappy to see his country become as dependent on foreigners as it had been under Batista but compensated with thundering anti-imperialist speeches right up until his death. Few were surprised he or his country's history books failed to mention the approximately twenty-five American volunteers who had fought with him up in the mountains. Most had left the country decades earlier, with only Richard Sanderlin and José Abrantes remaining in Cuba after the Bay of Pigs. Sanderlin stayed because his injured arm required regular operations and, in the autumn of 1964, he died undergoing yet another procedure in a Cuban hospital when his heart stopped under general anaesthetic. His family in America believed he was murdered by a Cuban government which suspected him of counter-revolution. The same year saw Herman Marks arrested for making obscene phone calls to journalist Jean Secon in New York. He was questioned the next August after breaking his leg falling from a tree where he'd been spying on a female neighbour as she took a shower. He moved back to Milwaukee, but in August 1966, the local police issued an arrest warrant after Marks was accused of indecent behaviour with a six-year-old girl. He went on the run and was never seen again, although some believe he moved to Mexico.

In December 1967, Thomas Spychala was thirty-eight years old and mentally disintegrating as he lived alone in Los Angeles. Five days before Christmas, he stole his neighbour's car and cruised the city, running red lights until a policeman pulled up beside him on a motorcycle. Spychala opened fire and left the officer dying in the street. He hijacked another car, took two hostages and drove to a pharmacy on the Pacific Coast Highway where he forced the clerk to hand over a vial of ant poison.

'I've already killed one man today,' said Spychala, 'and I don't want to kill anyone else but myself.'[2]

The poison failed to work and Spychala spent the next five years in a psychiatric institution before being ruled competent to stand trial. He was found guilty of murder and disappeared into the prison system. North Carolina native Jimmy Gentry had died of natural causes a few years earlier, having long abandoned both Cuba and his brief involvement in the counter-revolutionary movement.

'He stated he left Cuba when he felt there were too many communists in Cuba,' said the FBI file on Gentry, 'and the government was not functioning as promised.'[3]

Richard A. Witzler, who had briefly fought with Bill Morgan in the Escambray mountains before deserting, returned to Maumee and became a police officer. He married Ruth Hanneman and adopted her two children. On 20 November 1974, something inside him snapped and Witzler shot dead his stepson and stepdaughter, seriously wounded his wife and killed himself. Three years later, the journalist Herbert Matthews passed away in Adelaide, Australia, from a brain haemorrhage. He had never fired a rifle in anger, but his writing on behalf of the rebel cause was arguably more important than any individual volunteer to its eventual victory. As time rolled on and attitudes changed, Matthews's continued support for the dictatorship in Cuba got him labelled a communist stooge by many and made even the *New York Times* wary of publishing his material. Today, a marble monument stands remote in the Sierra Maestra beneath the wavering shadows of the trees to commemorate the place that Matthews first met Fidel Castro and made him a temporary hero to Americans.

Fellow journalist Robert Taber continued to work for CBS until his death in 1995 but is remembered today mostly for writing *The War of the Flea*, a 1965 bestseller about guerrilla warfare that tapped into the anti-establishment zeitgeist and allowed privileged hippies to imagine themselves as urban warriors. Someone who fought a guerrilla war for real was Second Front veteran Juan Espiritu, who campaigned against Castro from the Escambray mountains for two years before his 1963 capture. Behind bars, he recovered his admiration for the rebel leader and was occasionally beaten by other prisoners for praising the government. After four years, he agreed to cooperate with the prison authorities in exchange for his freedom and admitted to being a long-time CIA agent who had arranged the 1948 murder of Colombian politician Jorge Eliécer Gaitán. No one who knew Espiritu as a poorly paid kitchen worker during that period believed the confession, but accusations that Fidel Castro had been involved in Gaitán's death had recently resurfaced and Espiritu's words were intended to disperse them. Espiritu was working as a building contractor in Cuba by the early 1970s, then returned to America. He died in 2006 but remained loyal enough to the regime to repeat the CIA fantasies to Cuban journalists in his later years.

Neill Macaulay became a professor of Latin American history at the University of Florida. He published some important academic works but sold far more copies of his 1970 memoir *A Rebel in Cuba*, which described executing prisoners during the revolution in dispassionate detail but failed to mention his work with counter-revolutionaries in Miami. He retired twenty years later and spent his holidays visiting old comrades in Cuba for emotional reunions before his 2007 death. Mike Garvey and Charles Ryan also returned to the island and met with Castro on his seventieth birthday. Both had joined the Army after their time as teenage guerrillas, with Ryan serving for twenty-three years and fighting in Vietnam. Their friend Victor Buehlman, who had been a Marine and then a salesman, refused to accompany them in protest at Cuba's authoritarian government. Castro still seemed delighted to see the pair and they talked for hours.

'It was like he was a young man again, trying to overcome adversity,' said Garvey.[4] 'It took him back to old times when he was not carrying the weight of running the country. He was more at peace with himself when he was running a war.'

Buehlman died in late 2010, followed by Ryan two years later and Garvey shortly afterwards. Other volunteers are undoubtedly dead by now but have left little traces of their subsequent activities. Jack Nordeen departed Miami in 1961 after trying to interest Interpen in Nicaragua and vanished from the history books. Pilot Walter 'Jack' Youngblood was accused by conspiracy theorists of involvement in Martin Luther King's assassination, although his main business seemed to be smuggling marijuana into America. José Abrantes may have been the same man executed by the Cuban government in the early 1980s for his involvement in a drug smuggling operation run by corrupt officials. Ed Bethune might be the former Marine who went on to become a Republican member of the House of Representatives before retiring to write legal thrillers.

Only one American volunteer was definitely still alive in 2022: Donald Soldini studied economics at a university in Mexico City after getting expelled from Cuba and discovered he liked capitalism. He became a Miami-based entrepreneur whose interest in real estate made him very rich. Soldini revisited old comrades in Cuba from the 1970s, tried to build a replica of the Taj Mahal in South Florida in the 1980s and helped fund the restoration of a Second World War bomber in the internet age. He regrets nothing about his life and drives a Rolls-Royce.

● ● ●

Miami looks very different today than it did when the first Batista officials and their families arrived in early 1959 fleeing the revolution. The city has sprouted enough high-rises to give it the third-tallest skyline in the country, and the Port of Miami is the busiest in the world, funnelling cruise ships around the Caribbean and further afield. Most inhabitants are now Hispanic, with Cubans forming the largest slice. Hundreds of thousands have fled their homeland over the years to escape Castro's rule, taking to the sea in overcrowded and leaky boats to brave the sharks and other predators in the hope of starting a new life abroad. In 1980 alone, at least 125,000 arrived in the Mariel boatlift when the Cuban authorities temporarily opened their borders and then emptied out the prisons for good measure.

The cocaine boom of that time turned a city known for its hotels and sea fishing into a glazed-eye parody of the American Dream, as young and hungry exiles organised smuggling operations that made them millionaires overnight and left the bodies piled high. South and Central Americans muscled into the market and bloody drugs wars claimed so many lives that the Miami authorities had to lease refrigerated trucks to cope with the corpses. The Oliver Stone scripted 1983 movie *Scarface* summed up the period with its chainsaw-wielding cocaine cowboys and public shoot-outs outside pastel-coloured hotels.

Alongside the cocaine war was the ongoing fight against Castro's Cuba, although it ran at a lower intensity than before. The CIA had stepped away, but paramilitary groups kept training in the Everglades as the century ended, dreaming of the day when they could recover their homeland. Orlando Bosch remained a hero to many until his 2011 death despite a lifetime of action that frequently crossed the line from warfare to terrorism, such as the bombing of Cubana de Aviación Flight 455 that killed all seventy-three passengers and crew. The paramilitary missions wound down as the years went on, and by the time of Fidel Castro's 2016 death, the scene was reduced to a few older men with guns under their beds and fanaticism in their eyes.

The man whose overthrow had started this long battle was long gone. Fulgencio Batista had left his Dominican exile for Portugal and then Francoist Spain, where he died in 1973 after years of spending money and writing self-justifying memoirs. Most of the Americans who joined the counter-revolution are dead too, either young and suddenly or from diseases that wait a whole lifetime to strike. Ignatius Paul Alvick, one-time member of the Anti-Communist Legion, collapsed on a New York street from an undiagnosed heart condition in early 1963, only one day away from his twenty-sixth birthday. He had been working as a bit-part actor on television. Publisher and would-be privateer Lyle H. Munson died in 1973 at the age of fifty-five years old, leaving a wife, two daughters and a warehouse full of right-wing literature. He is remembered today mostly by conspiracy theorists who attach importance to his 1964 pamphlet 'Stifle the Legend', which suggests Lyndon Johnson or possibly communist Cuba had been behind President Kennedy's assassination.

Fellow writer Hans Tanner died two years after Munson in a murder-suicide. The Swiss motor journalist dropped out of the exile scene after Alex Rorke's disappearance to write books about Ferraris and rare firearms. He managed to get residency in America, left his wife and daughter and began living with a younger Cuban woman and her son. At his Los Angeles home, he liked to show off a collection of rare and antique weapons to visitors, including a hollowed-out book in which he claimed to have smuggled a pistol into Cuba during his counter-revolutionary days. His physical and mental health deteriorated after a cancer diagnosis. On 23 March 1975, he shot dead his girlfriend and then himself.

Later the same year, someone killed Rolando Masferrer in his driveway. The 57-year-old turned the key on his Ford Torino and a dynamite bomb scattered pieces of car and driver across the front lawn. Police responders recorded time of death at 10:58 in the morning of 31 October, while journalists noted that a week earlier Masferrer had written an editorial in his Spanish-language newspaper *Libertad* praising anyone who used terrorism against Castro.

'There's nothing that speaks more eloquently in all four corners of the world than dynamite,' he wrote.[5]

Clearly he was right. No one claimed responsibility for the death, but it was generally accepted that Cuban Intelligence had planted the bomb in revenge for Masferrer's activities over the years. In 1978, a more natural but still premature death came for 57-year-old

Austin Frank Young in Florida. The pilot had ended up in a Cuban prison after getting involved with Masferrer and the Biltmore Terrace Hotel crowd and was finally freed sometime in the late 1960s to rebuild his life.

Masferrer's colleague Mitch WerBell III sold weapons to the Afghan monarchy before its 1973 overthrow and was later acquitted of trying to sell silenced Ingram machine pistols to a federal agent; in the aftermath, he quit the arms business and moved into security and counter-terrorism training. He got involved in a 1975 plot with a group of American property developers to gain the independence of Abaco from the Bahamas, oversaw abortive coups in various Central American countries and was acquitted of involvement in marijuana smuggling. WerBell got ever more right-wing as he aged.

'Communism has no place in the western hemisphere,' he told a journalist.[6] 'Or any hemisphere. I am totally opposed to it and the spread of ideological germs and filth it brings.'

He became a security adviser to pornographer Larry Flynt in his later years, drank too much and died at sixty-five years old of heart failure in 1983; allegations he had been poisoned led to Flynt's brother-in-law being charged but acquitted after a wide-ranging inquiry that involved everything from the mysterious death of an obese prostitute to the murder of a producer involved in the *Cotton Club* movie. Alan Robert Nye, a less successful killer, died on 15 August 1984 of cardiac arrest and cirrhosis of the liver. He had moved back to Maryland after his experience in Cuba and worked for an aircraft company before becoming a newspaper editor of *St Mary's Beacon*. He never talked about his time behind bars in Havana.

The private detective Vincent J. Hanard, head of the short-lived Freedom Fighters of the Americas, lost his agency and moved on to annoying the FBI by impersonating a federal agent. He got two years' probation after a trial in which he represented himself, then demanded a retrial because of his incompetence as a lawyer. A lifetime of misadventures followed, including stints as a minister, funeral director, informant in a drug-smuggling case and bounty hunter. By 1985, Hanard was a shrunken, rasping sixty-year-old suing tobacco companies for selling the cigarettes that had given him emphysema. He lost the case and died shortly afterwards.

George Washington Tanner, founder of the Anti-Communist Legion, went on to be involved in various petty crimes, including car theft and burglary, before moving to Texas and dying in 1996 at seventy-one years old. He got a marble tombstone in the neat green grass of Fort Sam Houston military cemetery engraved with the words 'PFC/US Army/World War II'.

Bay of Pigs veteran Douglas Nelson Lethbridge Aguilera was freed with the rest of the prisoners in late 1962 and returned to America to sell infrared missiles for Mitch WerBell, get married several more times and eventually move to Caracas with a Venezuelan girl twenty years his junior. He worked for a company that exported cattle embryos, blamed any financial setbacks on an alleged lifetime of top-secret work for the CIA ('There has never been any relationship with him since his participation in Brigade 2506,' noted a quietly exasperated agency report) and was lucky not to be jailed after a bar fight with the son of an important judge.[7] He wriggled out of the charges and the history books. Boris Grgurevich, his one-time comrade in Brigade 2506, achieved some type of immortality when his hipster writer friend Terry Southern turned a conversation about the Bay of Pigs into a 1963 article for *Esquire* magazine. Initially proud of the piece, Grgurevich would come to believe he'd been exploited by Southern and would regularly turn up on the *Dr Strangelove* scriptwriter's doorstep demanding financial compensation.

Ed Arthur quit the Cuban gunrunning business in the summer of 1965 and returned to Ohio. The next year, he volunteered to fight in the Vietnam War, serving as a recon-scout with the First Cavalry Division and claiming to be the oldest door gunner in the Army. He was badly wounded when North Vietnamese forces blasted his helicopter out of the sky ('Being shot down was no fun – ha! They got us good,' he wrote to a friend with his usual cheerfulness) and spent time in hospital before re-enlisting in December 1969 in the safer role of instructor.[8] Back home, he joined law enforcement in Colorado for a long career fighting crime before passing away in 2015.

• • •

Most of those Americans who fought for and against Fidel Castro are long forgotten, except for an unlucky few taken up by conspiracy theorists obsessed with the death of President John F. Kennedy. The appearance of Loran Hall in the Garrison investigation first put Interpen on the radar, but Gerald Hemming's group became more widely known when the government voted to establish the 1976 House Select Committee on Assassinations (HSCA) to take a deep dive into the deaths of President Kennedy and Martin Luther King Jr. Prompted by public distrust of the official narrative and revelations of state-sponsored assassinations, the committee spent $6.5 million analysing ballistics, sound recordings, photographs, handwriting and pathology reports. Anyone with the slightest connection to the assassination or its ancillary conspiracy theories was interviewed under oath.

While some were reluctant to attend, Gerald Hemming seemed to relish the attention. He claimed to have spent the years since leaving Miami running guns from Mexico, attempting to free Americans captive in Cuba and training Black Panther militants while simultaneously establishing a base in Mexico for right-wingers to escape a civil war Hemming believed was looming. In the late 1960s, he and sidekick Roy Hargraves came up with a plot to start a bigger war by persuading defecting Cuban missile technicians to launch an attack on Guantánamo Bay naval base.

'They continually are devising irresponsible military plans that will never be put into effect because they lack the money, manpower, and necessary military equipment,' a source informed the FBI.[9]

By the early 1970s, Hemming was involved in arms dealing and private detective work, before joining a plot to assassinate the Guatemalan President, which collapsed after a conspirator got badly wounded in a firefight with unknown assailants. In 1977, Hemming appeared before the Select Committee to confuse everyone with his now habitual mix of truth, lies and misleading ambiguity. Committee members came away convinced Interpen had no involvement in the assassination but that nothing else Hemming said could be trusted, especially when he denied under oath ever meeting Lee Harvey Oswald and then told journalists the exact opposite afterwards.

A recently divorced Loran Hall made a better impression before the committee, explaining that assassination talk had been rampant during his mercenary days ('Back in 1963 … almost every meeting I ever went to I heard somebody plotting or talking about [how] somebody should blow Kennedy's head off') but denying any involvement.[10] Hall next made the headlines around 1990 when he, his daughter and three sons were arrested selling methamphetamine, allegedly to finance the rightist Contras in Nicaragua. He died five years later in Kansas.

Hemming outlived him by thirteen years. In 1980, he was arrested for smuggling marijuana into America for a Colombian cartel by light aeroplane and, after serving as his own lawyer, was sentenced to thirty-five years in prison. He got out after eight years and reinvented himself as a paralegal researcher with a sideline in talking up fantasies about the Kennedy assassination. He now claimed conspirators had planted bombs in Dealey Plaza to blow up the motorcade if the snipers missed; a second assassin in the Texas School Book Depository building had a separate contract to kill Governor John Connally; and the entire assassination was funded by the Trujillo family as revenge for the dictator's 1961 murder, which they blamed on the CIA. By Hemming's death in 2008, not even the most hardcore conspiracy theorists took him seriously.

Few Interpen veterans outlived him. Howard K. Davis had passed away in 2002 after years serving in the US Department of Homeland Security and US Customs and Border Protection. Steve Wilson died of a cerebral aneurysm while working as a steel worker in 1984 high above the Miami skyline. Ed Collins drowned while drunk on a 1964 fishing trip, an event Hemming predictably dramatised into a murder by Castro agents. Canadian William Dempsey of Interpen was briefly involved in a plot to rescue American businessman Joel Kaplan from a Mexican prison, where he was serving a sentence for murdering his business partner. The plot never went anywhere and Dempsey returned the money he had been advanced for the escape, to the astonishment of everyone involved. Joe Garman died in 2010 in Bowling Green, Kentucky, at eighty years old, after a long life spent as a gentleman farmer whose hobbies revolved around hunting and the outdoors. He was an enthusiastic member of the National Rifle Association.

Martin F. X. Casey died the following year at seventy-two years old. He had left the mercenary life behind and worked as everything from a journalist to a doctor's assistant among the rural poor in Central America and bag boy at a Miami supermarket. His wife had died twenty years earlier of a brain aneurysm and friends believed he never recovered from the loss. An attempt to write an autobiography only lasted twenty or so pages before petering out through lack of motivation. Casey did not have especially fond memories of his days as a soldier of fortune.

'There were a lot of plans made, a lot of broken dreams,' he told a journalist.[11] 'But there was never any money.'

Only Robert K. Brown outlived them all. After fighting in Vietnam, he engaged in various military adventures everywhere from Rhodesia to Bosnia but is best known for creating *Soldier of Fortune*, a popular magazine for mercenaries and those who liked to see themselves as such. In 2022, both *SoF* and Brown are still around.

• • •

In 1991, Hemming and Davis had a brief brush with a more glamorous kind of fame when they worked as 'technical advisers' on Oliver Stone's film *JFK*, a big-screen version of Jim Garrison's conspiracy theories based on the self-serving books written by the former New Orleans district attorney. Not everyone believed the thesis of a gay cabal in league with the far-right and the CIA, but the film's success pushed Congress to pass the JFK Assassination Records Collection Act, which began the process of declassifying millions of confidential assassination documents. By 2022, only a few still remained classified.

Nothing emerged to radically change the existing narrative or support conspiracy theorists who have variously blamed the assassination on Fidel Castro, Lyndon B. Johnson, Nikita Khrushchev, the Mafia, the CIA, Cuban exiles, Haitian paramilitaries, Rafael Trujillo's family, aliens, rogue Soviet agents, French settlers in Algeria, Robert Kennedy, Katangese secessionists, the father of Hollywood actor Woody Harrelson, partisans of murdered South Vietnamese President Ngô Đình Diệm, Kennedy's own chauffeur or Lucien Prévost, a Paris gangster who'd collaborated with the Nazis as part of the Bonny-Lafont gang and disappeared at the end of the war.

Frank Fiorini remained permanently in the theorists' crosshairs. Watergate had given him a public profile and the CIA connections of those involved in the burglary caught the attention of many on the left. In 1975, Alan J. Weberman and Michael Canfield published *Coup d'État in America: The CIA and the Assassination of JFK*, which claimed Kennedy had been assassinated by the agency because of his inaction during the Bay of Pigs. The authors were convinced Hunt and Fiorini had been in Dealey Plaza during the assassination, based on the pair's resemblance to some tramps photographed in the area that day. The alleged similarity wasn't startling and not everyone took the book seriously, especially after learning that Weberman was a former drug dealer and Bob Dylan obsessive who thought many of the singer's songs contained secret messages addressed to him personally. But in the growing world of conspiracy theorists, Fiorini became a prime suspect for those who wanted to believe right-wingers were the source of all evil in the world. His friend Joaquín Sanjenís became central to another, stranger conspiracy after dying in 1974 at sixty years old, not long after his AMOT group was dismantled by the CIA following accusations of drug running and other criminal activities. Some claim to believe Sanjenís faked his death and went on to murder former Beatle John Lennon in 1980 while posing as doorman to the Dakota apartment building.

Fiorini was asked to testify before the Select Committee on Assassinations in the mid-1970s, where his display of punch-drunk inarticulacy, deliberate or not, confused matters further. Some apparently accidental mistakes, such as the committee confusing Brigade 2506 for the International Anti-Communist Brigade, made things worse. Even as conspiracy theorists dreamed up new connective spiderwebs, Fiorini insisted he was a blue-collar Democrat with no link to the assassination. Witnesses have placed him at home in Florida on 22 November 1963.

Marita Lorenz also testified to the commission, but her evidence was dismissed as 'unreliable' after she claimed to have been a member of Operation 40 alongside Frank Fiorini, Alex Rorke, Orlando Bosch, Pedro Díaz Lanz, Gerald Hemming and Lee Harvey Oswald. Photographs proving this, she claimed, had all mysteriously disappeared. Lorenz testified to joining some of these men in a car convoy to Dallas just before the assassination, although everyone she named had alibis that placed them elsewhere. She later wrote several memoirs, notably *Yo Fui la Espía que Amó al Comandante* (*The Spy who Loved the Comandante*), that mixed truth about a rackety life of love affairs with Castro and various New York Mafia figures alongside less believable accounts of Frank Fiorini killing Kennedy, blowing up Rolando Masferrer and being responsible for Alex Rorke's disappearance.

Rorke had been officially declared dead by his wife in 1968, but

Geoffrey Sullivan's daughter would sue the Cuban government decades later, claiming the pilot had been executed in Havana. She won the case when the Cuban authorities refused to respond, but no compensation or information was ever forthcoming and in 2012 a federal court reversed the ruling. No trace of the blue-and-white Beechcraft aircraft has ever been found. Marita Lorenz died in 2019 at eighty years old, adamant to the last that her stories were true.

Fiorini ignored all the allegations and continued with his anti-communist crusade. He joined the United Cubans group, which claimed to be the legitimate government in exile, and organised various missions against Havana, as well as training rightist movements in Angola and Central America. In 1980, he was in Tehran failing to convince the new Islamic government to offer the United Cubans a base in exchange for guarding the frontier with Afghanistan. Later, he opened a video store in Miami that refused to stock any movies starring Jane Fonda or Vanessa Redgrave because of their support for the North Vietnamese during the war. Fiorini also met Palestinian leader Yasser Arafat, lectured a far-right Argentinean political group and continued to train Cuban exiles in the Everglades. Towards the end of his life, he began making notes about the Kennedy assassination that, perhaps unsurprisingly, pointed towards Oswald working for the Soviet Union. He died on 4 December 1993 and a crowd of exiles attended his funeral in the heart of Miami's Little Havana.

• • •

The Americans who fought for Castro's rebels were on the winning side but found themselves left out of the history books by a revolutionary government determined not to share credit for victory.

Disillusionment with the subsequent dictatorial regime saw at least seven of those twenty-five Americans switch sides and play some role in counter-revolutionary activities, ranging from Jimmy Gentry's minor intrigues to Frank Fiorini's lifelong war. Bill Morgan paid for his opposition to the regime with his life.

Most of Castro's American volunteers never talked publicly about their rebel days. The Cuban dictator remained a hate figure in the US until his death and it was no good trying to explain that things had been different up in the mountains sixty years earlier. Those on the counter-revolutionary side had less reason to fear speaking out but little to boast about. Apart from a few men like Frank Fiorini, Alex Rorke and those who followed Rolando Masferrer in the early days, most soldiers of fortune in Miami spent their time hanging around Bayfront Park and drinking beer when they weren't out in the Everglades training volunteers even less competent than themselves. The real fighting was done by Cuban exiles and their CIA paymasters, to whom the soldiers of fortune were just mice scurrying around the feet of giants, oblivious to the real story and desperate for a dropped crust. Eventually, the mercenary scene faded away and a violent, crazy chapter in American–Cuban relations ended, preserved only in distant memories, fading newspaper clippings and a warehouse stacked high with FBI reports.

On 16 April 2021, Raúl Castro stepped down as leader and handed power to sixty-year-old Politburo member Miguel Díaz-Canel. Exiles in Miami decided this meant Cuban communism was on the verge of collapse and celebrated in the streets, as they have done at every significant announcement out of Havana over the past sixty years. So far nothing seems to have changed.

NOTES

Reference numbers given for FBI, CIA and other agency documents relate to the President John F. Kennedy Assassination Records Collection. Dates contained within the titles of American documents appear in the US style of mm/dd/yy. All other dates are in standard UK format.

PROLOGUE: MISSING OVER CUBA: $25,000 REWARD

1 Ralph Blumenthal, *Stork Club: America's Most Famous Nightspot and the Lost World of Café Society* (Little, Brown & Co., 2000), p. 256.
2 Christopher Paul, et al., *Paths to Victory: Detailed Insurgency Case Studies* (RAND Corporation, 2013), p. 107.
3 Holthaus, Gerald George, 10/27/59 (FBI Document 124-10280-10182).
4 Memorandum on Interview with Alexander I. Rorke, 07/06/60 (CIA Document 104-10180-10057).

1: THE CITY OF SUPERMAN

1 Jim Hunt and Bob Risch, *Warrior: Frank Sturgis – The CIA's #1 Assassin-Spy, Who Nearly Killed Castro but Was Ambushed by Watergate* (Forge, 2011), p. 21.
2 Ibid., p. 30.
3 Alan J. Weberman and Michael Canfield, *Coup d'État in America: The CIA and the Assassination of John F. Kennedy* (Quick American Archives, 1992).
4 Arthur M. Schlesinger Jr, *A Thousand Days: John F. Kennedy in the White House* (Houghton Mifflin, 2002), p. 216.
5 Richard Skylar, 'Cuba's Lure-Legalized Filth!', *Suppressed* (February 1957).

2: INVENTING A CARIBBEAN PARADISE

1 Andrew St George, 'How the CIA Blew Away Trujillo', *Swank* (October 1975).
2 Jack B. Pfeiffer, 'Official History of the Bay of Pigs Operation, Volume III: Evolution of CIA's Anti-Castro Policies, 1959–January 1961' (CIA Document, 1979), p. 1.
3 Anthony DePalma, *The Man Who Invented Fidel: Castro, Cuba, and Herbert L. Matthews of the New York Times* (Public Affairs, 2006), p. 19.
4 Ibid., p. 51.
5 Herbert L. Matthews, 'Cuban Rebel Is Visited in Hideout', *New York Times* (24 February 1957).
6 Ibid.

3: TEENAGE REBELS

1   Paul Brinkley-Rogers, 'America's Yanqui Fidelistas', *Miami Herald* (10 January 1999).
2   Ibid.
3   Van Gosse, *Where the Boys Are: Cuba, Cold War America and the Making of a New Left* (Verso, 1993), p. 90.
4   Aran Shetterly, *The Americano: Fighting with Castro for Cuba's Freedom* (Algonquin Books, 2007).
5   Kestner, 'Raid Suspect Led Restless Life', *Norfolk Ledger-Star* (19 June 1972).
6   Andrew St George, 'Confessions of a Watergate Burglar', *True* (August 1974).
7   Brinkley-Rogers, 'America's Yanqui Fidelistas'.

4: THIS IS THE HARD CORE

1   *Rebels of the Sierra Maestra: The Story of Cuba's Jungle Fighters* (CBS Television Documentary, 19 May 1957).
2   Brinkley-Rogers, 'America's Yanqui Fidelistas'.
3   Ernesto 'Che' Guevara, *Diary of a Combatant* (Ocean Press, 2013).
4   Daniel M. Friedenberg, 'A Journey to Cuba', *Dissent* (Summer 1960).
5   Ruby Hart Phillips, *Cuba: Island of Paradox* (McDowell, Obolensky Inc., 1959), p. 325.
6   Gosse, *Where the Boys Are*, p. 91.
7   Brinkley-Rogers, 'America's Yanqui Fidelistas'.
8   Gosse, *Where the Boys Are*, p. 104 n. 79.
9   Brinkley-Rogers, 'America's Yanqui Fidelistas'.

5: IN THE BELLY OF A SHARK

1   Jay Mallin Sr and Robert K. Brown, *Merc: American Soldiers of Fortune* (New American Library, 1979), p. 6.
2   David Grann, 'The Yankee Comandante', *New Yorker* (28 May 2012).
3   Shetterly, *The Americano*.
4   Ibid.
5   Ibid.
6   Ibid.
7   Harold Flender, 'Cuba Libre', *New Leader* (3 March 1958).

6: TIGERS OF THE JUNGLE

1   Shetterly, *The Americano*.
2   Grann, 'The Yankee Comandante'.
3   Shetterly, *The Americano*.
4   Record of Person Discharged from the Armed Forces: Espiritu, John M., 07/24/44.
5   'Executioner is Ex-Convict', *New York Times* (31 March 1959).
6   Hickey, 'Man Without a Country', *St Louis Globe-Democrat* (27 August 1961).

7: PRIVATEERS AND PATRIOTS

1   A Petition to Congress, 07/19/58 (CIA Document RDP75-00001R000200350023-3).
2   Brinkley-Rogers, 'America's Yanqui Fidelistas'.
3   Thomas G. Paterson, *Contesting Castro: The United States and the Triumph of the Cuban Revolution* (Oxford University Press, 1994), p. 165.
4   Ibid.
5   Jay Mallin Sr, *Adventures in Journalism: A Memoir* (Kelbrenjac Publisher, 1998), p. 90.
6   Ruben Urribarres,'Cuban Air Force against Castro's Guerrillas', www.urrib2000.narod.ru/Mil2-3-e.html
7   Knowles, '"Privateer" Finds He is in Demand', *New York Times* (8 July 1958).
8   Gosse, *Where the Boys Are*, p. 89.

9   'Sebastopol Sailor in Hospital', *Press Democrat* (11 November 1958).
10 Lee Hall, 'Inside Rebel Cuba with Raúl Castro', *Life* (21 July 1958).
11 Report: Richard Meredith Sanderlin/Arrest, 01/28/59 (CIA Document 104-10221-10197).
12 Andrew St George, 'Cuban Rebels', *Look* (4 February 1958).
13 Hunt and Risch, *Warrior*, p. 40.
14 Larry James Bockman, 'The Spirit of Moncada: Fidel Castro's Rise To Power, 1953–59, www.globalsecurity.org/military/library/report/1984/BLJ.htm

8: TRAINING UP THE FIRING SQUAD

1   Neill Macaulay, 'I Fought For Fidel', *American Heritage* (November 1991), vol. 42, issue 7.
2   Ibid.
3   Neill Macaulay, *A Rebel in Cuba: An American's Memoir* (Wacahoota Press, 1999), p. 14.
4   Shetterly, *The Americano*.
5   Macaulay, 'I Fought For Fidel'.
6   'Nordeen Boy "Accidentally" Kills Brother', *Oshkosh Northwestern* (9 February 1956).
7   LEH, Prisoner, Havana, Cuba, 06/11/59 (FBI Document 124-10217-10076).
8   Dick Russell, 'Does This Man Know Who Conspired to Assassinate King?', *The Village Voice* (19 January 1976).
9   Macaulay, *A Rebel in Cuba*, p. 74.
10 Macaulay, 'I Fought For Fidel'.
11 Macaulay, *A Rebel in Cuba*, p. 53.

9: THE LAST DAYS OF OLD CUBA

1   Frank Argote-Freyre, 'In Search of Fulgencio Batista: A Reexamination of Pre-Revolutionary Cuban Scholarship', *Revista Mexicana del Caribe* (2001), vol. 6, no. 11.
2   Hunt and Risch, *Warrior*, p. 40.
3   Combs, 'Norfolk Man with Castro Reveals Part in Uprising', *Ledger Star* (31 January 1959).
4   Patterson may have been CIA agent Robert Weicha, who later admitted that he and most agency staff were pro-Castro at this time out of disgust at Batista's dictatorship.
5   Brinkley-Rogers, 'America's Yanqui Fidelistas'.
6   Macaulay, *A Rebel in Cuba*, p. 125.
7   Fulgencio Batista, *Cuba Betrayed* (Vantage Press, 1962), p. 131.
8   Ibid., p. 135.

10: THIS WAY FOR THE FESTIVITIES, LADIES AND GENTLEMEN

1   Macaulay, 'I Fought For Fidel'.
2   Shetterly, *The Americano*.
3   Blair Woodard, 'Intimate Enemies: Visual Culture and US–Cuban Relations, 1945–2000', PhD thesis, University of New Mexico (2010).
4   *Bohemia* (11 January 1959).
5   George Plimpton, *Shadow Box: An Amateur in the Ring* (Lyons Press, 2010).
6   Eduardo Sáenz Rovner, *The Cuban Connection: Drug Trafficking, Smuggling, and Gambling in Cuba from the 1920s to the Revolution* (University of North Carolina Press, 2009), p. 130.
7   Andrew Feldman, *Ernesto: The Untold Story of Hemingway in Revolutionary Cuba* (Melville House, 2019), p. 319.
8   Plimpton, *Shadow Box*.
9   Ibid.
10 Anthony Borgo, 'Alan Robert Nye', www.wrhistoricalsociety.com/alan-robert-nye
11 '"Stay Home, I Can Handle It" Whiting Prisoner Tells Mom', *Times from Munster, Indiana* (1959).
12 Havana Embassy: Political Matters Cuba, 04/14/59 (Department of State Document 2003-02-25 Grafeld-JHL).

13 Borgo, 'Alan Robert Nye'.

14 CIA Liaison Material: Ignatius Paul Alvick, 06/20/61 (FBI Document 124-90140-10029).

11: THREE FERRARIS ON YOUR TAIL

1 Eliot Kleinberg, *Palm Beach Past: The Best of 'Post Time'* (Arcadia Publishing, 2006).

2 NRO, Assoc, EMP, Anti-Castro Elements etc., 01/04/60 (FBI Document 124-10280-10177).

3 Hearings before the Select Committee on Assassinations: House of Representatives – Sturgis, Frank, 03/20/78 (HSCA Document 180-10088-10087).

4 Ibid.

5 Ibid.

6 Ibid.

7 Ibid.

8 Tully, '"Little Things" Tell It', *Knoxville News-Sentinel* (6 January 1959).

9 Hearings before the Select Committee on Assassinations: House of Representatives – Sturgis, Frank, 03/20/78 (HSCA Document 180-10088-10087).

10 'Dominican Republic: Three Men in a Funk', *Time* (9 February 1959).

12: THE DOMINICAN REPUBLIC AFFAIR

1 Shetterly, *The Americano*.

2 Hearings before the Select Committee on Assassinations: House of Representatives – Sturgis, Frank, 03/20/78 (HSCA 180-10088-10087).

3 'Parlor Bolsheviki Sharply Denounced at Club Luncheon', *New York Tribune* (7 March 1920).

4 'Billingsley Finds Stork Club Technique Can't Handle Daughter', *Star Tribune – Minneapolis* (26 December 1954).

5 Memorandum: Loren Eugene Hall, 08/21/59 (CIA Document 104-10217-10299).

6 'Horrors of Castro's Jails Told by Alexander Rorke', *Palm Beach Post* (29 January 1963).

7 Shetterly, *The Americano*.

8 'Dominican Republic: Blood on the Beach', *Time* (6 July 1959).

9 Miami File, 1959 (FBI Document Cuba 109-12-210 – Volume 6 – Serials 292-450).

10 Grann, 'The Yankee Comandante'.

11 Conversation with Alexander I. Rorke, 07/06/60 (CIA Document 104-10069-10195).

13: THIRTY SECONDS OVER HAVANA

1 Gosse, *Where the Boys Are*, pp. 110, 108.

2 Joseph Raymond Merola, Robert Ellis Frost, 03/30/60 (FBI Document 124-90110-10023).

3 Joseph Raymond Merola, Robert Ellis Frost, 02/24/60 (FBI Document 124-90110-10001).

4 Joseph Raymond Merola, Robert Ellis Frost, 03/30/60 (FBI Document 124-90110-10023).

5 Ibid.

6 Eliot Kleinberg, 'The Last Flight of Matt Duke', *Palm Beach Post* (4 September 2015).

7 MLO, REL, LTR, CASTRO, et al., 01/26/60 (FBI Document 124-10206-10261).

8 Haviv Schieber was the brains behind the Anti-Communist International, but most of the money came from Robert Speller, a hard-right New York publisher whose main interests seemed to be attacking communism, supporting the Katanga secession in Africa and socialising with various frauds who claimed to be surviving members of the Russian royal family; see my *Katanga 1960–63: Mercenaries, Spies and the African Nation that Waged War on the World* (History Press, 2015) for more on the secession and the role of Speller employee Philippa Schuyler.

14: NO CHILDREN, NO PETS, NO CUBANS

1 Amaury E. del Valle, 'Rolando Masferrer Rojas: ¡Voló en pedazos el "Tigre"!', *La Jiribilla* (16–22 April 2005).

2   Embassy, Habana to Department of State, Washington, 05/31/57 (FBI Records 124-90089-10249).
3   Humberto Fontova, *Fidel: Hollywood's Favorite Tyrant* (Simon & Schuster, 2012).
4   Gosse, *Where the Boys Are*, p. 144.
5   Warren Hinckle and William Turner, *Deadly Secrets: The CIA-Mafia War against Castro and the Assassination of JFK* (Basic Books, 1993), p. 47.
6   María de los Angeles Torres, *In the Land of Mirrors: Cuban Exile Politics in the United States* (University of Michigan Press, 1999), p. 73.
7   '2 Americans Slain by Cuban Squad', *Miami Herald* (17 October 1960).
8   Rolando Masferrer, 11/17/60 (FBI Document 124-90089-10060).
9   Ibid.
10 Ibid.
11 '23 Americans Sign Up for Invasion of Cuba', *Miami Herald* (25 December 1960).
12 Office Memorandum: Interview with Wilbur Gee, Seaman Patient at USPRS Hospital, Detroit, 08/22/61 (CIA Document 104-10071-10073).
13 Frank Anthony Sturgis, 04/24/61 (FBI Document 104-10221-10313).

15: NOW DIG! WE'RE FIGHTING CASTRO!

1   David E. Davis Jr, 'My Friend Hans Tanner', *Car and Driver* (March 2011).
2   Hans Tanner, *Counter-Revolutionary Agent – Cuba* (G. T. Foulis & Co., 1962), p. 4.
3   Rolando Masferrer, 02/20/61 (FBI Document 124-90089-10122).
4   '"My Boy Hates Fighting," Says Mother of Cuban Fighter', *Nashville Banner* (19 January 1961).
5   Frank Anthony Sturgis, 04/24/61 (FBI Document 104-10221-10313).
6   Classified Message, 03/31/60 (CIA Document 104-10177-10158).
7   Colegrove, 'Ex-Castro Big Wheel Returns to Miami for Different Reason', *Washington Daily News* (28 January 1961).
8   Macaulay, 'I Fought For Fidel'.
9   Tanner, *Counter-Revolutionary Agent*, p. 56.

16: PORK CHOP BAY

1   Terry Southern, 'How I Signed Up at $250 A Month for the Big Parade Through Havana Bla-Bla-Bla and Wound Up in Guatemala with the CIA: A hipster-mercenary's version of the Cuban Affair', *Esquire* (June 1963).
2   Gail Gerber and Tom Lisanti, *Trippin' with Terry Southern: What I Think I Remember* (McFarland, 2009), p. 69.
3   Southern, 'How I Signed Up at $250 A Month for the Big Parade Through Havana Bla-Bla-Bla and Wound Up in Guatemala with the CIA'.
4   Ibid.
5   Official History of the Bay of Pigs Operation Volume III: Evolution of CIA's Anti-Castro Policies, 1959–January 1961 (CIA Document), p. 223.
6   John Dille, 'This Was the Bay of Pigs', *Life* (10 May 1963).
7   Southern, 'How I Signed Up at $250 A Month for the Big Parade Through Havana Bla-Bla-Bla and Wound Up in Guatemala with the CIA'.
8   Dispatch: Interrogation of Cuban Refugees, 08/15/62 (CIA Document 104-10218-10006).
9   Gosse, *Where the Boys Are*, p. 197.
10 Dille, 'This Was the Bay of Pigs'.
11 Juan O. Tamayo, 'Juan Clark, Cuba scholar and Bay of Pigs vet, dies', *Miami Herald* (27 February 2013).
12 Eder, 'Cuba Bars US Volunteers', *New York Times* (20 April 1961).
13 Gosse, *Where the Boys Are*, p. 226.
14 DePalma, *The Man Who Invented Fidel*, p. 187.

15 Southern, 'How I Signed Up at $250 A Month for the Big Parade Through Havana Bla-Bla-Bla and Wound Up in Guatemala with the CIA'.

17: MERCENARIES IN THE MAGIC CITY

1 'Anti-Red Legion Seeks Volunteers', *Houston Chronicle* (1 May 1961).
2 Gans, '50 (All) Americans Want to Fight Fidel', *Miami News* (26 April 1961).
3 GPH, Interpen, Anti-Communist Legionnaires, 07/31/61 (FBI Document 124-10226-10450).
4 Interpen, Group, Anticommunist Legionnaires etc., 05/03/61 (FBI Document 124-10298-10239).
5 Ibid.
6 Miller, 'Anti-Castro Recruits from Houston Stranded in Miami', *Houston Chronicle* (15 May 1961).
7 'Would-Be Rebels Lingering Here', *Miami News* (17 May 1961).

18: INTERCONTINENTAL PENETRATION

1 Freedom Fighters of the Americas, Steve Wilson, 08/21/61 (FBI Document 124-90049-10001).
2 CIA Liaison Material: Ignatius Paul Alvick, 06/20/61 (FBI Document 124-90140-10029).
3 Weberman and Canfield, *Coup d'État in America*.
4 From Commanding Officer, Service School Command, US Naval Training Center, Bainbridge, Maryland, 09/05/58 (US Marines Document P11-1[2]).
5 Weberman and Canfield, *Coup d'État in America*.
6 Ibid.
7 Ibid.
8 Hemming Moves to Miami to Engage in Anti-Castro Ops, 31/03/61 (NARA Document 1993.06.30.15:16:25:900800).
9 'Soldiers-of-Fortune Training in Florida for Action in Cuba', *Miami Herald* (5 July 1961).
10 Alexander Rorke, 01/20/64 (FBI Document 124-9001910300).
11 Hearings before the Select Committee on Assassinations: House of Representatives – Sturgis, Frank, 03/20/78 (HSCA 180-10088-10087).

19: A REAL RAUNCHY GROUP OF MEN

1 Intercontinental Penetration Forces, 07/31/61 (FBI Document 2-1693).
2 Hearings before the Select Committee on Assassinations: House of Representatives – Sturgis, Frank, 03/20/78 (HSCA 180-10088-10087).
3 'Soldiers-of-Fortune Training in Florida for Action in Cuba'.
4 Don Bohning, 'Indoctrination U', www.washingtondecoded.com/site/2008/06/simkin.html
5 Frank Anthony Sturgis Neutrality Matters, 07/05/62 (CIA Document 104-10221-10174).
6 DePalma, *The Man Who Invented Fidel*, p. 191.

20: BOMBE CARIBIENNE

1 William Styron, *Havanas in Camelot: Personal Essays* (Random House, 2008).
2 Joseph A. Esposito, *Dinner in Camelot: The Night America's Greatest Scientists, Writers, and Scholars Partied at the Kennedy White House* (ForeEdge, 2018).
3 Styron, *Havanas in Camelot*.
4 Benjamin Schwartz, 'The Real Cuban Missile Crisis', *The Atlantic* (January–February 2013).
5 Ibid.
6 Alice L. George, *Awaiting Armageddon: How Americans Faced the Cuban Missile Crisis* (University of North Carolina Press, 2003), p. xiv.
7 Rich Halten, 'How The Cuban Missile Crisis Shaped Miami', www.wlrn.org/this-miami-life/2012-10-24/how-the-cuban-missile-crisis-shaped-miami
8 American Foreign Policy: Current Documents 1962 (Historical Division, Bureau of Public Affairs, 1962), p. 444.
9 Report of Investigation: Hemming, Gerald P., 02/15/62 (CIA Document 104-10120-10193).

10 Dorschner, 'Soldiers of Fortune', *Tampa Bay Times* (15 August 1976).
11 William Stuckey, 'Adventurer Works Hard to Establish Anti-Castro Base Near Covington', *New Orleans States-Item* (21 July 1962).

21: STRICTLY A NO-GOOD PUNK
1 Mike Wales, *Ed Arthur's Glory No More* (Dakar Publishing, 1975), p. 28.
2 Hearings before the Select Committee on Assassinations: House of Representatives – Sturgis, Frank, 03/20/78 (HSCA 180-10088-10087).
3 EIA, INTV, Americans for Freedom etc., 05/05/64 (FBI Document 124-10285-10206).
4 EIA, INTV, CHENNAULT, et al., 12/02/63 (FBI Document 124-10281-10199).
5 Operation JMPALM; Haitian Exile Activities at JMWAVE, 08/10/64 (CIA Document 104-10071-10202).
6 EIA, INTV, CHENNAULT, et al., 12/02/63 (FBI Document 124-10281-10199).
7 Hinckle and Turner, *Deadly Secrets*, p. 279.
8 EIA, INTV, CHENNAULT, et al., 12/02/63 (FBI Document 124-10281-10199).
9 Wales, *Ed Arthur's Glory No More*, p. 116.

22: INTO THIN AIR
1 Letter: Gerry Patrick to 'Dick' (3 February 1963).
2 To: Director; From: JMWAVE, 08/08/62 (CIA Document 104-10192-10099).
3 Alexander Rorke, Alexander Irwin Rorke Jr, 05/14/63 (FBI Document 124-90019-10174).
4 Meisler, 'Photographer Films Havana Bomb Drop', *Decatur Daily* (27 April 1963).
5 Alexander Rorke, Alexander Irwin Rorke Jr, 05/14/63 (FBI Document 124-90019-10174).
6 WJ, AIR, ASSOC, ANTI-COMMUNIST etc., 02/20/64 (FBI Document 124-10296-10045).
7 Ibid.
8 Hearings before the Select Committee on Assassinations: House of Representatives – Sturgis, Frank, 03/20/78 (HSCA Document 180-10088-10087).
9 Alexander Rorke, 6/24/63 (CIA Document 80T01357A).
10 Kirk, 'Two US Foes of Castro Missing on Mystery Flight', *New York Post* (4 October 1963).
11 Alexander Rorke, 12/24/63 (FBI Document 124-90019-10295).
12 Alexander Rorke, George W. Tanner Jr, 11/21/63 (FBI Document 124-90019-10287).
13 '$25,000 Offered for Lost Fliers', *New York Times* (11 February 1964).
14 Letter: Alexander I. Rorke Sr to Frank Fiorini (21 January 1964).

23: THE VIEW FROM THE TEXAS SCHOOL BOOK DEPOSITORY
1 Report of the President's Commission on the Assassination of President John F. Kennedy, Chapter VII (US Government Printing Office, 1964), p. 394.
2 Oswald, Lee, Post Russian Period, Employment, 02/14/78 (HSCA Document 180-10106-10002).
3 Paul Matzko, *The Radio Right: How a Band of Broadcasters Took on the Federal Government and Built the Modern Conservative Movement* (Oxford University Press, 2020), p. 86.
4 Letter: Fair Play for Cuba Committee to Lee Harvey Oswald, 05/29/63, https://texashistory.unt.edu/ark:/67531/metapth337534/m1/1/
5 Investigation of the Assassination of President John F. Kennedy: Hearings before the President's Commission on the Assassination of President Kennedy, Volume IV (US Government Printing Office, 1964), p. 147.
6 Investigation of the Assassination of President John F. Kennedy: Hearings before the President's Commission on the Assassination of President Kennedy, Volume III (US Government Printing Office, 1964), p. 144.
7 Scott P. Johnson, *The Faces of Lee Harvey Oswald: The Evolution of an Alleged Assassin* (Lexington Books, 2013), p. 9.
8 Leo Janos, 'The Last Days of the President', *The Atlantic* (July 1973).
9 J. Harry Jones Jr, *A Private Army* (Collier Books, 1969), p. 90.

24: THEY CALL HIM PAPA DOC

1   Robert K. Brown and Vann Spencer, *I Am Soldier of Fortune: Dancing with Devils* (Casemate, 2013).
2   'Bill Dempsey: The Silent Soldier of Fortune', *Hamilton Spectator*.
3   Masferrer and Counterrevolutionary Activities in General, 02/13/63 (CIA Document Rec-23).
4   Brown and Spencer, *I Am Soldier of Fortune*.
5   Millery Polyné, *From Douglass to Duvalier: US African Americans, Haiti, Pan Americanism, 1870–1964* (University Press of Florida, 2010), p. 195.
6   Fitzhugh S. M. Mulien, 'Where Haiti Stands', *Harvard Crimson* (3 October 1963).
7   Brown and Spencer, *I Am Soldier of Fortune*.
8   Ibid.

25: BAY OF PIGLETS

1   Matt Flegenheimer, 'Jay McMullen, CBS Investigative Journalist, Dies at 90', *New York Times* (12 March 2012).
2   St George had some experience of media outlets paying mercenaries to obtain stories: in the winter of 1962, *Life* had helped finance a mission by Cuban exiles, a right-wing millionaire and members of the CIA acting unofficially to extract some Soviet officers in Havana who allegedly wanted to defect; the mission appears to have been a set-up by the Cubans and the landing party disappeared without trace.
3   Gene Grove, 'The CIA, FBI and CBS Bomb in Mission: Impossible', *Scanlan's Monthly* (March 1970).
4   Gus Constantine, 'The Story of CBS and the Plot to Invade Haiti', *Washington Star* (26 February 1970).
5   House of Representatives Report on Network News Documentary Practices, 07/20/70 (HR Report no. 91-1319), p. 112.
6   Ibid, p. 145.
7   John Dorschner, 'Miami: Casablanca Of The Caribbean', *Miami Herald – Tropic Magazine* (4 April 1976).
8   House of Representatives Report on Network News Documentary Practices, 07/20/70 (HR Report no. 91-1319), p. 32.
9   Dorschner, 'Miami: Casablanca Of The Caribbean'.
10   Ediger, 'Night Lead Invasion', *Associated Press* (3 January 1967).
11   'Cuban Plotters Plot but US Keeps the Lid On', *San Francisco Sunday Examiner and Chronicle* (19 March 1967).
12   MASFERRER Prosecution, Miami, Florida, 04/02/67 (CIA Document WH/C 67–54).
13   REF: SAIGON 8251 (in 53602), 15/05/69 (CIA Document 104-10256-10082).
14   Anderson, 'CBS Films a Comic Opera "Invasion"', *Washington Post* (18 June 1970).

26: MR GARRISON INVESTIGATES

1   Burton, 'Three Californians Subpoenaed as Witnesses in Garrison's Kennedy Assassination Probe', *LA Free Press* (5 January 1968).
2   Patricia Lambert, *False Witness: The Real Story of Jim Garrison's Investigation and Oliver Stone's Film JFK* (M. Evans & Co., 1998), p. 89.
3   Fred Litwin, *On the Trail of Delusion: Jim Garrison, The Great Accuser* (NorthernBlues Books, 2020).
4   Lambert, *False Witness*.
5   'Playboy Interview: Jim Garrison', *Playboy* (October 1967).
6   Memorandum: Visit of GERRY PATRICK HEMMING and ROY HARGREAVES, 09/18/67 (Garrison Investigation Document: courtesy of Fred Litwin).
7   'Playboy Interview: Jim Garrison'.
8   Litwin, *On the Trail of Delusion*.

9   Interview with Loran Hall, 05/06/68, New Orleans, Louisiana (Garrison Investigation Document: courtesy of Fred Litwin).
10   'Probe Figure Howard Bares Trip to NO', *News Orleans States-Item* (27 February 1968).
11   Memorandum: Interview of GERRY PATRICK HEMMING, 05/08/68 (Garrison Investigation Document: courtesy of Fred Litwin).

27: DÉJÀ VU OVER PORT-AU-PRINCE
1   Dorschner, 'Soldiers of Fortune'.
2   Ibid.
3   Avila stayed in prison and later became an agent for Cuban intelligence, and then a double agent for the FBI when he made it back to America – see: Larry Rohter, 'Leader of Exile Group Tells of Spying for Cuba', *New York Times* (11 November 1992).
4   Hinckle and Turner, *Deadly Secrets*, p. 293.
5   Criminal Prosecutions against Cuban Refugees, 09/24/70 (NARA Document 1993.07.22.08: 42:15:590620).
6   Montalbano and Smith, 'Haiti Invasion Camp Raided in Everglades', *Miami Herald* (13 March 1969).
7   Dorschner, 'Soldiers of Fortune'.
8   Ibid.
9   Ibid.
10   Florcyk, 'Bomber Comes Home', *Free Press* (10 June 1969).

28: WEIRD TIMES AT THE WATERGATE
1   'Watergate Retrospective: The Decline and Fall', *Time* (19 August 1974).
2   St George, 'Confessions of a Watergate Burglar'.
3   Hunt and Risch, *Warrior*, p. 128.
4   Keith Sharon, 'The man who stayed late: The Watergate story you've never heard', *Mercury News* (17 June 2019).
5   'Ziegler, Baker, Others on "Third-Rate Burglary Attempt"', *Associated Press* (23 April 1994), https://apnews.com/article/5669edd4488063c863dd5ba72bb29746
6   Press Release: Statement to Press re Watergate, Schultz & Overby Law Firm (26 March 1973).

29: COMMUNISM, COCAINE, CONSPIRACIES
1   Kavitha Iyengar, 'The Venceremos Brigade: North Americans in Cuba Since 1969', *International Journal of Cuban Studies* (Winter 2015), vol. 7, no. 2.
2   'Death Wish – Wrong Man Dies', *San Francisco Examiner* (21 December 1967).
3   LEH, Prisoner, Havana, Cuba, 06/11/59 (FBI Document 124-10217-10076).
4   Brinkley-Rogers, 'America's Yanqui Fidelistas'.
5   'Ex-Batista Aide Killed by Bomb As He Starts His Auto in Miami', *New York Times* (1 November 1975).
6   WerBell Military Armament Corporation, Powder Springs, Georgia etc., 11/05/70 (CIA Document 104-10256-10076).
7   Sergio Arcacha-Smith, 06/09/67 (CIA Document 1994.05.09.10:51:44:000005).
8   Information from Rob Krott (26 November 2020).
9   Roy Emory Hargraves, Gerald Patrick Hemming, Internal Security – Cuba, 12/10/70 (FBI Document 104-10218-10109).
10   Hall, Loran Eugene: Testimony before Committee, 10/05/77 (HSCA Document 180-10118-10115).
11   Dorschner, 'Martin F. X. Casey, 72, a soldier of fortune', *Miami Herald* (18 January 2011).

BIBLIOGRAPHY

Anderson, Jon Lee, *Che Guevara: A Revolutionary Life* (Grove Press, 2010).

Angeles Torres, María de los, *In the Land of Mirrors: Cuban Exile Politics in the United States* (University of Michigan Press, 1999).

Arboleya, Jesús, *The Cuban Counter-Revolution* (Ohio University Center for International Studies, 2000).

Argote-Freyre, Frank, *Fulgencio Batista: From Revolutionary to Strongman* (Rutgers University Press, 2006).

Batista, Fulgencio, *Cuba Betrayed* (Vantage Press, 1962).

Beckemeier, Eric, *Traitors Beware: A History of Robert DePugh's Minutemen* (Lulu, 2007).

Blumenthal, Ralph, *Stork Club: America's Most Famous Nightspot and the Lost World of Café Society* (Little, Brown & Co., 2000).

Brown, Robert K. and Spencer, Vann, *I Am Soldier of Fortune: Dancing with Devils* (Casemate, 2013).

Colhoun, Jack, *Gangsterismo: The United States, Cuba, and the Mafia, 1933 to 1966* (OR Books, 2013).

DePalma, Anthony, *The Man Who Invented Fidel: Castro, Cuba, and Herbert L. Matthews of the New York Times* (Public Affairs, 2006).

English, T. J., *Havana Nocturne: How the Mob Owned Cuba ... and Then Lost It to the Revolution* (William Morrow, 2009).

Esposito, Joseph A., *Dinner in Camelot: The Night America's Greatest Scientists, Writers, and Scholars Partied at the Kennedy White House* (ForeEdge, 2018).

Feldman, Andrew, *Ernesto: The Untold Story of Hemingway in Revolutionary Cuba* (Melville House, 2019).

Flynn, Errol, *My Wicked, Wicked Ways: The Autobiography of Errol Flynn* (Cooper Square Press, 2002).

Fontova, Humberto, *Fidel: Hollywood's Favorite Tyrant* (Simon & Schuster, 2012).

Gosse, Van, *Where the Boys Are: Cuba, Cold War America and the Making of a New Left* (Verso, 1993).

Guevara, Ernesto 'Che', *Diary of a Combatant* (Ocean Press, 2013).

Hinckle, Warren and Turner, William, *Deadly Secrets: The CIA-Mafia War against Castro and the Assassination of JFK* (Basic Books, 1993).

Hull, Christopher, *Our Man Down in Havana: The Story Behind Graham Greene's Cold War Spy Novel* (Pegasus Books, 2019).

Hunt, Jim and Risch, Bob, *Warrior: Frank Sturgis – The CIA's #1 Assassin-Spy, Who Nearly Killed Castro but Was Ambushed by Watergate* (Forge, 2011).

Johnson, Scott P., *The Faces of Lee Harvey Oswald: The Evolution of an Alleged Assassin* (Lexington Books, 2013).

Jones Jr, J. Harry, *A Private Army* (Collier Books, 1969).

Kleinberg, Eliot, *Palm Beach Past: The Best of 'Post Time'* (Arcadia Publishing, 2006).

Lambert, Patricia, *False Witness: The Real Story of Jim Garrison's Investigation and Oliver Stone's Film JFK* (M. Evans & Co., 1998).

Liddy, G. Gordon, *Will* (Sphere, 1981).

Litwin, Fred, *On the Trail of Delusion: Jim Garrison, The Great Accuser* (NorthernBlues Books, 2020).

Lorenz, Marita, *The Spy Who Loved Castro* (Ebury Press, 2017).

Macaulay, Neill, *A Rebel in Cuba: An American's Memoir* (Wacahoota Press, 1999).

Mallin Sr, Jay, *Adventures in Journalism: A Memoir* (Kelbrenjac Publisher, 1998).

Mallin Sr, Jay and Brown, Robert K., *Merc: American Soldiers of Fortune* (New American Library, 1979).

Matzko, Paul, *The Radio Right: How a Band of Broadcasters Took on the Federal Government and Built the Modern Conservative Movement* (Oxford University Press, 2020).

Olson, Keith W., *Watergate: The Presidential Scandal That Shook America* (University Press of Kansas, 2016).

Paterson, Thomas G., *Contesting Castro: The United States and the Triumph of the Cuban Revolution* (Oxford University Press, 1994).

Paul, Christopher, et al., *Paths to Victory: Detailed Insurgency Case Studies* (RAND Corporation, 2013).

Perrottet, Tony, *Cuba Libre! Che, Fidel, and the Improbable Revolution That Changed World History* (Blue Rider Press, 2019).

Phillips, Ruby Hart, *Cuba: Island of Paradox* (McDowell, Obolensky Inc., 1959).

Plimpton, George, *Shadow Box: An Amateur in the Ring* (Lyons Press, 2010).

Polyné, Millery, *From Douglass to Duvalier: US African Americans, Haiti, Pan Americanism, 1870–1964* (University Press of Florida, 2010).

Sáenz Rovner, Eduardo, *The Cuban Connection: Drug Trafficking, Smuggling, and Gambling in Cuba from the 1920s to the Revolution* (University of North Carolina Press, 2009).

Sanderlin, Terry K., *The Last American Rebel in Cuba* (Author-House, 2012).

Schlesinger Jr, Arthur M., *A Thousand Days: John F. Kennedy in the White House* (Houghton Mifflin, 2002).

Shetterly, Aran, *The Americano: Fighting with Castro for Cuba's Freedom* (Algonquin Books, 2007).

Southern, Terry, *Now Dig This: The Unspeakable Writings of Terry Southern, 1950–95* (Open Road Media, 2012).

Stockton, Bayard, *Flawed Patriot: The Rise and Fall of CIA Legend Bill Harvey* (Potomac Books, Inc., 2006).

Styron, William, *Havanas in Camelot: Personal Essays* (Random House, 2008).

Tanner, Hans, *Counter-Revolutionary Agent – Cuba* (G. T. Foulis & Co., 1962).

Thomas, Hugh, *Cuba: A History* (Penguin, 2010).

von Tunzelmann, Alex, *Red Heat: Conspiracy, Murder and the Cold War in the Caribbean* (Simon & Schuster, 2012).

Turner, William Weyland, *The Cuban Connection: Nixon, Castro, and the Mob* (Prometheus Books, 2013).

Wales, Mike, *Ed Arthur's Glory No More* (Dakar Publishing, 1975).

Weberman, Alan J. and Canfield, Michael, *Coup d'État in America: The CIA and the Assassination of John F. Kennedy* (Quick American Archives, 1992).

INDEX